International Education and Schools

ALSO AVAILABLE FROM BLOOMSBURY

Anglican Church School Education: Moving Beyond the First Two Hundred Years, Edited by Howard J. Worsley
England's Citizenship Education Experiment: State, School and Student Perspectives, Lee Jerome

International Education and Schools

Moving Beyond the First 40 Years

EDITED BY RICHARD PEARCE

International School of London

B L O O M S B U R Y

LONDON · NEW DELHI · NEW YORK · SYDNEY

Bloomsbury Academic

An imprint of Bloomsbury Publishing Plc

50 Bedford Square	1385 Broadway
London	New York
WC1B 3DP	NY 10018
UK	USA

www.bloomsbury.com

Bloomsbury is a registered trademark of Bloomsbury Publishing PLC

First published 2013

British Library Cataloguing-in-Publication Data
A catalogue record for this book is available from the British Library.

ISBN: HB: 978-1-4725-1046-4
PB: 978-1-4725-1074-7
ePub: 978-1-4725-1290-1
ePDF: 978-1-4725-0914-7

Library of Congress Cataloging-in-Publication Data
International education and schools : moving beyond the
first 40 years / edited by Richard Pearce.
pages cm
Includes bibliographical references and index.
ISBN 978-1-4725-1074-7 (pbk.) – ISBN 978-1-4725-1046-4 (hardback) –
ISBN 978-1-4725-0914-7 (epdf) 1. International education. 2. International schools.
I. Pearce, Richard.
LC1090.I5543 2013
370.116–dc23
2013020841

Typeset by Integra Software Services Pvt. Ltd.
Printed and bound in Great Britain

CONTENTS

NOTES ON CONTRIBUTORS

Michael Allan has been in international education for more than 25 years, the last 10 in the Netherlands, and is at present Multicultural Coordinator at the International School of Amsterdam, The Netherlands. His initial research was in the area of cultural dissonance and inter-cultural learning at Oxford Brookes University, UK, which he continued with doctoral studies at the University of Bath, UK, in the field of cross-cultural discourse and multicultural pedagogy. He was Chair of the European Council of International Schools (ECIS) Cross-culture Committee and is the holder of the ECIS Award for the Promotion of International Education. He has extensive experience in writing and training for the International Baccalaureate (IB) and other channels of international education.

Tristan Bunnell has taught IB Economics at two of the pioneer IB international schools, in London and in Copenhagen. His doctoral research at the University of Southampton, UK, was in international schools and their public relations activity. He is a prolific writer and frequent peer reviewer for numerous academic journals. In the last 4 years he has written four books and numerous articles on the nature of international education and its relations to its context. He has also contributed to postgraduate programmes at the University of Bath, UK, and Deakin University, Australia.

Nicholas Brummitt is Founder and Managing Director of the International School Consultancy (ISC) Group, including ISC Research and ISC Worldwide. After graduating from the University of York, UK, and later Britannia Royal Naval College, Dartmouth, UK, he became involved with the international schools and was intrigued by their development and complexity. He realized that business predictions in the expanding field called for statistics and undertook research to record them. He has been researching the international schools market consistently since 1978.

Richard Caffyn is currently Principal at the International School Telemark, Norway. He has been Primary Principal at the International School of Milan, Italy, and had previously worked in the UK, Azerbaijan, Romania and Austria. He was Head of Research Support and Development for the IB Research Unit at the University of Bath, UK, and is a visiting research fellow at the university. His doctorate investigated the micropolitics and social dynamics of international school leadership and management, a topic about which he regularly writes and presents at conferences.

James Cambridge is an international education consultant. He teaches part-time at the International School of London, UK, and is an external member of the Centre for International and Comparative Studies at the University of Bristol, UK. He was formerly Head of Research Projects with the International Baccalaureate Research Unit and a visiting research fellow at the University of Bath, UK. He has previously worked in the fields of teaching, assessment, curriculum development, initial teacher education and continuing professional development, in the UK, the Middle East and Southern Africa, and has written and reviewed extensively.

Maurice Carder is an independent researcher and consultant on language matters in international schools, following a distinguished career in language teaching, most notably at Vienna International School, Austria, but also in seven other countries. He holds an Ed.D. from the Institute of Education, University of London, UK, and has been a pioneering advocate for bilingual education. He has been an examiner for IB Diploma language A2 and moderator for IB Middle Years Programme (MYP) language B, and has contributed to various IB projects concerned with languages. He has chaired the ECIS English as a Second Language (ESL) and Mother Tongue Committee and written books, chapters and refereed articles on bilingualism and language-related matters.

Mary Hayden is Director of the Centre for the study of Education in an International Context (CEIC) at the University of Bath, the major centre of its kind in the UK. She has taught, researched and supervised research in international schools and international education and was largely responsible for developing the MA course in international education at the CEIC. She is currently Head of the Department of Education at the University of Bath, UK. She has worked for the IB Organization as Research and Development Officer and is on the Advisory Board of the International Primary Curriculum. Having written extensively on topics of international education, she is editor of the *Journal of Research in International Education*, and a trustee of the Alliance for International Education.

Anne Keeling is Media Relations Representative, ISC Research. Her role is to present data to the press and media, as issues arise. She has been working within the international schools market for the last 6 years and also handles the media relations for Fieldwork Education and Teachers International Consultancy, two other companies that are well established within the international schools market. Her experience in media relations spans 25 years. She is a graduate of the University of Bath, UK.

Richard Pearce is a consultant in international education at the International School of London, UK, having worked there since its foundation, including 35 years teaching IB Diploma Biology. He has taught in the UK and the US, and was a co-founder and Chair of the ECIS Cross-culture Committee. His doctoral research at the University of Bath, UK, concerned the adjustment of cultural identity in internationally mobile children. He has contributed to cross-cultural training at schools and universities in 18 countries, and has written on matters of identity, culture and values.

Boyd Roberts has been involved in international education for over 30 years, including being head of two IB schools – St Clares, Oxford, UK, and Amman Baccalaureate School, Jordan. He has been a director of the Association of Recognized English Language Services and is on the executive committee of the Council for Independent Further Education. He is currently a consultant for the Oxford University Press IB Diploma Programme course companions and on the advisory board of Cambridge University Press IB publications. Following early retirement, his energies have been devoted to various projects concerned with global issues and global citizenship education, and he was until recently working for the IB as director of its community theme project. This commitment has led to the book *Educating for Global Citizenship: a practical guide for schools*, published by the IB in 2009, and to the International Global Citizen's Award.

Susan Shortland is Principal Lecturer in Human Resource Management (HRM) at London Metropolitan University, UK. She began her career in industrial relations research before moving on to head the CBI's Employee Relocation Council. She has also worked in a managerial and consulting role in international Human Research Management (HRM) at KPMG. She holds master's degrees from the Universities of Cambridge, UK, and Westminster, UK, and gained her PhD from the University of Westminster for research on women's participation in expatriation. She is author of five books on mobility and HRM and has written extensively on topics of international Human Resources (HR) and international relocation issues in both academic and practitioner journals.

Jeff Thompson, Emeritus Professor of Education at the University of Bath, UK, was the founding director of the CEIC, and has pioneered research in the field. He has held numerous posts in UK education, including chairing the Examination Appeals Board, the National Curriculum science working group and the British Association for the Advancement of Science. He was the founding editor of the *Journal of Research in International Education,* former Academic Director, Director of Research and Chair of the Examining Board of the International Baccalaureate Diploma. He is currently Chair of the Curriculum Advisory Board of the International Primary Curriculum and the International Middle Years Curriculum, Director of the International Board of the United World Colleges and immediate past chair of the Association for International Education.

David Wilkinson has been the founding head of the Mahindra United World College of India and of Li Po Chun United World College of Hong Kong, and Founding Deputy Head of the United World College of the Adriatic in Italy. He was one of the team that developed the IB Diploma Theory of Knowledge course, and has been an examiner. He was Chair of the International Baccalaureate Development Council for India until July 2009 and currently he is working as Founder and Chair of the Oaktree Foundation, building an IB school in Kolkata, India, and also developing a Pestalozzi school in Zambia. He has over 30 years of hands-on experience in the field of international education as a headmaster, examiner, curriculum developer and author.

Veronica Wilkinson is an educational consultant and IB Deputy Chief Examiner of English. Her international experience derived from working at and helping to found the United World Colleges in Italy (Duino), Hong Kong (Li Po Chun) and India (Mahindra), as well as in Thailand and Southern Africa, and led her to doctoral research at the University of Bath, UK, where she studied the effects on students' cultural attitudes and assumptions of an IB Diploma education. She has also been closely involved through the Oaktree Foundation in the founding of the Oaktree International School in Kolkata, India. This has been linked with her work for PestalozziWorld, including the development of the Pestalozzi Education Centre in Lusaka, Zambia.

ACKNOWLEDGEMENTS

My thanks are due to this patient, generous and collaborative team of expert contributors; they are the right people to consult on international education. My own learning has happened over the 40 years since the foundation of the International School of London and I owe a great personal debt to the generations of colleagues, parents and students who have been my tutors and interpreters. The present general manager, Mr. Amin Makarem, has been supportive throughout the production of the book. I owe a lifetime's debt to my family, whose tolerance and encouragement over many years has allowed me to develop ideas, albeit late in life. My tutor in cross-cultural matters has been Bernadette van Houten. These ideas were developed with the support of my supervisors, Jeff Thompson and Mary Hayden, and matured in debate with Jim Cambridge, Mike Allan and other members of the writing team. Vital help with the editing when I needed it was generously given by Chris Dunford. For the publishers, Rosie Pattinson has been positive and constructive at every stage.

INTRODUCTION

Early in 1972 the English educational press carried an advertisement for teachers to staff an 'International School of London' (ISL), which in due course would be offering the International Baccalaureate (IB) Diploma. Those of us who joined then were embarking on a new and little-known career. Expansion was rapid, under the headship of John Parkes and American ownership, until the building, rented from the Working Men's College, was full. The IB programme duly began in 1976. This, and involvement in the European Council of International Schools (ECIS), of which John Parkes became Board Chairman, provided a focus for deeper engagement with the emerging field. After 18 years, ownership was transferred to the Makarem family, who had a tradition of school ownership and management in Lebanon, and at last ISL had a building of its own. On the school's 40th anniversary the ISL group now has other schools, in Surrey, UK, and in Doha, Qatar, and has an established place in the very diverse international education scene which has emerged. This volume is offered as a compendium of reflections triggered by the anniversary, with the benefit of the school's own history and the experience of the expert contributors.

Michael Allan notes that all writing on international education seems obliged to begin by defining it. 'International education' is a floating signifier, a phrase without a circumscribed meaning which is invoked by a variety of users who feel that it gives a valuable impression of their projects. We can see that the field encompasses a huge diversity of institutions and practices and the task is to find any uniformity. We shall explore ways of talking meaningfully about some sectors of international education, and some international schools, because wherever generalizations *can* be made, theories can be deployed and practice can develop. The existence of this volume is evidence, on the other hand, of the intense personal commitment felt by each of the contributing authors, whose engagement has led them to the materially unrewarding but intellectually enriching studies of what they perceive as international education. There is vital research yet to be done on what we, the practitioners and students of international education, find so fascinating.

One reason why international schools are self-consciously concerned with their nature, like an adolescent in a permanent identity crisis, is that they are intrinsically exceptional. Whether teaching in English in a non-English-speaking environment, not following the local system, or founded either as a market alternative to local schools or from global idealism, they are always anomalous. Even where they are part of a group or brand, they are outsiders to their neighbours. This in turn makes the branding of international education as a whole, with its obligations to quality assurance, a problematic project.

To take one example of international school exceptionalism we can look at the curriculum. There is the instrumental curriculum which can be designed according to the visible requirements of the academic or commercial target to which the students are being aimed. Perhaps the choice will be the IB or another of the international options. This can be argued, concluded and explained. But what of the unwritten interstitial curriculum of peer learning, where social skills are acquired?

Schools are social institutions. We are social learners, if we accept the Vygotskyan view, and our actions and learning are conditioned by those key points which unite us with significant others. These group memberships and marks of membership may not be massive, but they allow us to identify with others, and so they define our social lives. Bond and Lun (2013) declare that 'of course, nations do not socialise children; parents do', to which I would add that peers have a great influence, and they are acquired at school. Peer learning is irresistible. What games are played, and what do they teach? There is language that we acquire in the playground *against* the will of our parents. It can be argued that our social and sexual learning came more from our peers than from our parents. In domestic schooling parents can select which peers will teach their children, by – especially in Britain – selecting the school community. In a plural school the society is unfamiliar and hard to gauge, and anyway offers a limited choice. Even the declaration that a school is 'child-centred' leaves open the matter of whose child is at the centre. Because there is so much less that we can take for granted, we need to look harder at international schools and to have more comprehensive ways of looking.

We have already remarked on the isolation of the international school from the local community, and it is this narrowing of the social world during expatriation which makes the school more salient than at home in the lives of children, and of their mothers, too. Group membership is of huge importance in some societies, which is a reason for the popularity of the Third Culture Kid paradigm (Useem and Downie, 1976), as it provides a group in which one can claim membership – although it is clear that a group of expatriates does not have the stability, history or uniformity of an authentic cultural community. Tajfel's work on minimal groups (Brewer, 1979) demonstrated that likeness is not a requirement for group loyalty, as many an expatriate can testify. Companionship on a desert island does not demand many shared interests, but it does lead to rapid learning.

Expatriate communities may be small, even claustrophobic, and at this scale there is a visible 'founder effect' (Mayr, 1963). A single person may have great influence, whether it is the 'old hand' or the charismatic role model. Alternatively, if the effect is negative, the influential figure may be a factor contributing to 'culture shock' (Furnham and Bochner, 1986). On this small scale there can be quantum effects which unbalance the average. The field of operations is intrinsically atomized and the particularities so specific that cases are seldom replicated, yet there must be generalizations if we are to make sense of the past and benefit from experience in the future. The particulate nature of international education, appearing for the most part a school at a time, fits it well to react appropriately in this milieu. It would be impossible to cover in one volume all the directions in which international education has diversified, any more than one could describe all the products and processes of biological evolution. What matters is an adequate way of describing the various starting points, the major lines that have prospered and the ecology of the environment in which they are developing. 'Globalization' is a word repeatedly cited, with the clear implication that there are economic and social factors which operate above the level of our usual national constraints.

Any historical account is of its time, and at one time some issues will be fluid and others stable. In 2013 there are two particular perceptible tensions whose resolution in the future is unclear. In any account of international education, the IB curriculum must have a central place. As the dominant badge of the non-national schools, these non-national programmes (which the editor has taught for 35 years) have been a rallying point for the movement. The IB has provided a normative model deployed in wider and wider contexts, offering highly regarded quality-assured international education throughout the world. In this role its growth has been spectacular, as recounted by Ian Hill, the Deputy Secretary-General from 2000 to 2012 (Hill, 2010), and by Tristan Bunnell (2013). In 1981 it was possible to invite all the IB biology teachers in the world to a weekend conference at Sèvres, in France, and in a few hours to rewrite the syllabus. Thankfully, things have moved on since then. Having no national political agenda, it has become the channel through which notions of 'internationalism' or 'globalism' have become visible in practice. But with the expansion of the IB into national systems it has met a new set of external influences to which it must react, and this will doubtless be formative of its future development. Can it satisfy all the demands upon it, or will it inevitably pursue a specific course, perhaps leaving alternative curricula to appear to meet other perceived needs?

A second, subtler, tension is between the 'internationalist' and 'globalist' visions (Cambridge and Thompson, 2004). These are expressed in a number of forms, and dealt with by several of the contributors, but core points may be distinguished: is it better to think of the world as being constituted by many nations, or as being one world regrettably divided into many nations? In some ways the first, internationalist, view reflects a European social democratic ideology of compromise and cooperation, while the globalist view has attractions for the more ambitious ideologies of the right wing or left wing, and of the New World. Can we, may we, build our ideal world, starting from here? What is so precious to us that we would not sacrifice it for a better future? Who should make the future, and for whom? These are issues much debated in some schools, and by many teachers; what difference will this make as those students grow into the world? As yet it seems that no world statesmen or women came from international schools because the routes to the top table are through success on national ladders. It can be a positive disadvantage in national politics to see the wider picture. Yet there are many in the schools who will try to pass on world-scale concerns through education, and it remains to be seen whether the discourses of internationalism and globalism will operate together or divergently.

In this volume the accounts give a sense of the flow of events at the time of writing, and of the trends which are associated with internal factors, such as the expansion of the community of international schools, and with the external forces of global economics and politics, as well as the 'cultural flows' (Hannerz, 1992) which bring influences from the major contributing communities. Contributors offer some traditional and some novel analyses in search of tools which will provide models for the future development. One thing we may expect is that international education will continue to develop in its own ways and directions, and future school leaders will need to decide which of the tools to use to analyse their situation.

The book is structured in three parts, which gives the reader a choice between sampling areas of particular interest and reading it as a continuous story. The parts are divided by the nature of the viewpoint that each takes. The first three chapters establish the historical outline, giving a taxonomy of international schools past, present and future, a detailed statistical account of their explosive growth and a portrait of the Human Resource (HR) policies that bring families into expatriation in the first place. The second part follows four of the major threads of their practice: the cultural diversity of students, the linguistic needs of a potentially bilingual community, the struggle to sustain individualized pedagogy in a large-scale education system and the global obligations of a worldwide community. The third part steps back and offers four types of analysis which may be useful in generalizing about an increasingly diverse community of schools: discourse can be analysed in all institutions and can be used to trace influences; the formative contributions of schools to the development of the IB are related; Bernsteinian analysis of pedagogical discourse gives a means of comparing internal philosophy with external influences; and finally mapping the internal social structure of schools can be used to illuminate the channels of power and influence.

Part one

The opening chapter lays out some essential information about the history of international education, through the eyes of two of the leading authorities. Jeff Thompson and Mary Hayden have made the University of Bath the prime centre of research and teaching in international education. Their Centre for the study of Education in an International Context (CEIC) is the first port of call for information or evaluations among researchers. From this vantage point they give a concise account of the present school scene and of its antecedents, and add some informed speculation about what the future may bring. Their classification of the current scene is illuminating, separating the three main streams of educational institutions that have used the title of 'international schools' on economic, historical and social grounds, but also examining the various claims to the existence of a discrete field of 'international education'. When their focus turns to the future they offer provocative metaphors for consideration of possibilities far beyond present horizons, imagining developments within social, commercial and political landscapes that are yet to come.

One problem of writing history is finding sources. Developments are happening at an exponential rate, as Brummitt and Keeling record. There is evidence of a localization, even a popularization, of 'international education' in the developing world. As the UN Millennium Goal of primary education for all recedes from reach, local markets and local entrepreneurs rush to supply the demand for quantity and quality in local terms, among those who can afford it. While close study has been made of the earliest pioneers, there has been no unifying body to chart the growth that has followed. By their diverse nature, new international schools often arise in the interstices between the old in this expanding universe, and even cataloguing their existence is an arduous task outside the remit of any existing body. Seeing this need, Nicholas Brummitt has established a niche consultancy which assembles and distributes data about these 'social factors' in the schools' ecology, in the vital area of potential competitors or collaborators. There may be many reasons why a school exists and various local factors to which it responds, but recording their presence and the services that support them is fundamental to any broad picture of the scene.

The economic context of international education is seldom examined by those working within the field. As culture has been overlooked because it is, as Trompenaars says, like water to a fish (Trompenaars and Hampden-Turner, 1997), so the HR needs of international commerce, which are a major demand driving the foundation of international schools, have been overlooked in the schools literature. Susan Shortland draws on data from the field of international HR to chart changes in the expatriation policies of Western multinationals. There is a rich vein of literature, relatively unknown among the schools, through which she explores the arguments for the role of international schools in company policies, and the risks, and even possible benefits, of expatriation in the eyes of the families. The consequences of company and family decisions have great importance for the schools, but only appear at a later stage. This original review raises questions about the way in which global commerce interacts with its service industries, and invites further investigation from either partner in this dyad.

Part two

International education is a broad stream, but in mapping its banks, its depths and its eddies we should not forget to study the water. The students passing through international education are various, and it is the range of needs which they and their families perceive that shapes the institutions. Pearce explores the discourse that has been used in 'mainstream' international schools to describe students, and finds from two specific sources that the constructs that have been used over the years reflect some curiously antiquated conceptualizations of student identity. Schooling is a normative process, and international teachers arrive with national training and norms, just as the students come with their own expectations of the role of a student. Is there in fact a recognizable discourse of international education in this scattered babel of practices? It is suggested that in the future so diverse a set of needs would be better served by a more particulate characterization of students, which calls for a better model of identity and an enhanced awareness of cultural diversity on the part of international educators.

Maurice Carder, a pioneer in promoting the linguistic pluralism that characterizes most of the non-Anglophone world, charts the flow and ebb of bilingualism in the organizations and curricula of international education. He finds that the inertia of Anglophone expectations has established in practice a monoglot community, with some 'foreign languages'. Perhaps it is precisely because of this monoglot mindset that Anglophones have needed to found special schools when they encounter the linguistic diversity of the outside world. It is curious that international schools pride themselves on the number of nationalities they contain, but find the number of languages those students bring to be an embarrassing and expensive problem. The dichotomous classification of 'English' and 'Foreign Languages' persists in some places, and there are still some schools that have a policy of employing only mother tongue English speakers, so that parity of esteem among languages is a distant prospect. Mother tongue teachers are a means of bringing polyglots into the teaching community, to the advantage of all, and Carder has proposals that could enfranchise the great variety of non-English-speaking children, as well as enriching the linguistic world of the English speakers.

The International Baccalaureate Diploma programme is in many ways central to the discourse of international education. It is a major outcome, responding to early perceptions of need, and as it has grown since the 1960s, it has had a formative influence on subsequent developments as an exemplar of the practice and the principles of international education. From its beginnings it has incorporated a high degree of the idealistic intentions. In his early article on the possible missions of international schools Matthews offered two alternative orientations, an idealistic mission or a pragmatic mission (Matthews, 1989), and it was clear which had priority in the IB. Taking one specific and recognizable early influence, the educational philosophy of Johan Pestalozzi, David and Veronica Wilkinson survey the evolution of the priorities of the IB. They observe, through IB publications, a change of balance from the laboratory stage in a limited number of enthusiastic institutions to the mass popularity of the programme in an expanding market. Seeking the accepting relationship between teacher and student that Pestalozzi felt essential for moral growth, they find that the best location for such a situation, the Theory of Knowledge course, has become pressurized by the need for standardized testing. They propose that there has been a movement towards prioritizing success in material directions, such as university entry, over the lifelong ideological humanitarian commitment of the student in earlier days. It is still possible for boarding institutions to pursue the wider mission, but the structure of the programme no longer intrinsically accommodates the 'education of the heart' which Pestalozzi advocated.

And what is the destination for which international education is preparing children? Is it offering to fit diverse children for a single, uniform and ideal world – the globalist mission – or for a peaceful world of many nations – the internationalist vision, to use Cambridge and Thompson's classic taxonomy (2004)? Is there one process or many; it certainly goes under a number of names? Roberts follows what is perhaps the most prominent thread of current discourse, global citizenship, and examines the emergence of an educational vision that looks beyond the provision of good citizens responding to national needs. This vision is rare in the sponsors of schools, and secondary to most expatriate parents, but it is widespread among those who choose to teach abroad. 'Internationalism' has been supported in recent decades by governments in domestic settings, aware of the need to survive and to compete in a world market. There are now contributions to this apparently idealistic campaign from many directions – national, international and supranational.

Part three

Michael Allan acknowledges the difficulties of finding valid tools for comparing so diverse a field. He offers an introduction to discourse analysis, a rigorous investigative tool which can be combined with the insights of Foucault to explore not merely the discourse but the structure of knowledge and power that it constructs. This can be used at any level in the system to explore the social imaginaries, the motivations and the distribution of power among the many players. This is applied to education policies in the Western nations and to the discourse of international education, taking the IB programme as an indicator of that discourse. He examines the role of the

IB and its relation to the discourses of globalization and internationalism, considering especially the interplay of national and supranational ideological forces. Recognizing that international education draws for its ideology upon national sources, dominated by Western Anglophone influences, he notes the predictable consequences for the access of non-English speakers to the arena. He concludes by drawing a further theme from the discourse which has arisen in the field, asking whether international education has managed to question itself sufficiently to establish a recognizable philosophy.

The IB, and in particular the IB Diploma programme, has emerged as an achievement of international education and consequently as the globally visible indicator of what is going on within it. Originating in the post-war period as an initiative of the largely British International Schools Association, the Diploma programme was opened to schools in the 1970s, and was extended by the Middle Years and Primary Years programmes in the 1990s. The essential history is well documented by Tristan Bunnell and others in this volume, supplementing the detailed history published over a period by Ian Hill, Deputy-Director from 2000 to 2012, and enriching the picture through an account of its dynamics. Bunnell in particular raises the question of the role of pioneer schools, with a detailed account of the early days. He shows that during the 1970s the schools were literally responsible for its survival, and acted as enthusiastic models and advocates for the programme, as well as playing active roles in its development which have now been taken in-house as the organization has grown.

How are we to generalize where there is such diversity? Cambridge finds Bernstein's taxonomy a useful lens, and applies it to the principal curriculum, the programmes of the IB, which has come to characterize a major stream of international education. Examining the distributive rules by which admission to IB Diploma programmes is controlled, applying the recontextualization rules to IB and home country history curricula and evaluative rules to the newly modified Middle Years Programme, he traces axes of tension on which the position of the programme is still uncertain. In conclusion he raises questions about the future relation of the IB to international schools in view of the powerful market demands of domestic school systems.

As well as the isolation of international schools from one another and from their host national environment, their operation is compartmentalized by invisible internal boundaries, as it is in any organization. The separation between an international school and its context, which has been advanced as almost the key characteristic, is a property of its outer boundary. But while we may speak about a school as a single institution, in reality there are also internal communities where dialogue is shared, and partitions which separate and make it possible for flows to be monitored. In such circumstances, together with the inevitable inequalities of power, every school has an internal political environment. Richard Caffyn traces the lines which may divide, and examines what parts of school life are contested in this way, using three examples of studies. These are realities, with many features which will be familiar to practitioners, and his approach gives us ways to trace them and ponder on their management. By controlling these boundaries the empowered groups define and filter the discourse within them, and manipulate policy to greater or lesser effect. This is another example of an analytic tool which is particularly apt for use in international schools.

References

Bond, M.H. and Lun, V.M.-C. (2013), *Citizen-Making: The Role of National Goals for Socializing Children*. Manuscript submitted for review. Hong Kong: Hong Kong Polytechnic University.

Brewer, M.B. (1979), 'Ingroup bias in the minimal intergroup situation: A cognitive motivational analysis', *Psychological Bulletin*, 86, 307–324.

Bunnell, T. (2013), 'International Baccalaureate and the role of the "pioneer" international schools', in R. Pearce (ed), *International Education and Schools: Moving Beyond the First Forty Years*. London: Bloomsbury, pp. 167–182.

Cambridge, J.C. and Thompson, J.J. (2004), 'Internationalism and globalisation as contexts for international education', *Compare*, 34(2), 157–171.

Furnham, A. and Bochner, S. (1986), *Culture Shock*. London: Methuen.

Hannerz, U. (1992), *Cultural Complexity: Studies in the Social Organization of Meaning*. New York: Columbia University Press.

Hill, I. (2010), *The International Baccalaureate: Pioneering in Education*, The International Schools Journal Compendium, Volume IV. Woodbridge: John Catt Educational Limited.

Matthews, M. (1989), 'The scale of international education', Pt I, *International Schools Journal*, 17, 7–17.

Mayr, E. (1963), *Animal Species and Evolution*. Cambridge, MA: Belknap Press of Harvard University Press.

Trompenaars, F. and Hampden-Turner, C. (1997), *Riding the Waves of Culture: Understanding Cultural Diversity in Business*. London: Nicholas Brealey Publications.

Useem, R.H. and Downie, R.D. (1976), 'Third-culture kids', *Today's Education*, 103–105.

PART ONE
A Historical Overview

CHAPTER ONE

International Schools: Antecedents, Current Issues and Metaphors for the Future

Mary Hayden and Jeff Thompson

Introduction

In celebrating the 40th anniversary of the International School of London (ISL) that has given rise to the publication of this book, we have set out to consider the international school sector from a macro perspective, charting developments over a number of years (including the 40 years of ISL's existence), raising issues that are current in the early twenty-first century and attempting to predict possible developments in international schools of the future. It may still be the case that, as Hayden and Thompson suggested in 2008, international schools are in many respects a well-kept secret, with the majority worldwide completely unaware of their existence. Education is, after all, still principally a national commodity. The links between education and national contexts are, however, increasingly being challenged, and not only by the growth in numbers of international schools around the world. Challenges also arise from the increase in numbers of educational programmes designed to be international rather than national in focus that are proving increasingly attractive in national, state-funded education systems. The demand for the International Baccalaureate Diploma in US high schools, for instance, and the popularity of the International Primary Curriculum in state-funded schools in England and Wales are just two examples of this recent phenomenon.

It is a cliché to say that the world is changing rapidly. But the speed and effects of that change are central to the changes in the international school sector that can be tracked over past years to the present, and that are key to the issues facing international schools today. Though international schools existed before the term 'globalization' was coined, the precursors to what we now know as globalization were undoubtedly instrumental in creating the early educational establishments we would now describe as international schools. And it is globalization and its effects that provide the context and the explanation for the growth and developments in the international school sector we witness today. In the next section we will consider some of the antecedents to those developments, which in turn will lead us to raise a number of issues germane to the international schools of the present, before proposing a number of metaphors for the potential future development of the international school sector.

International schools:
Where did they come from?

In order to trace the antecedents of a present-day phenomenon it is necessary first to be clear about the nature of that phenomenon. The lack of clarity about how to define the international school concept has been written about in a number of sources in recent years (see, e.g., Hayden, 2006) and will not be explored in depth in this chapter. Suffice to say that since no international body has the authority to adjudicate on whether or not a school may describe itself as an international school, the 'international school' label has to be interpreted cautiously. Not only are we unclear as to what we might find within the school, based on that label. Neither can we be certain that we would not find exactly the same characteristics in another school that chooses not to describe itself as an international school. Most international schools are privately funded, and marketing considerations are no doubt important, for many, in determining how the 'international school' label is or is not used in a particular context. That said, there is arguably one main characteristic found in all schools that describe themselves as international schools, or would be considered by others as deserving that label: they offer a curriculum that is not of the 'host country' (the country in which they are located). Until recently we would have included here a second common characteristic – that teaching staff are mostly not of the host country (see, e.g., Hayden and Thompson, 2011) – but as the international sector grows and diversifies this characteristic is changing, for reasons which will become clear later in this section.

Within the large number of institutions included in our broad definition of international schools today are arguably three main subgroups, which we choose to describe as follows:

- 'Type A' 'traditional' international schools: established principally to cater for globally mobile expatriate families for whom the local education system is not considered appropriate

- 'Type B' 'ideological' international schools: established principally on an ideological basis, bringing together young people from different parts of the world to be educated together with a view to promoting global peace and understanding

- 'Type C' 'non-traditional' international schools: established principally to cater for 'host country nationals' – the socio -economically advantaged elite of the host country who seek for their children a form of education different from, and perceived to be of higher quality than, that available in the national education system

In the section 'International schools: some current issues' we will discuss issues arising in these different subgroups as they are manifested today. First we will use them as a basis for tracing antecedents of the *status quo*, as follows.

'Type A' 'traditional' international schools

It is impossible to claim with any confidence exactly when the first school was established specifically to cater for the children of globally mobile expatriate families, but it was undoubtedly longer ago than we tend to imagine. It has not always been the case, of course, that globally mobile parents were accompanied by their children, and 'boarding schools' in at least some national systems were the norm over many years for the children of colonial administrators and other expatriates. In some contexts, where children did accompany such parents, schools were already in existence in the nineteenth century. What is now the Maseru English Medium Preparatory School in Lesotho, for instance, began in 1890 as the European School of Maseru, whose purpose was to cater for the children of traders, missionaries and officials of the British Administration of the then Basutoland (MEMPS, 1990). This is just one example of the early antecedents of the international schools more commonly thought of as having first arrived on the scene with the establishment of schools such as the International School of Geneva and Yokohama International School, both founded in 1924. Established earlier in the year than Yokohama International School, the International School of Geneva was perhaps the first international school to use that label in its title and is widely considered to have been the first international school of this type (Knight, 1999).

Until the relatively late twentieth century this type of school accounted for the vast majority of international schools in existence. With some variation over time, as the global environment has changed, such schools have continued to cater for expatriate children away from a 'home' national context, usually teaching through the medium of English, sometimes offering a national education system away from the home country and sometimes offering an international programme such as those of the International Baccalaureate. They may also accept local students (where such students are allowed by law to attend international schools), but their principal *raison d'être* is to support the expatriate community of their city or wider region.

'Type B' 'ideological' international schools

Again, it is impossible to say when the first school of this type was established, but, again, it was almost certainly earlier than we might have expected. These schools are different from those discussed above in that they do not exist to respond to a pragmatic market demand. Rather, they have been created specifically to bring young people together, based on an underpinning ideology arising from the belief that many of the problems faced by our world, and, in particular, those problems relating to violence, hatred and war, can be overcome – or at least alleviated – if young people are able to live and study together with those from different national and cultural backgrounds with a view to breaking down the barriers that so often arise through ignorance and prejudice. This subgroup of international schools (for whom such an ideology is their principal *raison d'être*) is much smaller in number than those we have described as Type A, with the most high profile of them being the group of United World Colleges worldwide (UWC, 2013). Originating with the establishment of Atlantic College in 1962, in 2013 there are 13 such colleges, bringing together students from around the world on scholarships to study and, usually, live together – based on the underpinning philosophy of Kurt Hahn and exemplified in the question asked by the then prime minister of Canada, Lester B Pearson, in his 1957 Nobel Peace Prize lecture:

> How can there be peace without people understanding each other, and how can this be if they don't know each other?
>
> (Lester B Pearson College of the Pacific, 1982, p.9)

There are arguably also earlier antecedents for this group of international schools. Hill (2012), for instance, traces the concept of international-mindedness (arguably the ideology on which the UWC are based) as far back as Comenius in the seventeenth century. More recently, what has elsewhere been described as possibly the first international school (Sylvester, 2002), Spring Grove International College, was established in west London in 1866 by a group including Charles Dickens, Cobden, Huxley and Tyndall with a vision to bring young people from different countries to study together. And indeed students (all boys) from a number of different countries (France, Germany, Spain, Portugal, India, North America, Brazil, Chile, Nicaragua and Bermuda) were brought together at Spring Grove, in a project that sadly only lasted until 1889 (Walker, 2011). Spring Grove was a tangible manifestation of a mid-nineteenth-century ideology that saw Charles Dickens proposing (in an article published in 1864) a series of international schools in Europe; a committee being set up by the commissioners of the Paris Universal Exposition of 1855 'to conduct an essay contest on the advantages of a school for pupils of various national origins' (Brickman, 1962 in Sylvester, 2002); and Cobden, as founder and chairman of the International Education Society, advocating international arbitration and disarmament and being one of the then leading advocates of free trade whose vision of international peace was expected to be realized by 'the creation of a new type of education which would enable the citizens of different countries to become international ambassadors' (Stewart, 1972).

'Type C' 'non-traditional' international schools

These international schools are, compared with those described above as Type A and Type B, relative newcomers to the scene. They have arguably only really emerged since the late twentieth century, as investors and entrepreneurs have identified a market in national economic elites who perceive international schools as providing a form of education superior to that available in their own national system. Usually English medium and offering internationally recognized programmes, such schools can be seen as a springboard to university entrance in, for instance, the UK or the US for those who perceive a Western education and fluency in English as a route to future success and prosperity in a globalized world. Such schools tend to be found in countries with an aspirational middle class, often in what might be described as the 'developing world'. Not all countries allow citizens to attend international schools in their home country, while some have changed their view on the acceptability of such access. Thailand, for instance, initially forbade its nationals from attending international schools but then chose to deregulate, since which time tremendous growth in the numbers of international schools has followed, with very many catering almost exclusively for Thai nationals (MacDonald, 2006). Growth of such schools in other countries as well as Thailand has almost certainly accounted for the large increase in numbers of international schools worldwide in recent years. Elsewhere in this volume, for instance, Brummitt and Keeling report ISC Research as suggesting that, between 2000 and 2013, numbers of international schools worldwide have grown from 2,584 to 6,400 (Brummitt and Keeling, 2013), though data are not available from either this source or elsewhere to support our hypothesis that this overall growth can be accounted for largely within what we have described as 'Type C' international schools.

Unlike the Type A and Type B subgroups, it is not clear what the antecedents of Type C international schools might have been. One possibility is the Type A international schools themselves, which, in some countries – though founded initially to cater for the globally mobile – had over time come to cater increasingly for economic elites of the host country. Another possible antecedent, though not international in focus, is the private school sector that already existed in many national contexts as a means of catering for those with aspirations for their children to experience a form of education perceived to be superior to that available in the state-funded sector, partly because of the quality of the infrastructure and facilities and partly because of its inaccessibility to the majority of the population.

International schools: Some current issues

The international school sector, then, has in recent years not only grown rapidly; its growth has been accompanied by increasing diversity as, for varying reasons, the experience of a form of education that is international rather than national becomes increasingly attractive. While such a form of education might have begun as a necessity for children located away from, and unable to access, their home education systems (as provided by Type A schools), it has moved into also being an education of choice for ideological (Type B) and pragmatic (Type C) reasons. This increased diversity brings with it an increased difficulty in making any sort of generalization across the sector. Indeed it throws into question the very use of the term 'sector' or 'system' in the context of international schools.

In 1995 Hayden and Thompson argued that 'for the most part, the body of international schools is a conglomeration of individual institutions which may or may not share an underlying educational philosophy' (1995, p. 332). Since 1995 the situation has changed somewhat, though it is still the case that the majority of 'international schools' – particularly in Type A – are individual institutions catering to a local market need. What has changed markedly since 1995 is the rapid growth in the number of (largely Type C) international schools developed as part of a particular international network. Groupings in Type B schools include the United World Colleges and, in a broad definition of 'international', the European schools created in 1953 for the children of employees of what we now describe as the European Union (Schola Europaea, 2013). Groupings of largely Type C schools arguably include, *inter alia*, Cognita, Nord Anglia, GEMS and Taaleem. A growing and increasingly influential aspect of this phenomenon is the number of schools established as international offspring of well-established and prestigious schools from national systems; in the vast majority of cases, England. Harrow School in west London, for instance, opened the first Harrow International School in Bangkok in 1998 and in

2013 has two further Harrow International Schools located in Hong Kong and Beijing. Others in this rapidly growing grouping of schools that Bunnell describes as based on a 'model of hyper-capitalism' (Bunnell, 2008) – of which Harrow and Dulwich College are the pioneers – include Wellington College, Shrewsbury School, Repton School and Brighton College, among many others. Similar in principle but different in kind are the 'family groupings' developing from some international schools. TASIS schools, for instance, are found in England, Puerto Rico and Switzerland, while, in its 40-year history, the ISL has grown from being one school in London to including schools in Surrey and Doha. The American Community Schools (ACS), meanwhile, have also recently added a Doha branch to their UK locations of Cobham, Egham and Hillingdon, and Sherborne School has similarly opened a branch in Qatar.

Type B schools may not have seen many changes in recent years, while Type A schools have continued to grow in number but not to the same extent as Type C. Interesting in this context are those schools that have shifted their type over time in response to changes in the environment, invariably from Type A to Type C. The ESF schools in Hong Kong, for instance, originally founded to cater for the children of expatriates away from their home country have, since the 1997 handover of Hong Kong from the UK to China, reinvented themselves to cater now also for Hong Kong Chinese students. Other examples undoubtedly exist of Type A international schools gradually responding to increasing demand from host country nationals by shifting the expatriate/host country student balance towards the Type C category. Indeed, in some contexts such has been the demand from host country nationals that a quota system has had to be introduced to ensure that the school's original mission of catering for expatriates is protected.

As the rapid growth and increasing diversity in the 'sector' has become marked, it is arguably now the case that the *only* characteristic all international schools can be argued to have in common is that the curriculum offered is not of the home country. Generalizations that might once have been made about the multicultural nature of student populations, or about teaching populations consisting largely of 'overseas hire' teachers, no longer apply in all such schools. Indeed as larger numbers of 'host country teachers' develop expertise in international programmes such as the International Baccalaureate, the need to appoint 'overseas hire' teachers for their international experience diminishes – a point to which we shall return later.

Perhaps we should now not only avoid using the word 'sector' or 'system' in this context but also find another way of describing the different groupings that avoids implying – through use of the common term 'international school' – that they have much in common at all. That said, there are a number of issues with which many international schools in one or other category will identify, which are discussed as follows.

Nature of the curriculum

As noted, schools in any of the categories above will offer a curriculum not of the country in which they are located. This might be the national programme of another country, such as British international schools offering GCSE and A level, or may be one of the international programmes that have developed since the 1960s. The International Baccalaureate Diploma, first offered in 1970 (Peterson, 1987), has been followed by international versions of national programmes, such as, *inter alia*, the International GCSE, Advanced Placement International Diploma, and more recently, the newly developed International Baccalaureate Middle Years Programme, International Baccalaureate Primary Years Programme, International Primary Curriculum and International Middle Years Curriculum. Thompson's categorization of such programmes according to their origins (exportation, adaptation, integration, creation) is helpful (1998), while their growth in popularity in national contexts – though not central to the theme of this chapter – has been analysed by Hayden (2012). That the leading, or only, language in which each of these programmes is offered is English raises a related issue for international schools with respect to their language of instruction.

English-medium international schools

If a broad umbrella definition of international schools includes schools away from their home country offering the curriculum of that country to expatriate children of that country (Hayden, 2006), then French lycées and other national schools outside their home country are included. It would not be true to claim then that all international schools are English-medium and, in some parts of the world (such as Latin America), many schools fitting this definition are bilingual. The vast majority of international schools are, however, English-medium, with developments in recent years including a growth in the proportion of students attending such schools for whom English is not their first language (Carder, 2007) and for whom, indeed, developing fluency in English may be the primary reason for choosing to attend an international school (MacKenzie et al., 2003). Not only is it the case therefore that international schools increasingly include among their teaching staff experts in English as an Additional Language or English as a Second Language (ESL) who run specialist support services. It is also the case that mainstream teachers without a specialism in this area may be teaching classes where the majority of students are not first language speakers of the language of instruction. Although programmes such as ESL in the Mainstream (Unlocking the World, 2013) have become increasingly popular in response to a need for support in this area, it is undoubtedly the case that too many international school teachers are expected to cope without specific training, and in some schools students may not be as well supported as they and their parents might expect to be the case.

A related issue of concern to some experienced international school educators is the effect on young children of moving from a home environment of one, two or even more languages (depending on the first language of parents and other care-givers) into a school environment where other languages are used, with (possibly) an expectation that young children's natural adaptability and resilience mean that they will somehow 'cope'. For many, the long-term benefits of bi- or multi-lingualism are marked; for some, though, a concern – expressed by, for instance, Kusuma-Powell (2004) and Murphy (2003) – is that an everyday facility in many languages masks a lack of sufficiently deep facility in any one of these languages, with an associated detrimental effect being absence of the ability to move from the concrete stages of cognitive development to abstract conceptualizations. Perhaps an issue of concern for only a small number of children, and most likely to be found in Type A international schools, this is nevertheless an area in which more research is needed.

Teachers in international schools

Hayden and Thompson (2011) have analysed a number of issues relating to teachers in international schools today and the skills they might be expected to require for international schools of the future. Among the issues highlighted by Hayden and Thompson is the growing difficulty of teacher recruitment noted by many international school leaders. As the international school 'sector' changes, so does the nature of the population of teachers to be found in such schools. Until recently in many international schools would have been found teachers from the three distinct categories highlighted by, for instance, Garton (2000):

- host country nationals
- 'local hire' expatriates
- 'overseas hire' expatriates

with the nature of the salary and benefits package often improving in moving from the first of these categories to the third. At least one reason behind the prevalence of this categorization, however, lies in the expectation that expatriates will have expertise in areas not found in host country teachers including, for instance, experience of teaching an international programme such as IGCSE, or the IB Diploma. As numbers of schools offering such programmes have increased, and as increasing numbers of host country nationals have been recruited to teach on those programmes, so has it become the case that recruiting expatriates to teach international programmes may not be as essential as it was once believed to be.

Increasingly, therefore, international schools may have large numbers of host country nationals on the teaching staff. Before we conjure up a vision, however, of most international schools (of whichever type) having experienced such change, it is important to remember another relevant factor. While it may be that the increasing difficulty of recruiting teachers for international schools noted by many Heads and Principals is ameliorated to some extent by the growing availability of experienced host country teachers, parental pressure cannot be ignored in what are almost exclusively private, fee-paying schools. Host country and expatriate teachers may have equal levels of experience in a particular programme, but in many cases the perceived prestige of children being educated by an expatriate rather than a host country teacher, or by a native English speaker rather than a non-native speaker, will create parental pressure on the Head and Board which can be difficult to resist – particularly in a context where international schools are in competition and parents have choice. Rightly or wrongly, for as long as it remains the case that international schools are catering for globally mobile aspirational middle classes seeking an educational advantage for their children, it may well remain the case that overseas hire expatriates have an advantage over their often equally well-qualified and experienced host country counterparts.

In this section we have highlighted just some of the issues currently prevalent in international schools of the early twenty-first century. The next section will move from a consideration of the current situation to speculation about what international schools might look like, and what issues might be of relevance to them, in the future.

What the future might hold: Changing contexts

To try to predict what the future might hold could be considered brave, if not foolhardy, and it is a rash author who would claim high levels of confidence in any attempt to suggest what the future might have in store. In the current context of rapid changes in society, national and global, it could be considered unwise to attempt to propose what might happen even next week. We therefore offer the suggestions and proposals that underpin the remainder of this chapter not in the expectation that they will be taken as holy writ, or that readers will believe them to be based on a greater ability to foresee the future than is the gift of any other researcher or practitioner with an interest in this area, but rather in the hope that they will stimulate reflection and discussion. If readers find some of our proposals unconvincing, but are prompted to reflect on why they are unconvincing and in doing so to propose alternatives, then this section will have served its purpose.

We begin with the premise that we cannot extrapolate from the *status quo* and assume the future will bring 'more of the same'. Changes in even the past 10 years suggest that that is unlikely to be the case. Though without any real rationale other than the 40-year anniversary of the ISL celebrated by this book, our predictions will be located within the coming 40 years. We hope that some younger readers may be able to judge the accuracy of our predictions by re-reading this chapter in 40 years' time!

Why schools?

One fundamental question that surely needs to be asked in any consideration of the future of education is whether schools – whether international or national – will continue to exist. Schools as we currently know them – where young people come together in buildings, divided into groups by (usually) age and interacting with teachers who have expertise in promoting learning – have arguably developed in this form as a means of preparing young people for adult life in a way that would not be possible if they were educated by their parents and other family members alone. In less developed societies and in earlier times, the young could have learned the skills required, of hunting or homemaking for instance, from their parents. The more developed society has become, the more knowledge and skills it has acquired, and so the more necessary has it become for the young of that society to be educated by specialists and individuals who are themselves highly educated and able to support the next generations in the acquisition and development of those skills and knowledge.

But if we have developed systems over the years for the sharing of knowledge and skills through face-to-face interaction in what we describe as schools and classrooms, the assumption that these systems continue to be the most appropriate means of facilitating learning is already being challenged by rapid advances in technology which mean that young people's knowledge and skills are increasingly developed through interaction not only with parents and teachers but also with individuals, databases and other features of the internet. As a consequence, children increasingly have knowledge and skills that are neither learned from their parents and/or teachers nor shared by their parents and teachers. The widespread accessibility of the internet has massive consequences for society of which we are only just becoming aware. In some educational contexts, the benefits of easy internet access are being harnessed. YouTube clips and other internet-based resources can be used effectively in lessons, while the International Baccalaureate, for instance, is already offering online versions of its Diploma Programme courses (Allen, 2011). Such organizations are part of a growing move, stimulated by the internet, away from the notion that learning must happen in particular geographic locations.

Our first suggestion, therefore, is that during the next 40 years such trends will continue to grow, and in so doing will challenge the assumption that, for learning to take place, the learners need to congregate in buildings with their 'teachers'. We are not envisaging that schools as we know them will disappear. There are of course other purposes served by schools in relation to the socialization of our young, and other social forms of learning developed through physical interaction that would not take place if every student were to be based all day in the family home interacting with electronic devices. But while the rationale for schools as buildings might remain strong in local village or town communities, will that rationale be so strong in the context currently served by Type A international schools, of globally mobile families whose children move from school to school, country to country, at frequent intervals? If the *raison d'être* of international schools founded to cater for mobile expatriates has been to provide a form of education not available in the local education system, might not such a form of education be provided to the child moving with parents to different locations worldwide, but interacting throughout their formal schooling years with an online education provider – with the benefit of continuity of experience, however frequent the physical relocation? It is not difficult to imagine a scenario where international schools as we now know them are replaced – or supplemented – by 'virtual' international schools, where virtual teaching is provided to groups of students scattered around the globe, interacting not only with their virtual teacher(s) but also with other students through online fora that stimulate discussion and debate. For generations brought up on Facebook and other social media sites, being part of a virtual rather than physical school community would surely not be as strange a phenomenon as it appears to those of us educated more formally in earlier times.

The effects of globalization

Linked to the rapid developments in technology that may challenge the very concept of schools are the many changes and developments arising from and influencing what might be described as globalization. The work of Friedman (2005) has been much quoted in this context, suggesting that since approximately the year 2000 we have been in the so-called 'third era' of globalization, where individuals (rather than countries, or multinational companies) collaborate and compete globally. The world is shrinking, says Friedman, from 'small' to 'tiny', with globalization now being driven not by Europeans and Americans (as in eras 1 and 2) but by more diverse groups – giving rise to his assertion that 'the world is flat' (2005). Rischard referred to such aspects of globalization ('the new world economy') as being one of the two large forces that will change the world as we know it by about 2020, the second being the 'demographic explosion' taking the population of our planet from around 5 billion in 1990 through around 6 billion in 2002 to a proposed 8 billion between 2020 and 2025 (Rischard, 2002). Around 95% of the 2 billion by which the population will grow by about the year 2025, says Rischard, will be in developing countries, and most will flock to the cities, with about 60 cities worldwide (twice the number in 1990) having more than 5 million inhabitants. Taken alongside the developing economies of, for example, the BRICS countries (Brazil, Russia, India, China and South Africa), it is not difficult to envisage a scenario where what we have termed 'Type C' international schools will grow rapidly in number (in those countries where host country nationals are allowed to attend them) as they prove increasingly attractive to the growing 'middle classes' who are losing confidence in the home education system and/or who seek a competitive edge for their children through a Western form of education (Lowe, 2000).

Not least of the characteristics of international schools likely to prove attractive to those seeking a 'Western' form of education for their children is the English-medium education provided. There can be little doubt that English is now the dominant international language, with estimates that in 2005 there were 1.5 billion users worldwide of whom roughly one-third each are native speakers, speakers of English as a Second Language and speakers of English as a Foreign Language (Gray, 2006). The same researcher suggests that by 2015 approximately half the world's population (about 3.5 billion) will either speak or be learning English, while Thomas (pers. comm.) suggests that bilingualism, in the form of English plus mother tongue – currently the norm for educated elites worldwide – is likely to become the norm for many more, in the short term at least. Gray (2006) suggests, however, that in subsequent years these numbers will decrease as other languages become increasingly widely spoken internationally. We propose that the demand for English-medium international schools offering a 'Western' form of education to the host country socio-economically advantaged will continue to grow strongly in the near future (and perhaps for the 40 years about which we speculate). We recognize, however, that a predicted decline in the dominance of English as the global *lingua franca* – though perhaps not until after the 40-year lifespan of our crystal ball – is likely to have an effect on the international school sector. What that effect might be we cannot predict, as the popularity of the English-medium 'Western' schooling is linked not only to the dominance of English as an international language but also to the prestige of English-medium universities such as Harvard, Yale, Oxford and Cambridge to which many of the global middle classes aspire. How might changes in the global dominance of English affect international schools? As already noted, English-medium education is currently the reason for many parents choosing an international school for their child (MacKenzie et al., 2003). Quite what the impact might be of a decline in the dominance of English is beyond the capability of our crystal ball. It is worth noting, however, that an impact of some sort there will undoubtedly be.

What, then, of the schools we have described as the 'Type A' international schools? If those (Type C) catering for host country elites seem likely to grow in number, is the same likely to be true of those more traditional international schools – largely catering for globally mobile expatriates? Here we can envisage two possible scenarios. In Scenario 1, the developing global economy will lead to increased numbers of multinational organizations having larger numbers of regional bases and growing numbers of globally mobile employees. The careers of such employees will be based on short periods spent in different locations, thus necessitating (notwithstanding our speculation that schools as buildings may have a limited lifespan) growing numbers of international schools to cater for those for whom the local education system is not appropriate, and for whom an English-medium education offering globally recognized programmes is attractive. In this scenario, the numbers of 'Type A' international schools will continue to grow.

In Scenario 2, multinational organizations will continue to exist and may indeed continue to grow in number. But instead of growth leading to increased numbers of employees and their families leading globally mobile lifestyles, in this scenario we envisage such organizations reducing the numbers of their employees flying around the world. Increasingly sophisticated technology will reduce the necessity for regular face-to-face contact, while global security concerns will mean professionals are less willing to travel or to live in some parts of the world, and increasing fuel costs together with concern for the environment will make frequent travel less attractive. We find difficult to judge which of these two scenarios is the more likely. What seems certain, however – whichever predicted scenario turns out to be more accurate – is that the growth in 'Type A' schools will be overtaken by the growth in 'Type C' schools. We feel confident in predicting that, for the foreseeable future at least, the proportion of 'Type A' international schools in the international school sector as a whole will decrease.

National systems of education

In attempting to envisage what the future might hold for international schools, it should be noted that what might once have been a dichotomy whereby international schools offer international education and national schools offer national education has been gradually breaking down. It has been argued elsewhere (Hayden and Thompson, 1995) that international schools do not necessarily offer international education: arguably some international schools essentially offer a national form of education transplanted to a different geographical location. It can now more confidently also be argued that many national schools no longer offer a purely national form of education, for a number of reasons. Immigration leading to developed countries becoming increasingly multicultural, together with the effects of globalization, has led schools to recognize the necessity for education to prepare young people – whether or not they plan to leave their national context in adulthood – for a future where interdependence of countries is the norm and actions in one part of the world influence what happens in another. Growing numbers of national schools, both state-funded and independent, in different national contexts, are now offering what might be described as international programmes, such as the International Primary Curriculum and those of the International Baccalaureate (Hayden, 2012), and/or are introducing an international dimension to the curriculum in some other way (Hayden, 2011; Hayden and Thompson, 2013) with a view to encouraging the development in students of broader, more international, perspectives. We envisage that the future will see further developments in this respect, with national forms of education increasingly including international dimensions in recognition that the future for which school-age students are being prepared can no longer be assumed to be constrained by national boundaries. One consequence of such a development is that if ever international schools had a monopoly on international education, that will no longer be the case. If a major reason for parents to send their child to an international school is, currently, in order that they should experience an international form of education, then competition in this respect from national schools could lead to a reduction in the demand for an international school education. Other factors are clearly at work of course, but changes in national education systems cannot be ignored in terms of their possible knock-on effects on the international school sector.

Pragmatic and ideological perspectives

Closely linked to differences within international schools currently, and likely to remain as major factors in international schools of the future, are two themes clearly identifiable as running through any consideration of these schools. Matthews (1989) argued that two types of international school exist that could be described as ideology-driven (founded in order to further international understanding and cooperation) or market-driven (all other international schools that have arisen from the needs of expatriate communities). More recently, and as Matthews himself has argued since, it may be 'more realistic to envisage the grouping of international schools as representing a spectrum, with the ideological at one end and the market-driven at the other' (Hayden, 2006, p. 17), with most international schools reconciling both sets of characteristics to varying degrees. In our classification above, Type B schools are defined as principally ideology-driven. Type A schools, meanwhile, reconcile both sets of characteristics to different degrees, while Type C schools are principally pragmatic in rationale and implementation. Similar concepts, but using different terminology, were described by Cambridge and Thompson (2004) in referring to globalizing and internationalist perspectives, the latter being identified with the promotion of peace, international understanding, cooperation and international mindedness. The globalizing perspective, meanwhile, sees international schools as a form of globalization 'spin off', providing a form of education that 'may be compared with other globally marketed goods and services such as soft drinks and hamburgers, a reliable product conforming to consistent quality standards throughout the world' (Cambridge and Thompson, 2004) which is attractive to both globally mobile expatriates and national socio-economic elites. The 'globalising current' of international education, says Cambridge, is 'influenced by and contributes to the global diffusion of the values of free-market capitalism…expressed…in terms of quality assurance, through the application of international accreditation procedures, the spread of quality standards and the global certification of educational qualifications' (Cambridge, 2002). Hayden (2006) and Hayden and Thompson (2008) used the terms 'pragmatic' and 'ideological' to describe very similar concepts, suggesting that international schools will demonstrate different balances of the two influences. We will draw on these two concepts in the next section.

Metaphors for international schools

What follows are four different metaphors for international schools that we propose might be conceived within the next 40 years. Whether or not any or all of them emerge will depend upon the balance of factors already discussed within this chapter, as well as on factors that we have not foreseen. As stated earlier, we do not claim to have any certainty about our predictions. Rather, we hope that they will stimulate discussion and debate – and perhaps disagreement and challenge – which will make a positive contribution to our understanding of this increasingly influential sector.

The 'hotel chain' metaphor

This metaphor is based upon an assumption that continued extensive growth in the international school sector will be accompanied by increased availability of choice in curriculum programmes designed to be international in focus, thus leading to enhanced competition in the international school marketplace. International schools will continue to be principally English-medium, we envisage, and growth in numbers of international schools will be accompanied by the establishment of new international universities/higher education institutions which provide training for large numbers of teachers intending to work in the international school sector. Using this metaphor, growth in the international school sector can be represented as accompanying developments in the global economy that will lead to increased numbers of multinational organizations, globally mobile expatriate professionals and expatriate children seeking an English-medium international school education. We envisage this situation as essentially optimistic, leading to what we describe as the 'hotel chain' metaphor for international schools; effectively a global business providing different levels of international school education to suit the wide range of parental (and employer) capacity to pay.

This notion (of, for instance, international schools classified as standard/ mid-range/deluxe or 3*, 5*, 7*) is, of course, not entirely new. The GEMS group of schools worldwide already operates something similar (GEMS, 2013). In the 'hotel chain' metaphor, pragmatic dimensions tend to have a higher profile than the ideological, and issues arising include those of quality assurance across the burgeoning sector and its subgroups.

The 'exclusive' metaphor

This metaphor, we envisage, will apply to a context where many national systems of education have developed to incorporate a significant international dimension to the curriculum. The possibly reduced size of the market for international schools then renders them more of a niche market. A continuing shortage of teachers and administrators (Heads, Principals), plus the possible growth in dominance of languages other than English as world languages, would lead to what we describe as the 'exclusive' metaphor for international schools where the pragmatic and ideological are more or less evenly balanced. In this model we envisage an increase in numbers of new international curriculum/assessment/certification programmes being developed to satisfy the 'credentialist' demand for high-stakes, high-status qualifications which become a curriculum of preference compared with other, non-international, programmes on offer. Quality assurance, accreditation, authorization and audit of schools would be organized and monitored in this context, we suggest, through a peer-controlled 'World Education Assembly', and students educated through the international school sector would tend to pursue their further studies through an international system of elite higher education institutions/universities with a focus on research and development.

The 'spa resort' metaphor

This metaphor is based on the notion of education reaching large numbers of *individuals* at a distance. All individuals will have direct access to the wide range of appropriate 'knowledge bases' and 'skill development programmes' which will be created, some of which already exist. Thus the case for schools to exist *per se*, in the traditional forms to which we have become accustomed, will be much reduced in impact. Collaboration would be developed between schools that provide expertise in specific areas, as specialist schools linked into the 'network' of international schools. In this scenario, individual students would be brought together for periods of shared interaction through, for instance, 'summer schools', short courses and study breaks. A number of world languages will be commonly used, and there would be variety in the languages used more widely. Regional networks would be developed of, for instance, small, one-semester institutions and summer school providers, generating opportunities for developing social skills, relationships and affective and physical development. The diverse programme of activities offered would be coordinated by a central administrative bureaucracy. In what we have described as the 'spa resort' metaphor for international schools, the ideological dimension would have greater prominence in curriculum planning than the pragmatic dimension.

The 'food court' metaphor

In this fourth of our metaphors we propose that there will be greater recognition of the importance of reducing the distinctions in status that have existed, in many parts of the world, between what might be described as 'academic education' and various patterns of 'vocational' or 'professional' education. This metaphor incorporates the high value that will be placed on academic understanding as well as on concurrent professional and vocational skill development, with preparation for further study, potential employment and lifelong learning providing an appropriate balance to meet changing demands globally. The emphasis in this scenario, which we describe as the 'food court metaphor', will be on meeting individual preferences and needs, allowing wide choice across traditional academic, professional and vocational 'subject streams', together with the design of curricula that incorporate concurrent academic and vocational study by any individual student. Schools here will demonstrate institutional flexibility for the introduction of new material and innovations in pedagogy, while pragmatic and ideological dimensions will be more or less evenly balanced in their influence. International schools described by this metaphor will ensure that close social interaction is maintained between students within different programmes and will provide opportunities for innovative curriculum planning.

Conclusion

In this chapter, we have outlined some of the antecedents to the international sector as it is now, traced some relevant developments and changes, and highlighted some of the issues and challenges facing international schools today. We have also attempted to predict, without claiming any great certainty in the accuracy of our predictions, some possible characteristics of the international school sector of the future.

Forty years ago, which international schools could have predicted the changes there were to be in the world and the nature of the curriculum they would be offering today? Those international schools in existence 40 years ago and still here today, including the ISL, have developed and flourished not only because in the 1970s they were offering an attractive and high quality form of education, but also because they have moved with the times in such a way as still to be able to offer an attractive and high quality form of education in 2013. Such flexibility has allowed the ISL, for instance, to introduce new international programmes; to develop expertise in and promote recognition of the importance of responding to the particular needs of globally mobile students through, for instance, the provision of mother tongue programmes; to open new branches of the school internationally; and to contribute to the promotion of international education by collaborating with other like-minded individuals and institutions through networks such as the Alliance for International Education, hosting conferences aimed at the furtherance of international mindedness through education (AIE, 2013). None of us can predict with any confidence what the future holds for international schools or, indeed, for the rapidly changing world more generally. What seems likely, however – whether or not any of our predictions turn out to have accuracy – is that the international schools of today that are still in existence in 40 years' time will be those that are sensitive to the rapidly changing environment and needs of students, and are as flexible in modifying the form of education offered as have been the international schools of 40 years ago that are still so successful today.

References

Allen, K. (2011), 'Extending access to the diploma programme: IB courses online', in M.C. Hayden and J.J. Thompson (eds), *Taking the IB Diploma Programme Forward*. Woodbridge: John Catt Educational, pp. 91–104.

Alliance for International Education. www.intedalliance.org (Accessed 3 March 2013).

Brummitt, N. and Keeling, A. (2013), 'International schools: charting the growth', in R. Pearce (ed) *International Education and Schools: Moving Beyond the First Forty Years*. London: Bloomsbury, pp. 25–36.

Bunnell, T. (2008), 'The exporting and franchising of elite English private schools: the emerging "second wave"', *Asia Pacific Journal of Education*, 28(4), 383–393.

Cambridge, J.C. (2002), 'Global product branding and international education', *Journal of Research in International Education*, 1(2), 227–243.

Cambridge, J.C. and Thompson, J.J. (2004), 'Internationalism and globalisation as contexts for international education', *Compare*, 34(2), 157–171.

Carder, M. (2007), *Bilingualism in International Schools: A Model for Enriching Language Education*. Clevedon: Multilingual Matters.

Friedman, T. (2005), *The World is Flat: a Brief History of the Globalized World in the 21st Century*. London: Allen Lane (Penguin).

Garton, B. (2000), 'Recruitment of teachers for international education', in M.C. Hayden and J.J. Thompson (eds), *International Schools and International Education: Improving Teaching, Management and Quality*. London: Kogan Page, pp. 85–95.

GEMS. (2013), http://www.gemseducation.com/gems-schools/ (Accessed 3 March 2013).

Gray, K. (2006), *The Globalisation of English*. Public lecture given at the University of Bath, 8 February.

Hayden, M.C. and Thompson, J.J. (1995), 'International schools and international education: a relationship reviewed', *Oxford Review of Education*, 21(3), 327–345.

Hayden, M.C. (2006), *Introduction to International Education: International Schools and their Communities*. London: Sage.

Hayden, M.C. (2011), 'Transnational spaces of education: the growth of the international school sector', *Globalisation, Societies and Education*, 9(2), 211–224.

Hayden, M.C. (2012), 'A review of curriculum in the UK: internationalising in a changing context', *Curriculum Journal*, 24(1), 8–26.

Hayden, M.C. and Thompson, J.J. (2008), *International Schools: Growth and Influence*. Paris: UNESCO International Institute for Educational Planning.

Hayden, M.C. and Thompson, J.J. (2011), 'Teachers for the International School of the future', in R. Bates (ed), *Schooling Internationally: Globalisation, Internationalisation and the Future for International Schools*. London: Routledge, pp. 83–100.

Hayden, M.C. and Thompson, J.J. (2013), 'International mindedness: connecting concepts to practice', in L. Stagg (ed), *International Mindedness: Global Perspectives for Learners and Educators*. Rochester: Urbane Publications. (in press)

Hill, I. (2012), 'Evolution of education for international mindedness', *Journal of Research in International Education*, 11(3), 245–261.

Knight, M. (1999), *Ecolint: A Portrait of the International School of Geneva 1924–1999*. Geneva: International School of Geneva.

Kusuma-Powell, O. (2004), 'Multilingual, but not making it in international schools', *Journal of Research in International Education*, 3(2), 157–172.

Lester B. Pearson College of the Pacific. (1982), *Adventures in High Endeavour: People Understanding People. The Story of Lester B. Pearson College of the Pacific*. Toronto: Brownstone.

Lowe, J. (2000), 'Assessment and educational quality: implications for international schools', in M.C. Hayden and J.J. Thompson (eds), *International Schools and International Education: Improving Teaching, Management and Quality*. London: Kogan Page, pp. 15–28.

MacDonald, J. (2006), 'The international school industry', *Journal of Research in International Education*, 5(2), 191–213.

MacKenzie, P., Hayden, M.C. and Thompson, J.J. (2003), 'Parental priorities in the selection of international schools', *Oxford Review of Education*, 29(3), 299–314.

Matthews, M. (1989), 'The scale of international education', *International Schools Journal*, 17, 7–17.

Maseru English Medium Preparatory School. (1990), *Maseru Prep 1890–1990: The School in the Sky*. Maseru: Maseru English Medium Preparatory School.

Murphy, E. (2003), 'Monolingual international schools and the young non-English speaking child', *Journal of Research in International Education*, 2(1), 25–45.

Peterson, A.D.C. (1987), *Schools Across Frontiers: The Story of the International Baccalaureate and the United World Colleges*. La Salle, IL: Open Court.

Rischard, J.F. (2002), *High Noon: 20 Global Problems, 20 Years to Solve Them*. New York: Basic.

Schola Europaea (2013), http://www.eursc.eu/index.php?l=2 (Accessed 3 March 2013).

Stewart, W.A.C. (1972), *Progressives and Radicals in English Education, 1750–1970*. London: Macmillan.

Sylvester, R. (2002), 'The "first" international school', in M.C. Hayden, J.J. Thompson and G.R. Walker (eds), *International Education in Practice: Dimensions for National and International Schools*. London: Kogan Page, pp. 3–17.

Thompson, J.J. (1998), 'Towards a model for international education', in M.C. Hayden and J.J. Thompson (eds), *International Education: Principles and Practice*. London: Kogan Page, pp. 276–290.

United World Colleges. (2013), www.uwc.org (Accessed 3 March 2013).

Unlocking the World. (2013), *ESL in the Mainstream*. http://www.unlockingtheworld.com/programs/esl-in-the-mainstream (Accessed 3 March 2013).

Walker, G.R. (ed) (2011), 'Introduction: past, present and future', in *The Changing Face of International Education: Challenges for the IB*. Cardiff: International Baccalaureate pp. 1–17.

CHAPTER TWO

Charting the Growth of International Schools

Nicholas Brummitt and Anne Keeling

Introduction

Forty years ago, international schools were, at best, sporadic; in many areas of the world, non-existent. Today, most major cities worldwide have at least one prominent international school if not several.

Throughout the past 40 years, international schools have changed in all but name, becoming a market force that, in many ways, is driving education globally. This chapter considers this growth.

Researching the market

ISC Research has been formally charting the development of the international schools market since the year 2004, and Nicholas Brummitt, Chairman and Founder of the International School Consultancy Group (of which ISC Research is a part), has been researching the market since 1978. The company is the only independent organization to work with and to analyse the data of the entire market. The sheer volume of information, and the number of people interested in the market, made it very clear that a single source of comprehensive and up-to-date information was required. This led to the formation of ISC Research.

The market itself is cause for debate as the term 'international schools' garners a range of definitions. Since 1978 ISC Research has included a school on its international schools database if it delivers a curriculum to any combination of infant, primary or secondary students, wholly or partly in

English outside an English-speaking country. There are, of course, exceptions to this; for example, American schools in the United Kingdom, British schools in America and also schools in countries such as India, Pakistan and several in Africa where English is one of the official languages. Schools in these countries are included if they offer an international curriculum.

Forty years ago

Forty years ago, the market was very different to the one it is today. The international schools that existed then did so to meet the needs of an expatriate market and the schools were few and far between. The Tenby International School in Miri on the northwestern coast of Borneo was one of them (Mainwaring, 2012). It was, until recently, one of the schools owned by the Shell oil company. The school, which was originally known as Piasau School, has existed since 1922. Shell's Head of Education Services, Henk van Hout, describes its emergence:

> Shell discovered the first oil field in Borneo near Miri at Canada Hill in 1910. This was an onshore field that was active until 1972, when it was closed. According to Piasau School itself, the earliest record of a Shell school for expatriates at Miri dates back to 1922.

He explains the motivation for the school.

> A key concern for many oil field workers, whether based offshore or onshore in a remote location, is how to maintain a family life, particularly if the oil worker has a young family. Regular, quality time with your family becomes complicated if you are working halfway across the world from them. Oil and gas operations in remote locations often do not have the kinds of facilities nearby that are required by a young family. However, some of the world's biggest oil and gas companies do make provision to ensure that even in remote operations they can maintain a family life.

And this is how Piasau School was established.

> It was only in 1968 that the school took off in a big way with the discovery of nearby offshore oil and gas fields. In 2012, the school was taken over by Tenby International and continues to provide a valuable education service in the community.

This is a typical reason why many of the first international schools were established. For these early international schools, an expatriate intake dominated, a national curriculum (based on the priorities of the founders) was used, the school was invariably small and limited in resources and most were not for profit. This bears little resemblance to the international schools of today. The demographic breakdown, learning approach and business model have all changed and it is no longer a small market catering for a niche group. The international schools market is now big business and is recognized as such by a broad range of providers, investors and suppliers.

The numbers

The international schools market has changed beyond recognition in the past 40 years and has experienced sustained, significant growth for the last 13 years.

In 2000 there were 2,584 international schools worldwide teaching 988,600 students and employing 90,000 full-time teaching staff. The countries dominating the market at that time were Spain (with 99 international schools), the United Arab Emirates (with 97 international schools), Hong Kong (70 international schools) and Thailand (55 international schools), but there was little evidence of any regional domination. Although still predominantly a provision for expatriates, by 2000 an increasing number of international school places were being taken by local children).

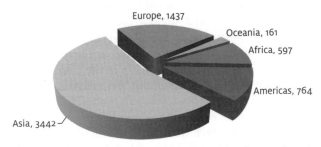

FIGURE 2.1: *Number of international schools in each region*
Source: © ISC Research Ltd

Six years on (2006), Asia was beginning to dominate the market and by 2008 had 2,361 international schools – 49% of the total market. The countries fuelling the growth were the UAE, China and Japan. Europe was the other strong region with 1,205 international schools – 25% of the market – resulting from growing numbers in Spain, Germany and the Netherlands. Today (2013), the total market has increased to 6,400 international schools teaching 3.2 million students and employing 300,000 full-time teaching staff.

Asia continues to dominate (Figure 2.1). The top five countries leading the international schools market today – all of which are in Asia – are the UAE, Pakistan, China, India and Japan; each with over 200 international schools.

The UAE alone has 376 schools. Thirty-two countries worldwide have over 50 international schools; 16 of these are located in Asia (Figure 2.2).

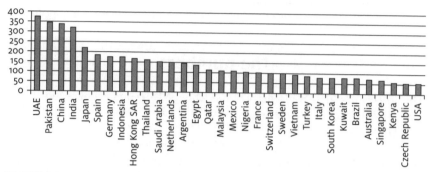

FIGURE 2.2: *Countries with more than 50 international schools*
Source: © ISC Research Ltd

The Middle East (Western Asia) is currently the largest of the five Asian sub-regions and the growth of international schools here in recent years has been phenomenal. In 2000, along with the 97 international schools in the UAE, there were just 21 international schools in Qatar and 37 in Saudi Arabia. By 2009 these figures had increased to 251 schools in the UAE, 91 schools in Qatar and 86 schools in Saudi Arabia. Just 4 years on, by the beginning of 2013, those figures had rocketed again to 112 international schools in Qatar, 155 in Saudi Arabia and 378 in the UAE. In total there are now 1,069 international schools throughout Western Asia teaching 926,533 students.

However, even with such expansion, a number of cities in Western Asia continue to experience the fact that demand for places at international schools outstrips supply. Dubai, Abu Dhabi and Doha all currently have significant supply problems, to such an extent that some relocating expatriates with families are now demanding confirmation of school places before accepting new transfers (Figure 2.3). By 2020 ISC Research predicts that worldwide there will be over 10,000 international schools with over 5 million students.

The market demographics: A transformation

Perhaps the biggest change in the international schools market – other than the overall growth – is the demographic breakdown of the student population. While the market today still caters for expatriate families with the total number of expatriate students continuing to grow year on year, demand for places has mostly been fuelled by local families.

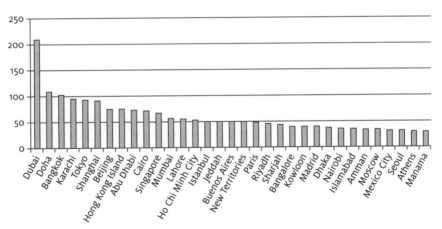

FIGURE 2.3: *Cities with 30 or more international schools*
Source: © ISC Research Ltd

Enrolment is increasingly dominated by the richest 5% of non-English-speaking parents looking for places at international schools in their own countries. This has come about as a result of an increase in wealth. As their income increases, an English-medium international school education becomes high on the list of priorities for many families. The main reason for this is that it is now widely accepted that for students who have attended international schools there are tremendous opportunities at the world's top universities, many often competing for the best students. Not only is this as a result of learning through the English language, but it is also because of the quality of teaching and learning that many international schools provide.

'Parents of the next generation are looking towards international schools to satisfy the need for critical thinking rather than learning by rote', says Clive Pierrepont (Keeling, 2011), Director of Communications at Taaleem, which owns and manages 13 international schools in Dubai and Abu Dhabi. The parents clearly see international schools as a route through for university opportunities.

It is this recognition, coupled with increased income, which is making attendance at an international school a real possibility for wealthier local families. The result of this is that today local children fill 80% of international school places, a complete reversal of 30 years ago when 80% were filled by expatriate children.

There are a few countries that are exceptions to this rule, where local children are not permitted to attend international schools. China is one example. Chinese children (meaning those with Chinese passports) at present must attend a Chinese curriculum school and foreign-owned schools cannot currently accept Chinese passport holders. As a result, the vast majority of English-medium international schools cater solely for expatriates. However, some Chinese children – those who have a foreign-born parent – do have the opportunity to attend an international school and some of the Chinese private schools do now offer an international curriculum, especially at the 16–18-year age group.

Also, due to the recent weakening of regulatory barriers in China, it is much easier for Sino-foreign joint ventures to operate. Over the last 4 years (since 2008), this has resulted in considerable growth in foreign programmes offered by English-medium sections within China's domestic schools, and more and more students are opting out of traditional Chinese curriculum programmes in order to increase their chances of attending North American, Australian and British universities.

Needless to say, there has still been huge growth in international schools in China. In the year 2000, there were just 22 international schools in the whole of China, supporting the learning needs of 7,268 children. By June 2010, this had increased to 260 international schools with 119,319 students. Today, there are 338 international schools in China, including 91 located in Shanghai and 76 in Beijing, with a total enrolment of 184,073 students and employing a total staff of 18,319.

As for the future of the international school market in China, no one at present really knows what's going to happen there; it all depends upon the regulations. If the rules are ever changed to allow Chinese passport holders to go to non-Chinese international schools, the number of international schools will grow dramatically. There are 200 million Chinese children who need schools and an increasing number come from wealthy Chinese families. The proportion of these children wanting an internationally oriented education will be very hard to satisfy with the current provision in China.

Big business

Another significant change in the international schools market in recent years has been the increase in the number of schools run for profit. Forty years ago, international schools were largely a non-profit phenomenon. Now, however, most international schools are for profit and the future will continue to be dominated by profit-making schools and school groups.

A number of multinational groups of schools already exist and appear to be moving from strength to strength. This includes GEMS with schools in many parts of the world; Taaleem with schools throughout the UAE and partnerships in other Middle East countries; WCL with schools in the US, the Middle East and Europe; Nord Anglia with schools in China, Thailand and Europe; and Cognita with schools in the UK, Europe and Asia. Also, ESOL is based in Cairo with schools in a number of Middle East countries and Yew Chung Education Foundation has schools in Hong Kong, China and the US. The one thing that nearly all these groups have in common is that they are expanding aggressively by either buying existing schools, expanding existing operations or starting new schools, and in so doing creating a powerful new sector within the market.

> As a group we are continuing to experience strong growth. Each year we look at two or three new projects. This year could include projects outside the UAE, within the MENA (Middle East and North Africa) region. We've been approached by a number of organisations from several of the GCC (Gulf Cooperation) countries about opening new operations but the motives have to be considered and establishing a good new organisation requires a long growth J-curve. (Pierrepont, Taaleem Group, pers. comm.)

There are also schools with campuses in several countries. These include an increasing number of UK private schools with international operations, such as Shrewsbury College in Bangkok, Wellington College in Tianjin (China), Brighton College in Abu Dhabi, Repton in Dubai, Haileybury in Almaty (Kazakhstan), Epsom College in Kuala Lumpur and Marlborough College in Malaysia, as well as enterprises such as Harrow International Management Services which has schools in Beijing, Bangkok and Hong Kong, and Dulwich College Management International with schools in Shanghai, Beijing and Suzhou (China) and in Seoul (South Korea). A variety of business models have been adopted to establish and support these overseas branches, from joint ventures and royalty fees to operating and managing the international sites directly from the parent school. All these schools have benefited from the reputation of their parent schools in Britain and are currently experiencing great success. More UK private schools are considering international operations too.

International schools are profitable. Today, based on annual fee income alone, the international schools market is generating £20.8 billion. Within 10 years, this figure is predicted to increase to £30 billion. Even during the global recession, the market was affected very little and, at the worst times still achieved a 6% annual growth. The next few years will be dominated by the race to keep up with demand. A significant number of brand new international schools are in the planning stages and many existing schools are expanding their capacity to cope with demand (Figure 2.4).

Many countries now realize the value of the economic contribution made by a well-established and high-spending international school community and, as a result, are actively encouraging growth. One current example of where this is happening is Malaysia, a country which aspires to be the educational hub for its region. By easing regulations, including taxation, and providing land and buildings in development zones, Malaysia has already attracted the likes of Marlborough College as part of EduCity, a world-class education hub under long-term development in Iskandar Malaysia, and more UK private schools and international schools are expected to follow suit. India, China and Korea are other countries also encouraging development.

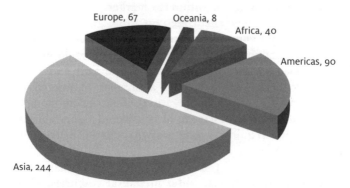

Number of schools

Europe, 67   Oceania, 8

Africa, 40

Americas, 90

Asia, 244

FIGURE 2.4: *Market growth, February 2012–February 2013*
Source: © ISC Research Ltd

A change in the learning

Curricula offered in international schools are changing too. No longer is the market dominated by a straightforward UK or American curriculum, although these are still used (entirely or in part) by almost half of the international school market. It is the international options which are now becoming a more popular choice by many schools. Forty-five per cent are currently choosing to use (all or in part) such curricula as the International Baccalaureate, the International Primary Curriculum or the Cambridge International Programmes.

The impact of increased demand

Dramatic growth nevertheless does come at a cost. The recruitment and retention of suitably qualified staff are getting harder for many schools and are likely to get much worse.

In 2000, there were a total of 90,000 full-time staff employed by international schools. Today that number has more than tripled to 300,000. The vast majority of these are expatriate teachers – qualified, experienced, English-speaking teachers largely coming from the UK, New Zealand, Australia, South Africa, Canada and the US. By 2022 ISC Research predicts that demand for qualified, English-speaking teachers will have reached 529,000.

Dr Mark Hensman is the Chief Operations Officer and Director of Schools for Harrow International. As the overall number of international schools increase, Hensman (Wigford, 2010) says that Harrow International recognizes the need to maintain the very high standards of its teaching staff in order to remain a first choice for prospective parents.

We know that the Harrow name engenders a sense of confidence. But we recognise that we must work hard to maintain that reputation and believe that the career paths we offer are a way of retaining existing staff (Harrow currently holds a 90% retention rate). As for the new recruits to the international arena, because of being Harrow and teaching to the National Curriculum for England, we want to attract teachers from the UK. We know that we'll have to be creative in our marketing approach into the future as competition for good quality candidates gets tougher.

This issue of the supply and demand of high-quality candidates is an issue that every international school is currently facing and it is an issue that will continue while the number of international schools continues to expand. The problem that ISC Research is hearing from specialist recruiters everywhere is that the candidate pool isn't expanding quickly enough. The internationally experienced, top-quality teachers and leaders are in extremely high demand. Although more teachers now realize the opportunities, both professionally and personally, of working internationally, the pool of available candidates is barely keeping pace with demand. International schools can no longer attract high numbers of applicants simply due to their location. Because of the wealth of options now available to them, candidates can be more discerning and base their selection on other factors such as salary and benefits package, reputation of the school, career potential and support for family.

Clive Pierrepont explains the issues of recruitment at Taaleem (Keeling, 2012):

The supply of teachers is definitely more challenging as a result of the growth in the market, especially for the cream of the crop such as qualified, experienced IB and British teachers, the type of teachers we want to attract. It's important for us to show good candidates the quality of life that they can get there; the location and lifestyle, and also the professional development opportunities and career potential, as well as the fact that we're a caring organisation. This fact is important for both hiring staff and for attracting our new students. The fact that we are part of a group with an established reputation is an enormous advantage; it's essential for recruiting good quality staff and attracting students.

The future of the international schools market

Regardless of this expansive growth in the market, demand for international school places is still not matched by supply. ISC Research has identified that many schools are increasing capacity as quickly as they can. In addition, there are many new developments; for example, the dramatic growth of English-medium sections in locally owned, private Chinese schools and also plans recently announced by the Gulf States to invest US$200 billion for up to 6,600 new schools and 1,200 university campuses by 2020.

Growth of the market over the next 10 years looks significant. Without taking into consideration the potential new developments and simply basing predictions upon the continuing market demand, calculating from historical development alone (at a conservative 6% growth rate), ISC Research predicts that within 10 years (by 2022) the number of international schools will expand to 11,331; the number of students will increase to 6.2 million; the number of staff to 529,000; and the annual fee income will reach almost $60 billion.

The next ten years will, without doubt, see dramatic growth in the international schools market. Demand continues to come from the expanding expatriate market and, more significantly, the increasing number of wealthy local families who are recognising the benefits of an English-medium education for their children. Almost two thirds of the growth in the current market is as a result of this increase in demand from local nationals and this looks set to continue and expand. The development in the market as a whole is resulting in a booming supply chain.

The booming supply chain

It is as a result of the market growth that many organizations which traditionally looked to national schools for their business are turning more of their attention internationally. Leading English-speaking universities and colleges around the world are increasingly keen to recruit students from the international schools who by definition are relatively well-off, have studied in English to a high standard and the majority of whom choose not to attend the universities available to them in their home countries. There is a developing supply chain from a range of sectors, too. Finalsite, a US company that provides online environments to schools, is one company that has seen a rapid change in its international business in recent years. 'In 2007 we had just one international school client', says Director of International Operations Clive Ungless (Keeling, 2012).

> For an international school, it only takes one other school to start up in the same location and you've suddenly got huge competition. It's staggering to look at a particular city to see what competition is out there for the schools. For these schools, prospective parents are trawling the websites to make their judgements before ever stepping foot into the building. That's where we can help and, as a result, 25% of our business is today with the international schools and we see no sign of it slowing down.

For Pearson Education, the international schools market is one that the education resource supplier has been developing for over 10 years. 'It's now a very important market for us', says Lisa Evans, Senior Marketing Communications Manager, explaining how the company has had to respond to the market's shift in demographics (Keeling, 2012).

> The increased number of local children attending international schools is impacting the number of students who are learning where English is their second language. This is influencing the way we prepare materials and resources for this market, producing more that are suitable for incorporating ESL teaching within one single resource.

And for Apply to Education, a Canadian-based company providing an online recruitment programme, the international schools market has had a significant impact on business. 'I'm amazed at how the international schools market has developed over the past year or two', says Account Manager, Kelsie McPherson. 'It's a very large network of schools that is growing very rapidly; particularly some of the regional groups. We see definite growth potential based on the demand for our software to support schools with their recruitment procedures.'

So what of the future? It looks very bright. These days ISC Research is approached continually for demographic studies and market reports; this suggests public recognition of a very healthy market. In some countries growth is being driven from the highest level. We predict that the market in the future will be dominated by for-profit international schools which will be bilingual to varying degrees with more of an emphasis on local language and culture but, at the same time, increasingly international in terms of curriculum and outlook. The continued growth will increase competition for the best teachers as well as the best students. Also, with so many new schools, the difference between the best and the worst will increase, making it vital that as many as possible subscribe to recognizable standards of international education. Location, standards, facilities, Unique Selling Point (USP) and good marketing, along with salaries for teachers and fees for students, will all play a crucial part in the success of every school in the future.

(The International School Consultancy Group includes ISC Consultancy, ISC Worldwide and ISC Research. ISC Research is the only organization that supplies data and market analyses covering the world's English-medium international schools, data that it has been tracking for over 20 years. The latest market updates plus individual school information, news, statistical overviews and country reports are all available from www.iscresearch.com.)

References

Keeling, A. (2011, May), 'Demand outstrips supply at many Dubai international schools', *International Schools Magazine*, 14, 1, 37.

Keeling, A. (2012, October), 'Prospecting for gold', *British International Schools Magazine*, 1, 6–7

Mainwaring, J. (2012, June), 'Shell schools: supporting expat families', *Rigzone*. http://www.rigzone.com/news/article.asp?hpf=1&a_id=118761

Wigford, A. (2010, October), 'Responding to recruitment', Teachers International Consultancy Newsletter. http://www.ticrecruitment.com/schools/case-studies/mark-hensman-harrow-international-school-recruitment

CHAPTER THREE

The Effects of Children's Education and Supporting Organizational Policy and Practice on Corporate Expatriation

Susan Shortland

Introduction

This chapter explores the impact of organizational provision for children's education on the willingness of employees and their families to undertake corporate expatriation. By reviewing the academic and practitioner literature on this issue, it highlights potential impediments to families' international mobility and the outcomes for employers and assignees with children in relation to the changing nature of the types of assignments undertaken.

This chapter also reviews the extant literature with regard to trends in employer policy and practice to support educational provision for expatriates' children either in the host country or at home during the period of the assignment and practice to extend education support after repatriation. While international schools are one potential benefit in relocation policy supporting children, decision-making in respect of undertaking expatriation with children rests not only upon available schooling and its quality but also upon other factors relating to children's well-being. This chapter therefore sets educational issues within the broader organizational context of the requirement to recognize and support family welfare, highlighting the family challenges deemed critical to international mobility and the effects of family concerns on assignment refusal.

This chapter highlights the financial and practical support offered by organizations to internationally mobile families and how such support has developed over the years. Having set the scene with respect to employer provision, this is then examined through the viewpoint of assignees themselves. Drawing upon research into female expatriates' mobility, the chapter examines the degree of emphasis placed by women assignees on educational provision for their children in their expatriate participation decision. In contrast to the rhetoric that suggests that having children precludes women's international mobility, it is proposed that relocation policy supporting children potentially acts as a facilitator of women's expatriation – either as lead assignees or as accompanying spouses/partners.

Expatriate compensation: The requirement to address children's education

Some of the very earliest literature in respect of global mobility recognizes the 'major adjustments for families, wives and children. The sacrifices are often great and, for some families, outweigh the rewards forthcoming – at least in personal terms' (Perlmutter, 1969, p. 17). In recognition of this, expatriate compensation packages have historically addressed family issues such as education concerns by making provision for children's schooling (Julius, 1982) and, in the main, continue to do so (although less generously) today.

Organizations must manage conflicting priorities in determining their expatriate compensation: costs have to be controlled but packages are required to be sufficiently competitive to attract, retain and motivate assignees whilst preserving equity (Sims and Schraeder, 2005). While acknowledging the difficulties in achieving this balancing act, the authors note that employers also aim to keep assignees 'whole' – in essence they should achieve no overt gain or loss on expatriation. Maintaining 'wholeness' is clearly a potential minefield where the host location has an infrastructure significantly less well developed than that of the sending country (facilities, healthcare, schools and so on being limited in provision and/or quality). Yet, even in developed host countries, the ability for employers to keep assignees 'whole' can be severely challenged. With respect to children's education, for example, language and curriculum differences between the home- and host-country school systems can present considerable barriers to family mobility, potentially damaging children's examination achievement and future access to further and higher education options. The availability and quality of pre-school childcare assistance is also an area of concern for working parents.

It is therefore unsurprising to find that children's adjustment and schooling, as well as childcare availability, affect willingness to relocate internationally (Dupuis et al., 2008; Hutchings et al., 2010; Tharenou, 2008; Tzeng, 2006; Zhu et al., 2006). This is particularly the case when expatriation involves moves to developing or culturally dissimilar countries (Tharenou, 2003, 2009).

In Warneke and Schneider's (2011) research, expatriates were asked to select the top five most important elements of the expatriate compensation package relevant to the assignment take-up decision. Their findings place schooling for accompanying children in fourth place (41%) after salary (71%), support for the accompanying partner (60%) and a reintegration guarantee (58%). Of course, while employer packages typically provide assistance with children's education to some degree, receipt of this benefit depends upon individuals' circumstances, which helps to explain the discrepancy between employer provision figures, ranging from 60% to 96% (Cartus, 2007, 2012; ORC Worldwide, 2007, 2008) (see Table 3.1), and receipt by assignees, recorded at 29% (Suutari and Tornikoski, 2001).

When interpreting the data here (and in the other tables presented in this chapter) it is important to remember that the various expatriate consultancies draw upon their client bases; as a result samples are unmatched and may focus to varying degrees on different world regions. As such, care is needed in interpreting – and generalizing from – the results. Cartus and GMAC/Brookfield, for instance, draw their data mainly from their US and European client organizations. ORC Worldwide (now Mercer) data tend to reflect a wider geographical spread, including, as well as US and European organizational responses, a higher proportion of replies from Asia-Pacific-based firms (in particular Japanese companies). It is notable that when Japanese employer responses are included in the data collection, the proportion of organizations providing education assistance is noticeably higher. Given the potential difficulties that Japanese children are likely to

Table 3.1: Expatriate children's education: a summary of employer provision

Year	Employers making provision (%)	Source
2004	72	Cartus, 2007
2006	96	ORC Worldwide, 2007
2007	80	Cartus, 2007
2008	95	ORC Worldwide, 2008
2010	80	Cartus, 2012
2012	60	Cartus, 2012

have both linguistically and culturally in attending local (non-Japanese) schools, this discrepancy in results between survey providers becomes understandable; Japanese assignees abroad need to use Japanese national schools and hence policy provision to address this is required from their Japanese employers. Given this context there is a consequent knock-on effect on published survey data.

Allard (1996) reports that schooling costs for expatriates' accompanying children have traditionally been met by organizations, with international schools used because they can provide continuity in curriculum and language. Although the current trend is to reduce costs, the use of international schools is still most prevalent (Perelstein, 2010). This practice arguably follows Sims and Schraeder's (2005) 'wholeness' mantra – that assignees (and, by appendage, their children) are no better or worse off than had they remained at home (financially and/or educationally). Allard (1996) also notes that the use of international schools makes re-assimilation into the home-country school easier on return at the end of the assignment.

Yet international schools provide a unique social context (Pearce, 1998). They potentially present a highly positive experience for assignees' children as they are acknowledged as having high standards, being frequently populated by children of the internationally mobile personnel who are usually the brightest and best within the workforce (hence their selection for an assignment). Studying abroad exposes children to multi-lingual and multi-cultural experiences, broadening their persona. Exposure to different cultural and behavioural norms helps them to develop a new cultural frame of reference, creating a 'third culture', which affects their perceptions of their 'internationalness' and potentially provides these 'third-culture kids' with a source of competitive advantage over home- or host-country non-mobile children when they enter the global job market as young adults (Selmer and Lam, 2004). Whilst acknowledging the difficulty of keeping assignees 'whole', it might therefore be argued that assignees whose children attend international schools as a result of their parents' mobility are, in fact, better off. This is particularly the case if, as Allard (1996) suggests, their companies foot the bill.

Notwithstanding this, an alternative perspective must be considered. Having undertaken this educational experience, children's reintegration into home-country schools can be more difficult. Local, state systems may appear (or be) inferior, friendships need to be built/rebuilt and readjustment is required to the educational system and culture. Indeed, homecoming has been described as 'a bitter-sweet experience'. Older age group children are reported as having 'difficulty in letting go of their "internationalness" and settling back in...Education provision for younger school age children...as an area of major concern' (University of Westminster/CBI, 1993, p. 18).

Given the competitive nature of university entrance, parental concern over educational continuity to maximize examination success is high. It is therefore to be expected that even when compensation packages that provide payment for children's education are offered, those with high school-aged children are the most reluctant to take up an international assignment (Dupuis et al., 2008; Tharenou, 2009).

Alternative assignments as facilitators of expatriate mobility

Assignment status (accompanied or unaccompanied) is linked to length, pattern and location and is driven by business need and cost considerations (Cartus, 2010; CBI/Deloitte and Touche, 1996). Long-term assignments are generally offered as accompanied postings while alternatives such as short-term assignments are, in the main, unaccompanied (ORC Worldwide, 2009). By their very nature, commuter and rotational assignments and international business travel are unaccompanied (CBI/Deloitte and Touche, 1996; Welch et al., 2007). There is increasing evidence that lengthy expatriation is declining (Morley et al., 2006; Scullion and Brewster, 2001) and the percentage of relocating employees with children is falling (Brookfield, 2009, 2010, 2011, 2012; deValk, 2004; GMAC, 2008) (see Table 3.2).

Instead, organizations are increasing their use of alternative types of assignments (Weichert, 2012). For example, short-term assignments (defined as between 3 and 12 months in length) cut costs (Anonymous, 2006); reduce the 'out of sight, out of mind' syndrome (Konopaske and Werner, 2005; Starr and Currie, 2009); help reduce problems of re-integration on repatriation (De Cieri et al., 2009); and address concerns over children's education which might form barriers to mobility (CBI/Deloitte and Touche, 1996). Due to short timescales of separation, employees are able to work abroad without having

Table 3.2: Expatriates accompanied by children: a summary of recent employer data

Year	Expatriates accompanied by children (%)	Historical average	Source	Notes
2008	51	57	GMAC (2008)	51% also in 2003/2004; 62% in 1994
2009	49	57	Brookfield (2009)	
2010	47	56	Brookfield (2010)	
2011	47	55	Brookfield (2011)	
2012	43	56	Brookfield (2012)	

to move their families (Forster, 2000). Yet, expatriates suffer stress particularly through family separation and lack of family support (Starr and Currie, 2009; UCL/CBI ERC, 1991). While Brown (2008) notes that both long-term and short-term assignments increase stress on family members, this is potentially a more widespread problem for short-term assignees as around three-quarters of all short-term mobility is unaccompanied (ORC Worldwide, 2006).

Besides long-term and short-term assignments, expatriation also takes the form of 'flexpatriate' style international mobility (Mayerhofer et al., 2004a, 2004b). For example, commuter and rotational assignments involve unaccompanied, frequent international mobility. Deploying individuals on such patterns is increasing (Cartus, 2010; Scullion and Brewster, 2001). Yet frequent travel and family separation are stressful to individuals (Ivancevich et al., 2003; Mayerhofer et al., 2004b; UCL/CBI, 1991; Welch et al., 2007), affecting health and wellness (Demel and Mayrhofer, 2010). Flexpatriation's requirements for repeated mobility and flexibility cause family conflict (Welch et al., 2007), straining and ultimately destabilizing nuclear-centred families (Carnoy, 2001).

It might therefore be argued that while accompanied long-term international mobility is disruptive to children's education and other family issues, short-term, commuter and rotational assignments create destabilization and stress through frequent travel, family separation and reunion. Mobility, regardless of assignment length, is, by its very nature, a disruptive phenomenon for individuals and their families. To encourage individuals with young and older age children to consider an alternative to a long-term international assignment, the employer's package may need to address education concerns. Indeed, Cartus (2007) reports that in 2007, 29% of developmental assignment policies made provision for children's education assistance and 16% of short-term assignment policies also did so – a potentially surprising finding given that such forms of mobility are less frequently accompanied. Indeed, discussion in employer forums today appears to suggest increased assignee pressure to undertake short-term mobility on accompanied status.

Family challenges to international mobility and reasons for assignment refusal

An analysis of organizational policy and practice is presented here to establish first employers' perceptions of the criticality of children's education and other family issues to expatriate mobility and second the financial and practical organizational support given to address children's education.

Drawing upon data from the past 5 years, Table 3.3 suggests that concerns over children's education do not present a critical assignment management challenge to employers once schooling is in place and employees are on assignment. However, encouraging families to rise to the challenge of relocating their children's schools so as to take up an assignment in the first

Table 3.3: Criticality of organizational provision for expatriate children's education: a summary of recent employer data

Year	Children's education considered as a critical family challenge to companies (%)	Concerns over children's education as a critical assignment management challenge (%)	Source	Notes
2008	13	4	GMAC (2008)	
2009	13	4	Brookfield (2009)	
2010	15	4	Brookfield (2010)	
2011	29	1	Brookfield (2011)	29% 'very critical'; 50% 'high importance'
2012	35	2	Brookfield (2012)	35% 'very critical'; 55% 'high importance'

place has become a 'very critical' issue (Brookfield, 2009, 2010, 2011, 2012; GMAC, 2008). Over one-third of employers (35%) reported that children's education presented their companies with a 'very critical' family challenge in 2012, up from 29% in 2011 (while 55% and 50% respectively noted this issue being of 'high importance') (Brookfield, 2011, 2012). For comparison, 13% and 15% reported children's education as a critical family challenge in 2008/2009 and 2010 respectively (Brookfield, 2009, 2010; GMAC, 2008). This potentially might be explained by the suggested and actual reductions taking place in employer support for children's education (ORC Worldwide, 2007, 2008; Perelstein, 2010).

In respect of issues that are predicted to affect the success of future assignments, concerns about schooling are not considered to be a real threat. Yet 23% of the respondents in Cartus's (2102) survey reported these as a potentially serious challenge and 46% said these were a real but manageable concern. Only 31% said schooling concerns were not a serious concern. Almost half (46%) reported that school availability or quality had a significant impact on the employer's ability to attract employees to new assignments and 18% reported these factors as reasons for turning down an assignment.

Besides children's education, other family challenges that have traditionally acted as a brake on mobility appear increasingly critical to employers. As shown in Table 3.4, spouse/partner resistance to international relocation was cited by almost half of organizations (48%) as a critical

Table 3.4: Family challenges deemed critical to international mobility: recent employer data

Year	Spouse/partner resistance to international relocation (%)	Family adjustment (%)	Degree of difficulty of destination location (emerging economy, isolation) (%)	Cross-cultural adjustment (%)	Inability to speak the language (%)	Spouse's/partner's career (%)	Assignment length (%)	Support for other dependent family members (%)	Source
2008	13	13	12	11	10	10	9	9	GMAC (2008)
2009	15	15	11	12	9	9	9	7	Brookfield (2009)
2010	15	15	11	12	8	9	8	7	Brookfield (2010)
2011	47	32	25	14	12	12	4	4	Brookfield (2011)
2012	48	38	21	12	11	10	3	-	Brookfield (2012)

Table 3.5: Family concerns cited as reasons for assignment refusal: recent employer data

Year	Family concerns (%)	Source
2008	89	GMAC (2008)
2009	92	Brookfield (2009)
2010	83	Brookfield (2010)
2011	34	Brookfield (2011)
2012	34	Brookfield (2012)

family challenge, while family adjustment was deemed a critical challenge by 38% in 2012 (Brookfield, 2012). Both issues increased in terms of their reported criticality from 13% in 2008 (GMAC, 2008). The nature of the assignment location became a more critical family challenge too. This was cited by 21% in 2012, compared with just 11% in 2008 – reflecting the increased trend for international assignments to be located in non-Western, emerging economies (Brookfield, 2012; GMAC, 2008). Yet, there was little change in the level of family challenge presented by cross-cultural adjustment, inability to speak the host-country language or the effect of the relocation on the spouse's/partner's career – around one-tenth of organizations recorded these issues as critical family challenges both in 2008 and in 2012. It is notable that assignment length and support for other dependent family members appeared to present less of a critical family challenge to international mobility over the same period – perhaps reflecting the shortening of assignment lengths (Brookfield, 2012; GMAC, 2008).

Despite some family issues appearing more critical as challenges to international mobility, employers appear to have managed these effectively as there is evidence of a fall in assignment refusal due to family concerns in recent years. As shown in Table 3.5, family concerns as a reason for assignment refusal reached a peak – being cited by 92% – in 2009 but have fallen to 34% by 2011/2012 (Brookfield, 2009, 2011, 2012). Of course, the changing nature of assignment types – with the rise in alternative assignments not requiring family mobility – might also help to explain this trend.

Organizational support for expatriate children's education

Figure 3.1 provides a timeline analysis based upon qualitative survey data as available from 1989 through to 2002 from the perspective of UK-based

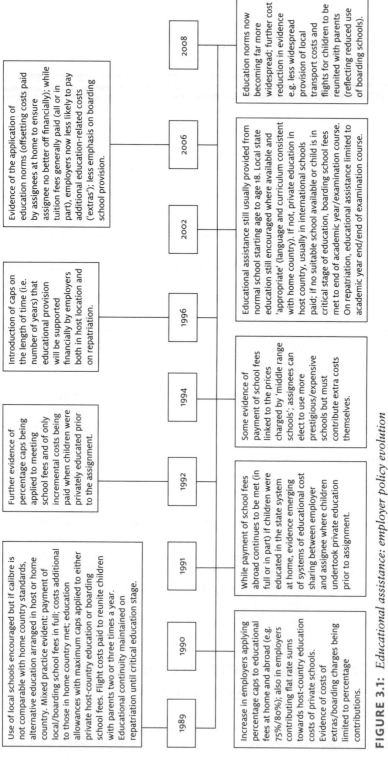

FIGURE 3.1: *Educational assistance: employer policy evolution*
Sources: CBI ERC (1989, 1990, 1991, 1992, 1994, 1996); IDS (2002); ORC Worldwide (2007, 2008).

organizations (CBI ERC, 1989, 1990, 1991, 1992, 1994, 1996; IDS, 2002) and quantitative data for 2006 and 2008 (ORC Worldwide, 2007, 2008) drawn from survey responses submitted by US-, European- and Asia-Pacific-based organizations. These data summaries indicate how organizational relocation policy for long-term assignments has evolved over two decades.

It can be seen that although practice in 1989 was quite varied in terms of policy content (with employers fully meeting local or boarding fees, additional costs incurred or applying educational allowances to a maximum limit), in the main provision was made for alternative education arranged in the host or home country if local host-country schools were considered to be of lower calibre. In addition, coverage of education to ensure continuity on repatriation was standard (CBI ERC, 1989).

As the timeline progresses, there is increasing evidence of employers applying limits to funding children's education costs. In 1990, it became more common for employers to limit their education contribution for host-country education and boarding to a percentage of the cost or to make flat-rate contributions towards it, rather than paying the full fees (CBI ERC, 1990). By 1991, there was evidence that employers sought to share education costs with parents if their children were educated privately in their home country (CBI ERC, 1991). By 1992, further evidence of capping of school fees and just incremental costs being met if children were privately educated was presented (CBI ERC, 1992).

In 1994, the emphasis shifted to the quality of the schools used: employers began to limit their contributions to the fees set by middle-range schools; if parents elected to use elite schools, they would need to pay the additional costs themselves (CBI ERC, 1994). By 1996, time limits were in evidence in employer's policies: school fees would only be met for a specified number of years if assignees were on very lengthy assignments. This suggests the beginning of the practice of localizing assignees' benefit packages and including education costs within the phasing-out or take-away of expatriate compensation elements (CBI ERC, 1996).

By 2002, although the use of local host-country schools was still encouraged where these were 'appropriate' and international school fees were paid (to some degree) if these were not deemed suitable, there appeared to be evidence of the beginning of the trend to discourage the use of boarding schools. It is notable that employer policy by this point frequently limited payment for these to the end of the academic year or to the completion of a critical stage in examinations, not for the duration of the assignment (IDS, 2002). Employers, it appeared, wished to encourage families to relocate together, rather than split up for educational reasons. Whether this policy change was taking place as a direct cost-reduction strategy (recognizing the high costs of boarding) or a 'nod' towards reducing family separation and stress (with knock-on implications for productivity and associated costs) was not clear though.

One of the key trends identified in the period from 2006 to 2008 concerns the application of education norms (ORC Worldwide, 2007, 2008). Under the keeping 'whole' home country-based expatriate remuneration approach, employers make a deduction for education costs met by assignees in their home countries; the employer contribution therefore addresses additional costs only – and these are mainly limited to tuition fees. Company cutbacks by 2006 also suggest that additional costs (extras such as bussing costs, textbooks and school trips) were no longer refunded as standard practice. Boarding school costs were also less commonly met by employers (ORC Worldwide, 2007). By 2008, education norms were gaining even greater prominence and cost reductions were being applied to travel costs to reunite families (reflecting the decreased provision of boarding) (ORC Worldwide, 2008). For example, between 2006 and 2008 the percentage of employers applying an education norm increased from 9% to 24% and those paying no travel expenses to reunite families rose from 8% to 18%. The percentage of employers paying local transport costs fell from 63% to 56%, while those meeting the cost of textbooks fell from 57% to 51% and school trips from 10% to 8% (ORC Worldwide, 2007, 2008).

Together with the cost-saving strategies mentioned already, Perelstein (2010) suggests cutbacks that employers might consider to reduce education costs yet further, including eliminating payment for extras such as music lessons and lunch costs and negotiating reductions in penalty fees for early withdrawal and multiple child discounts (from the same family or company) with international schools. It is clear that while employers recognize the need to assist with expatriate children's education, the future lies in leaner policy provision. Of course the question arises as to the extent that cost reduction can be achieved without compromising the facilitation of international mobility or other objectives such as expatriate localization. For example, 2% of employers cited children's education as their single biggest localization challenge in 2012 (Cartus, 2012).

Cartus (2012) reports that children's education assistance was offered as part of long-term assignment policy by 80% of companies in 2010, but this dropped to 60% in 2012 – a 20% reduction. However, this fall does not necessarily represent a take-away of provision; it could reflect a generational change – younger more mobile assignees are taking up assignments, generating cost savings for employers. The fall in policy provision cannot therefore necessarily be interpreted as a reduction in expatriate support. The decline in the percentage of assignees with accompanying children may be correlated with a shift to a younger-age assignee profile (Brookfield, 2012). Such assignees simply do not require children's education assistance and hence assignment policies are less likely to include such provision.

Yet the 'chicken and egg' effect is hard to disentangle. Does the current younger-age assignee profile reflect a deliberate effort on the part of employers to select personnel who can best meet the business objectives of the foreign posting? Or are assignees with children less willing to relocate because educational support has been trimmed back such that the assignment becomes unattractive to them? And the 'crunch question', is the reduction in provision for children's education counterproductive in that the best talent for the overseas role is sacrificed for cost trimming? If the potential expatriate and the spouse/partner are unhappy with the provision made for their family, the assignment may not be accepted, may not be extended or may fail. A further question concerns whether there is a gendered effect on willingness to expatriate linked to children's education provision. These issues are explored in the following sections.

Gendered effects on expatriate mobility

Hallett and Gilbert (1997) find that college-educated women assume that having a career and a family are both possible, while Coyne (2002) suggests that care-giving responsibilities can limit the realization of employment potential for both men and women. Yet women still bear primary responsibility for family life and caring for children (Gordon and Whelan-Berry, 2004). Both home-country management and societal assumptions indicate that a woman's primary role is 'that of a mother, not international manager' (Linehan and Walsh, 2000, p. 57). Hence, it is women's commitment that is doubted once they become mothers (Linehan and Walsh, 2001). From the organizational perspective, children are seen as impediments to women's careers (Wood and Newton, 2006) and family ties as obstacles to overseas assignment availability and consequently promotion (Linehan and Scullion, 2002).

The guilt and conflict derived from the way society defines parental roles force women to make choices, compromises and experience greater sacrifices to reduce work–family conflict than men pursuing international careers (Linehan, 2002). Time spent with children provides greater feelings of work–family balance for mothers than for fathers (Milkie et al., 2010); women recognize foregone career opportunities through time spent with children but are happy with the choices made (Gallhofer et al., 2011). Indeed, women expatriates state that having children reduces their willingness to accept an international posting (Stroh et al., 2000). Hence, while work environments remain insufficiently flexible to enable women to balance international careers and family responsibilities (Linehan and Walsh, 2001), it might be suggested that women are likely to find having children is a major restriction to their expatriation.

Women assignees' views on organizational policy provision

Shortland's (2012) research, conducted within two medium-sized oil and gas exploration and production firms, examined organizational policy on education provision for expatriates, the views of 14 Human Resource (HR) professionals responsible for policy design and implementation, survey returns from 71 female expatriate policy recipients (a 76% response rate) and in-depth interviews with 26 female assignees (drawn from the survey respondents). These data provided evidence to suggest that organizational interventions via expatriate relocation policy can act as a facilitator of women's mobility as expatriates in their own right as well as in an accompanying working spouse/partner capacity.

Examining the findings in detail, provision was made in both organizations' policies for education assistance for legally dependent children in the host location or boarding in the home country and transport for children to visit parents, applicable to expatriates on long-term assignments. One company's written policy extended education assistance to expatriates who took their children with them on short-term assignments; expatriates on unaccompanied long-term or short-term assignments leaving children at home with their partners were entitled to travel costs for children to visit them abroad. Neither organization made educational provision for children of assignees on flexpatriate-style rotational or commuter assignments. The high importance placed on schooling by women for their assignment participation was clearly understood by HR. They highlighted provision of school search, payment of school fees and education assistance being given on repatriation. With respect to repatriation support, education consultants were used to identify suitable schools when assignments ended prematurely and assimilation tutoring was also supported financially.

The survey responses indicated that seven women received school search assistance and nine the children's education allowance. Three women received education assistance on repatriation. Survey respondents were asked to rate the importance of policy elements to their assignment participation, using a three-point classification: 'very important', 'important' and 'not important'. All said the education allowance and repatriation assistance were 'very important'. Five assignees considered school search assistance as 'very important'. One assignee reported that she received support on repatriation with social and family issues, although she said that this was not important to her expatriate participation. All assignees were on long-term assignments.

In relation to the profile of the survey participants, 17 women (24%) had children; 7 women had only 1 child; 5 each had 2 and 3 children. The 32 children ranged in age from babies under 1 year old to adults aged 18 or over. Twenty-two of the children were under 11 years; 6 were aged between 18 and 26; while only 4 were aged between 12 and 16. This aligns with the findings in the extant literature indicating that assignment participation declines to accommodate children's schooling at critical education stages (Dupuis et al., 2008; Tharenou, 2009).

Twelve women were accompanied by all of their children; three by some but not all of their children (leaving the older children behind). Two women were not accompanied by their children (one had grown-up children; the other had left a teenage child behind while on a short-term assignment).

While Brookfield (2012) reports that 43% of expatriates (all-industries, non-gender specific data) have accompanying children, only 21% of the women assignees in the 2 case-study firms did. This suggests that women's expatriate participation may be affected negatively once they have children, possibly explained by the nature of exploration and production work environments in the oil and gas sector (challenging and remote locations). Indeed, with respect to location factors, potential education opportunities for children were reported as current assignment disincentives by 6% of the survey respondents, but only one woman reported turning down a previous assignment for this reason. The following quote was typical: 'whether you can go to these countries, you have to establish whether the schools are actually of a standard that you are prepared to accept.'

Unexpectedly, and in contrast to the extant literature which suggests having children reduces willingness to take up assignments or precludes expatriation (Dupuis et al., 2008; Hutchings et al., 2010; Tharenou, 2008; Tzeng, 2006; Zhu et al., 2006), 11 assignees reported on family responsibilities influencing their assignment participation decision positively. They gave examples of how expatriate housing close to the workplace combined with low cost, high-quality childcare (particularly in the Far East) enabled them to combine full-time work roles (in an expatriate capacity) with motherhood which they said they could not have done in their home countries where long commutes and hours of work could not easily be combined with childcare responsibilities. Examples were even given of women stating the underlying driver for taking up expatriation was having children:

I was working part-time before I left, because we had three very young children…so I was looking at either going part-time permanently and putting my career on hold really, which is effectively what you do in this type of job, and/or changing so that we could make things work for us.

Indeed, it was recognized that international schools were excellent and, as such, participation in expatriation by mothers could be facilitated through access to them: 'some of the best education in the world for children is in these international schools…there are many good reasons to be an expat'.

Thus, motherhood did not appear to have a detrimental effect on assignment participation *per se*, but any likely disruption to their children's education or lives generally was taken into consideration. For example, primitive healthcare was cited as an assignment disincentive by 11% of the survey respondents; mothers, in particular, reported being less likely to accept future postings if the destination posed health risks to children. Access to medical facilities was considered very important; and there was considerable concern over emergency facilities in less developed and isolated locations. Poor security was also reported as an assignment disincentive by 11%. Once again, women with children were less prepared to accept postings to high security risk regions: 'I certainly wouldn't want to take my family to (West Africa). People do, but I probably wouldn't feel too happy about that.' 'I did turn down an opportunity to go to (South America) due to the safety and security issues for my family.' The assignees were cognizant of the value of educational support in facilitating their international mobility: '…the school fees get paid, which I think is a huge bonus'.

However, at critical stages of education, generous organizational policy did not always provide sufficient incentive to remain internationally mobile. Assignees spoke of their career paths and putting them 'on hold' while children were in secondary education (unless they were willing to use boarding schools), being free to pursue them through expatriation once they had grown up: 'when kids get to the age of 11…you want them to be in…one school for the entire period, so you might want to get based in the (home country) for those six or seven years'. The timing of assignments also became an increasingly sensitive issue to women with children of school age: 'you can't show up and put your kid in a school the next day'.

Overall though, the organizations' international assignment policies supported children's education well, facilitating the take-up of long-term assignments in particular. The findings indicate that women with pre-teenage school children were not obliged to 'choose' between a career and family life as the literature might imply (Linehan and Walsh, 2000), although during teenage years, assignment take-up was reduced by children's educational concerns.

In summary, while the assignees did engage in international assignments as new mothers, mothers of young children, when teenage children were accommodated in boarding schools and when their children were grown up, they noted that assignments could not be undertaken if this jeopardized time spent with children or disrupted their stability, education, welfare, health or happiness. While the assignees wished to maintain their careers, these were viewed as secondary to family life and the expatriation locations, lengths, patterns and status and supporting organizational policy had to be appropriate to raising a family.

Reducing educational support

The effect of negative organizational policy change on education provision on assignees' willingness to undertake expatriation is not reported in the literature. Yet Shortland's research (unpublished) suggests that any reductions in education support are likely to impact upon assignment take-up and continuation negatively. For example, one of the case-study firms in her research announced reductions in expatriate education support that involved such actions as providing assistance only from age 5 upwards (no longer for pre-school); providing support for education on repatriation shared with repatriating assignees (i.e. no longer fully company-funded) and limiting this to children aged 11+; treating education fees on repatriation as taxable benefits; and removing school transport costs. While this did not affect current assignees, it was to be imposed on new assignments and assignment extensions.

The women assignees who were interviewed believed that the changes to repatriation support in particular would detrimentally affect assignment take-up and willingness to extend assignments by both male and female expatriates in the future. The key issue concerned the costs involved if assignees had to meet these themselves:

> the vast majority of expats...have children under the age of 11...who will have to pay school fees, so they may well vote with their feet...one person I know has got two children under the age of 11, and he will have to factor all that in and he will have to take a (£ tens of thousands) overall reduction in his package, changing overnight...he was deciding whether to extend or not and he will make a different decision now.

The message to employers has to be to consider the elements of education support that can be trimmed back with potentially minimum effect on assignment acceptance. Perelstein (2010) suggests the 'extras' might be ripe for cutbacks. Yet, eroding fees can have a potentially unintended, disproportionate, negative impact on assignment acceptance and extension, particularly when such employer actions hit the group of parents most likely to have children accompanying them on assignment – namely those with children in the under-11 age group.

Conclusion

Employer provision of support for expatriate children's education is a critical factor in international relocation and assignment resourcing. It is also a dynamic issue that has seen evolving organizational practice over the decades as employers juggle the competing pressures of cost containment while facilitating assignee mobility. There is no doubt that children's education presents a challenge to employers moving an assignee with family responsibilities. Over the years there has been increasing emphasis on the use of unaccompanied short-term and flexible assignments to address business needs, but with the by-product of minimizing disruption to spouses'/partners' careers/incomes and children's schooling. Yet there is evidence that such mobility is damaging to family relationships and employers cite increased employee pressure to address accompanied status and education issues for flexpatriation as well as traditional expatriation.

Employers have reduced their support for expatriate children's education for many years now, both in respect of the percentage of organizations including it in policy declining and in terms of those that do offer it reducing the benefits available. There has also been, over the years, a fall in the proportion of assignees taking children with them on assignment. There may be a correlation between decreased education support and/or the increasing use of alternative single-status types of assignments and declining family mobility; and/or the trend may reflect a change in assignee profile as the selection of younger, highly mobile assignees becomes more prevalent. Whether or not whittling down education support is a cause of reduced international family relocation is not clear. Yet the provision of education and other expatriate policy elements does appear to encourage mothers to accept international relocation while the cutting back of fee payments (on expatriation/repatriation) does seem to present a likely cause of reduced willingness to relocate internationally. Employers need to take heed of this; cutting expatriate children's education support too far could result in direct relocation policy cost savings but at the expense of an assignee-resourcing strategy that precludes/excludes talented staff that place their children's schooling and future careers ahead of their own.

References

Allard, L.A. (1996), 'Managing globe-trotting expatriates', *Management Review*, 85, 39–43.

Anonymous. (2006), 'International short-term assignments remain popular', *Expansion Management*, 21(7), 16.

Brookfield. (2009), *Global Relocation Trends: 2009 Survey Report*. Chicago, IL: Brookfield Global Relocation Services/National Foreign Trade Council.

Brookfield. (2010), *Global Relocation Trends: 2010 Survey Report*. Chicago, IL: Brookfield Global Relocation Services.

Brookfield. (2011), *Global Relocation Trends: 2011 Survey Report*. Chicago, IL: Brookfield Global Relocation Services.

Brookfield. (2012), *Global Relocation Trends: 2012 Survey Report*. Chicago, IL: Brookfield Global Relocation Services.

Brown, R.J. (2008), 'Dominant stressors on expatriate couples during international assignments', *The International Journal of Human Resource Management*, 19(6), 1018–1034.

Carnoy, M. (2001), 'The family, flexible work and social cohesion at risk', in M.F. Loutfi (ed), *Women, Gender and Work: What is Equality and How do We Get There?* Geneva: International Labour Organization, pp. 305–326.

Cartus. (2007), *Emerging Trends in Global Mobility: Policy and Practices Survey, 2007*. Danbury, CT: Cartus.

Cartus. (2010), *Global Mobility Policy and Practices Survey: Navigating a Challenging Landscape*. Danbury, CT: Cartus.

Cartus. (2012), *2012 Trends in Global Relocation*. Danbury, CT: Cartus.

CBI/Deloitte and Touche. (1996), *International Short-Term and Commuter Assignments*. London: CBI Employee Relocation Council/ Deloitte & Touche.

CBI ERC. (1989), *Survey of Domestic and International Relocation Policies*. London: CBI Employee Relocation Council.

CBI ERC. (1990), *Survey of Domestic and International Relocation Policies.* London: CBI Employee Relocation Council.

CBI ERC. (1991), *Survey of Domestic and International Relocation Policies.* London: CBI Employee Relocation Council.

CBI ERC. (1992), *Survey of Domestic and International Relocation Policies.* London: CBI Employee Relocation Council.

CBI ERC. (1994), *Survey of Domestic and International Relocation Policies.* London: CBI Employee Relocation Council.

CBI ERC. (1996), *Survey of Domestic and International Relocation Policies.* London: CBI Employee Relocation Council.

Coyne, B.S. (2002), 'Has care giving become the new glass ceiling? A cross-cultural comparison of UK/US responses by lone parents with sole care-giving responsibilities', *Human Resource Development International,* 5(4), 447–466.

De Cieri, H., Sheehan, C., Costa, C., Fenwick, M. and Cooper, B.K. (2009), 'International talent flow and intention to repatriate: an identity explanation', *The International Journal of Human Resource Management,* 12(3), 243–261.

Demel, B. and Mayrhofer, W. (2010), 'Frequent business travellers across Europe: career aspirations and implications', *Thunderbird International Business Review,* 52(4), 301–311.

deValk, P. (2004), 'The global mobile workforce', *Workspan,* 47(12), 40–42. http://proquest.umi.com (Accessed 28 March 2006).

Dupuis, M.-J., Haines III, V.Y. and Saba, T. (2008), 'Gender, family ties, and international mobility: cultural distance matters', *The International Journal of Human Resource Management,* 19(2), 274–295.

Forster, N. (2000), 'The myth of the "international manager"', *The International Journal of Human Resource Management,* 11(1), 126–142.

Gallhofer, S., Paisey, C., Roberts, C. and Tarbert, H. (2011), 'Preferences, constraints and work-lifestyle choices: the case of Scottish chartered accountants', *Accounting, Auditing & Accountability Journal,* 24(4), 440–470.

GMAC. (2008), *Global Relocation Trends: 2009 Survey Report.* Woodridge, IL: GMAC Global Relocation Services/National Foreign Trade Council.

Gordon, J.R. and Whelan-Berry, K.S. (2004), 'It takes two to tango: an empirical study of perceived spousal support for working women', *Women in Management Review,* 19(5), 260–273.

Hallett, M.B. and Gilbert, L.A. (1997), 'Variables differentiating university women considering role-sharing and conventional dual-career marriages', *Journal of Vocational Behavior,* 50(2), 308–322.

Hutchings, K., Metcalfe, B.D. and Cooper, B.K. (2010), 'Exploring Arab Middle Eastern women's perceptions of barriers to, and facilitators of, international management opportunities', *The International Journal of Human Resource Management,* 21(1), 61–83.

IDS. (2002), 'International assignments'. *IDS Studies.* Special issue, 728 (May). London: Incomes Data Services Ltd.

Ivancevich, J.M., Konopaske, R.T. and DeFrank, R.S. (2003), 'Business travel stress: a model, propositions and managerial implications', *Work & Stress,* 17(2), 138–157.

Julius, C. (1982), 'The human problems of working overseas'. in B. Lewis (ed), *The Management of Expatriates.* London: Institute of Personnel Management, pp. 8–60.

Konopaske, R. and Werner, S. (2005), 'US managers' willingness to accept a global assignment: do expatriate benefits and assignment length make a difference?' *The International Journal of Human Resource Management*, 16(7), 1159–1175.

Linehan, M. (2002), 'Senior female international managers: empirical evidence from Western Europe', *The International Journal of Human Resource Management*, 13(5), 802–814.

Linehan, M. and Scullion, H. (2002), 'The repatriation of female international managers: an empirical study', *International Journal of Manpower*, 23(7), 649–658.

Linehan, M. and Walsh, J.S. (2000), 'Work-family conflict and the senior female international manager', *British Journal of Management* 11(special issue), 49–58.

Linehan, M. and Walsh, J.S. (2001), 'Key issues in the senior female international career move: a qualitative study in a European context', *British Journal of Management*, 12(1), 85–95.

Mayerhofer, H., Hartmann, L.C. and Herbert, A. (2004a), 'Career management issues for flexpatriate international staff', *Thunderbird International Business Review*, 46(6), 647–666.

Mayerhofer, H., Hartmann, L.C., Michelitsch-Riedl, G. and Kollinger, I., (2004b), 'Flexpatriate assignments: a neglected issue in global staffing', *The International Journal of Human Resource Management*, 15(8), 1371–1389.

Milkie, M. A., Kendig, S.M., Nomaguchi, K.M. and Denny K.E. (2010), 'Time with children, children's well-being, and work-family balance among employed parents', *Journal of Marriage and Family,* 72(5), 1329–1343.

Morley, M.J., Heraty, N. and Collings, D.G. (2006), 'Introduction: new directions in expatriate research', in M.J. Morley, N. Heraty, and D.G. Collings (eds), *New Directions in Expatriate Research*. Basingstoke: Palgrave Macmillan, pp. 1–17.

ORC Worldwide. (2006), *2006 Survey of International Short-Term Assignment Policies*. New York: ORC Worldwide.

ORC Worldwide. (2007), *2006 Worldwide Survey of International Assignment Policies and Practices*. New York: ORC Worldwide.

ORC Worldwide. (2008), *2008 Worldwide Survey of International Assignment Policies and Practices*. New York: ORC Worldwide.

ORC Worldwide. (2009), *2009 Survey of Short-Term and Commuter International Assignment Policies*. New York: ORC Worldwide.

Pearce, R. (1998), 'Developing cultural identity in an international school environment', in M. Hayden and J. Thompson (eds), *International Education: Principles and Practice*. London: Kogan Page, pp. 44–62.

Perelstein, E. (2010), 'Expatriate education policies: reducing costs the smart way', *Innovations in International HR*, 36(2), 10–11.

Perlmutter, H.V. (1969), 'The tortuous evolution of the multinational corporation', *Columbia Journal of World Business* 4(1), 9–18.

Selmer, J. and Lam, H. (2004), '"Third-culture kids" Future business expatriates', *The International Journal of Human Resource Management*, 33(4), 430–445.

Scullion, H. and Brewster, C. (2001), 'The management of expatriates: messages from Europe?' *Journal of World Business*, 36(4), 346–365.

Shortland, S.M. (2012), '*Women's participation in expatriation: the contribution of organisational policy and practice. A Case Study of the Oil & Gas Exploration & Production Sector*'. London: University of Westminster.

Sims, R.H. and Schraeder, M. (2005), 'Expatriate compensation: an exploratory review of salient contextual factors and common practices', *Career Development International*, 10(2), 98–108.

Starr, T.L. and Currie, G. (2009) ' "Out of sight but still in the picture": short-term international assignments and the influential role of the family', *The International Journal of Human Resource Management*, 20(6), 1421–1438.

Stroh, L.K., Varma, A. and Valy-Durbin, S.J. (2000), 'Women and expatriation: revisiting Adler's findings', in M.J. Davidson and R.J. Burke (eds), *Women in Management*. London: Sage, pp. 104–119.

Suutari, V. and Tornikoski, C. (2001), 'The challenge of expatriate compensation: the sources of satisfaction and dissatisfaction among expatriates', *The International Journal of Human Resource Management*, 12(3), 389–404.

Tharenou, P. (2003), 'The initial development of receptivity to working abroad: self-initiated international work opportunities in young graduate employees', *Journal of Occupational and Organizational Psychology*, 76(4), 489–515.

Tharenou, P. (2008), 'Disruptive decisions to leave home: gender and family differences in expatriation choices', *Organizational Behavior & Human Decision Processes*, 105(2), 183–200.

Tharenou, P. (2009), 'Self-initiated international careers: gender differences and career outcomes', in S.G. Baugh and S.E. Sullivan (eds), *Maintaining Focus, Energy, and Options Over the Career*. Charlotte, NC: Information Age Publishing, pp. 198–226.

Tzeng, R. (2006), 'Gender issues and family concerns for women with international careers: female expatriates in Western multinational corporations in Taiwan', *Women in Management Review*, 21(5), 376–392.

UCL/CBI ERC. (1991), *Survey on Stress and International Mobility*. London: University College London/ CBI Employee Relocation Council.

University of Westminster/CBI. (1993), *Survey on Repatriation Assistance*. London: University of Westminster/CBI Employee Relocation Council.

Warneke, D. and Schneider, M. (2011), 'Expatriate compensation packages: what do employees prefer?' *Cross Cultural Management: An International Journal*, 18(2), 236–256.

Weichert. (2012), *Alternative International Assignments Survey Results 2012*. Morris Plains, NJ: Weichert Relocation Resources.

Welch, D.E., Welch, L.S. and Worm, V. (2007), 'The international business traveller: a neglected but strategic human resource', *The International Journal of Human Resource Management*, 18(2), 173–183.

Wood, G.J. and Newton, J. (2006), ' "Facing the wall" – "equal" opportunity for women in management?' *Equal Opportunities International*, 25(1), 8–24.

Zhu, W., Luthans, F., Chew, I.K.H. and Li, C. (2006), 'Potential expats in Singaporean organizations', *Journal of Management Development*, 25(8), 763–776.

PART TWO
Emerging Themes

CHAPTER FOUR

Student Diversity: The Core Challenge to International Schools

Richard Pearce

Introduction

Does a teacher working in an international school do anything more than they were trained to do at home? The incessant drive to define 'international education' could be seen as an attempt to claim a distinctive practice where in fact there is nothing distinctive but the location, an *apologia pro sua via*. If there is some distinctive feature of the situation it needs to be identified and recognized, in order that appropriate practice can be designed.

This chapter takes the position that the crucial characteristic of international schools is the diversity of their students, and it is to this that practice should be responding. It is important to discover what constructs teachers use to categorize the students' various needs. These constructs should be visible from the way students are described, and they will reflect the implicit model of identity which underlies the kind of pedagogy that is being used. We shall consider the changes in the discourse concerning the nature of students within international education over the last 40 years and examine how and why ideas have changed.

Identity as commonly used in psychology is our perception of what is persistent in the person's tendencies to act, as they progress through time and space. These tendencies have accumulated historically through the life of the subject, and societies have devised collective education systems to contribute to this in socially approved ways. The case will be made that in general teachers have performed international education according to the national models in which they have been trained, and it has frequently been based upon outdated models of identity. A more modern conceptualization of identity will be proposed which could help teachers to develop more effective strategies in situations, as in international schools, where child and environment are of different social characters.

The teacher and the student

The need for a match between teacher and learner is taken as fundamental to learning, as Bruner noted (1985, p. 28):

> I agree with Vygotsky that there is a deep parallel in all forms of knowledge acquisition – precisely the existence of a crucial match between a *support system* in the social environment and an *acquisition process* in the learner. I think it is this match which makes possible the transmission of the culture.

Festinger in proposing his Cognitive Dissonance Theory (1957) remarked on the tendency in cultural dissonance for subjects to withdraw from the source of emotional discomfort, a stage of culture shock which sorely impedes learning in international schools. In Vygotsky's terms, it is necessary that the teacher and learner should use a common set of 'mediational means' (Wertsch, 1985). This is more than just sharing a common working language; it concerns roles, understandings of the world and perceptions of responsibilities. For international schools there must be a challenge to establish and sustain an effective relationship between teachers and learners who have grown up with different conventions of communication, and differing understandings of their roles. To examine this we shall try to trace the dominant discourses concerning the nature of student identities in international education since 1972. These are influenced by internal and external factors. As the schools have developed it is to be expected that they will admit different populations of client families, presenting different challenges, and in any era the domestic agendas that framed the teachers' training will have established their social and educational focus. The discourses are therefore shaped by client populations, educational policy in the training nations and to a variable extent by the host-country situation. Of these three, ironically it is the immediate environment that is likely to be the least influential.

Origins

Sources of the discourse

International educators, despite the widely shared rhetoric of international-mindedness, are principally trained according to the national norms and expectations of their home country (Leach, 1969). The vast majority of teachers have domestic qualifications and upbringing, which are the normative basis for their daily work. It can hardly be otherwise. The Council of International Schools (CIS) requires for its recruitment fairs that all enrolling teachers should produce evidence of a national qualification. The requirements state: 'Candidates need to have specific experience teaching in one or more of the following curriculum models: United States, United Kingdom Type National, Canadian, Australian, or New Zealand. Experience with Advanced Placement or International Baccalaureate programs is a plus' (CIS, 2013).

A second element which teachers may bring to international schools is their personal ideology and motivation for choosing the field. It has been remarked that all international school teachers are risk-takers. This could be mere curiosity, or it may be a specific commitment to internationalist or globalist causes. Teacher self-selection is a question that sorely needs research.

Third, there may have been specific training for work in international education, but beyond the curriculum-oriented courses of the International Baccalaureate (IB), this is a scarce experience. At an estimated 6,400 international schools there must be of the order of 300,000 teachers (Brummitt and Keeling, 2013). The total output of teachers undertaking specialist postgraduate or undergraduate courses in international education is severely limited, although increasing. There are now pre-service courses, such as those at George Mason University in the US (http://fasttrain.gmu.edu/) and Hogeschool Fontys, Sittard, in the Netherlands (http://fontys.nl/Over-Fontys/Fontys-Lerarenopleiding-Sittard.htm), or postgraduate courses, such as those at the University of Bath, UK (www.bath.ac.uk/ceic/), and the University of New England, Australia (Hayden, 2007; Maxwell et al., 2004). There is in-service training such as the ECIS International Teacher Certificate (ITC) (Snowball, 2007), and some course-specific training such as for the IB or IPC programmes, but the great majority of teachers have only domestic system training. Far greater numbers, including those who later go abroad, will have been in contact with recent initiatives for 'international education' in domestic systems, but these schemes have been prompted by national needs and framed by domestic perceptions. As well as national professional training, we shall in due course look at national conceptualizations of 'international education'. We shall note some explicit topical concerns, particularly in the US and the UK, and later examine the concepts which are implicit in them.

Influential trends in the US

According to the US constitution education is the responsibility of the states, which guard this jealously from federal government intervention. This means that while the arena of educational debate may be national, the arena of educational action is local. This situation has been described by Turner

(1985, p. 105) as 'freedom to be unequal'. However, federal funding may be given where national needs are perceived, and this has happened in several significant instances. The launch of Sputnik in 1956 precipitated a dramatic rush for education projects in the US, in order to make up a perceived deficit in technological know-how and world knowledge. The National Defense Education Act (NDEA) of 1958 sought to promote the nation's role in the world. According to a later review (Wiley, 2001):

> NDEA heralded a major US commitment to devoting new attention to the world beyond its borders – first, to teach more of the uncommonly taught foreign languages, and then to learn in depth about the histories, societies, cultures and political systems of the key foreign powers as well as the rapidly multiplying 'Third World' nations.

The stated aim has been to compete more effectively in world markets and to maintain global economic dominance. International aims continue to be prominent in the explicit aims of American teacher training, but the intention is only reaching practice to a limited extent (Shaklee and Baily, 2012). In the context of international education, Leach observed that the favoured American roles abroad are as missionary or as leader (1969):

> It is extraordinarily difficult for Americans to approach other cultures on the basis of equality. The United States is composed of people whose ancestors rejected other cultures to take their part in the pragmatic new world.

Local initiatives to support the Gifted and Talented (GAT) in order to promote industrial competitiveness were given federal funding from the NDEA, but the provision was sporadic until the publication in 1972 of the Marland Report, which drew attention to the diverse nature of the provision, and its small size (Marland, 1972).

There followed a decade of increased funding and the provision of services (Foreman-Haldimann, 1982), but this was eroded by two later initiatives, one following the report 'A Nation at Risk' (Gardner, 1983), promoting broader funding of lower achievers, and the Jacob Javits Act of 1988, which led to the diversion of some of the GAT funding towards research and away from district-level interventions. The 'No Child Left Behind' (NCLB) programme of George W. Bush in 2001 further moved the emphasis towards equality of support for the underprivileged, a cause with strong resonances in the US.

Perhaps, the US policy which has been most relevant for international schools is multicultural education. Developing from the post-Civil War need to give equal status to all citizens, it was characterized in the 1960s by a tension between recognizing distinct underprivileged groups respectfully and responding to their demands to share the facilities of the dominant society. Education being subject to local democracy, one or the other priority could dominate locally. In time accusations of moral relativism and dilution of standards swung the pendulum of popular opinion away from multiculturalism. At this time the NCLB initiative became a popular device for funding any groups with particular needs. In recent decades the Hispanic minority has shown more inclination to remain distinct, but nevertheless the traditional question still dominates, and teachers from the US predominantly approach cultural matters in terms of minimizing difference, with social uniformity as a prime aspiration.

A late arrival on the scene has been differentiated teaching (Allan and Tomlinson, 2000; Tomlinson, 1999), which gives the freedom to consider a variety of needs, though framed for the accommodation of a range of performance levels. The word has recently entered the international education vocabulary, and the concept seems likely to be valuable.

In summary, US education has inbuilt sensitivity to any division, having a tradition of assimilation and bitter experience of 'separate but equal'. Various federal initiatives have given opportunities to respond in varied ways, for the gifted, for low achievers and for a variety of learning styles (Kolb, 1976), and more recently 'differentiation' provides a framework for dealing with diversity. It seems probable, and supported by experience, that although the domestic agenda of internationalism is driven by competitiveness, those who choose to teach overseas are more likely to see their mission as bringing aid and a way of life to other countries.

Influential trends in the UK

In England and Wales, the Labour government in the 1970s was completing its move towards comprehensive secondary education, and the development of common examination systems at 16 years. By the time the Conservatives came into power in 1979 the academically selective education system dating from the 1944 Act was largely relegated to the small (7%) independent sector and a few conservative local authorities, and the teaching profession was divided between traditionalists who favoured the former meritocratic system and modernists who prioritized the enfranchising of the underprivileged. Dramatic changes were introduced in 1988 and the ensuing years, as the Thatcher government took power from local authorities and introduced a more critical attitude to inspection and supervision, in a campaign to raise standards. In England child-centred primary education reached a high point in the 1980s, which is reflected in the IB PYP and MYP programmes, but it has been reined in by more easily monitored teaching methods since then. A massive increase in university participation brought many families who had no class expectation of Higher Education into what they – and successive governments – saw as an instrumental system of preparation for employment. Many were disappointed after graduation, as it coincided with a decline in manufacturing and other industries.

In the post-colonial period immigration to the UK has been problematic. Without the constitutional framework which commits the US (at least theoretically) to admit and assimilate newcomers, social divisions have progressively developed, and in the cities education has dealt with issues of language and cultural difference in a piecemeal fashion. Urban teachers are aware of the issue, but no national initiatives have consistently been effective. There has been a multicultural education movement, but it has been opposed as tokenism by the political left and as dilution of standards by the right.

Like the US, England and Wales have initiatives to 'internationalize' education in preparation for global economic activity, such as the Gateway project to link every primary school with a school abroad, originally through the British Council. This has not had much effect on teacher training or the work of teachers in international schools abroad.

It is instructive to see what concepts are implicated in the practice into which English-trained teachers will have been inducted. The 1944 Education Act was based upon an essentialist view of intelligence, such that ability could be measured at the age of 11 and appropriate education provided. Indeed, Jones (1985) observed that 'In a comparative analysis, essentialism comes out as the peculiarly British approach to the curriculum.' Applied to models of identity, essentialism sees human capacities as innate, and education according to ability a reasonable response to diversity. Selection or streaming of academic students for IB Diploma courses is normal.

To summarize, English education has not been doctrinaire but has a long tradition of tension between the meritocratic and the democratic, the one accepting separation, the other opposing it. Recent attempts to bring the market to bear on education have increased pressures on teachers, and in such an atmosphere teaching overseas has been seen by some as an attractive alternative. They are more likely to see their hosts as equals, the closer the country is to Britain.

The influence of other international teachers

Canada, Australia, New Zealand, South Africa and other countries have provided many teachers at international schools; in some cases schools still prefer their staff to be mother tongue speakers of English. These other Anglophone countries have produced many classroom teachers, but they may have had less influence at an administrative level because the two main trading nations have tended to look to their own national models when founding and framing the schools. The pendulum has not swung as strongly against multiculturalism as in the US, especially in New Zealand and Canada, where vocal minorities have demanded plural responses. Australia and South Africa have more recently developed creative pluralistic strategies, and all of these traditions contribute richly.

Some international schools are less connected. Bates (2010, p. 263) declares:

The explosion in the number of international schools in developing countries over the past two decades can be seen as a direct result of this thirst both for positional advantage in the home country and for the race up the hierarchy of desirable states.

Since they are more locally based, in origin and in clientele, the majority of these schools have not substantially contributed to the wider discourse, though they are numerically important in the actual world population of schools.

There is a growing awareness of the importance of mother tongue instruction and its consequences for regional identifications, which are championed in the 14 European schools (Savvides and Faas, 2014) and pioneered at the International School of London, among others. This is ideally practised by teachers from the respective home systems, and fosters the norms of the home system, which those teachers themselves model. In general, the meritocratic tradition of central and southern Europe has no problem accepting differentiated education. A final normative source, independent of governmental pressures, is the curricula such as the IB or IPC systems. However, Doherty (2009) has elegantly shown in Australian examples how local perceptions have variously influenced its embodiment in practice.

Having reviewed the concerns of various national systems, it is worth remembering the self-selecting nature of the teachers, which will tend to reinforce the nature of the community as it attracts more of those people who find its present character attractive.

Evidence of the discourse

Sources of the data

Studying the history of international education is problematic. Quite apart from the diverse applications of the term, its scattered distribution, in outlying schools with many geographical and social settings, has always made data collection difficult. Lacking the unifying bodies for the normative processes of legislating, sponsoring, funding, training and inspecting that a national system provides, one must seek records through what are effectively opportunity samples. In turn, this will demand a rigorous consideration of the character of the sample.

Michael Allan sets out the role of discourse in studying international education (Allan, 2013), and Richard Caffyn considers the boundaries which separate the discursive communities in international schools (Caffyn, 2013). From a third angle, employing Bernstein's pedagogic device, James Cambridge describes the reinterpretation of knowledge as it passes from one discursive group to another on its way into practice (Cambridge, 2013). In discussing the history of the discourse of international education one must examine exactly what group is yielding the data. Indeed, it is worth considering to what extent there is an actual discursive community in international education. Where do teachers or other levels of practitioners converse professionally?

In national education systems conformity of policy is most often exerted through the design of the curriculum. Doherty and Mu (2011) point out that in transfer from ministry to classroom there is a series of reinterpretations, or 'recontextualizations' (Bernstein, 2000), according to the understanding and ideology of the successive participants. We cannot research what happened in 40 years of classrooms, but we can examine the records of debate within several layers of the apparatus of international education.

In international schools practices may be transmitted or standardized through the process of accreditation. Accreditation is a form of standardization adopted in the US because of the lack of national examinations. Since the merit of a student is shown by the grades awarded by that school or school district, the universities have formed regional boards to evaluate normatively the standards which each school is applying. Accreditation of international schools takes place through the US American college accreditation groups and the CIS, until 2003 a wing of the ECIS, which conducted its first accreditation in 1972. In recent years the CIS and North-Eastern Association of Schools and Colleges (NEASC) have collaborated on a common framework, which therefore accommodates US American expectations. The CIS self-study documents ask schools to review their own provision for various functions which CIS takes to be essential to the operation of a school. Certain functions are taken as universal, but the evaluation is made on the terms which the school has chosen and publicly advertised, and hence related to discourse. Changes in CIS documents were not used as a source, because they only evolved in a limited number of steps.

A second source through which the discourse within international schools can be analysed is the training programmes of the ECIS. The major event is the annual conference, held each November, on the lines used in independent schools in the US for the collective organization of training. An examination of conference programmes shows what topics are selected for collective training by ECIS. The ECIS has committees which promote training in specific subjects or other areas of expertise. The first of these was founded in 1977 and committees have since been added according to the perceptions of the day, showing the development of focus. Committees are invited to comment on proposals in their area of interest, but are only entitled to select one out of ten or more speakers. That presentations are selected by one or two administrators of ECIS in the light of previous conferences gives an inbuilt conservatism. However, the programme does change annually, and with up to 300 presentations gives an opportunity for finer-focused examination.

ECIS also organizes its own in-service training programme for the International Teacher Certificate (ITC), with extensive assistance from Cambridge University International Examinations (http://www.internationalteachercertificate.com/26 February 2013). This was initiated in 2007, and despite being fundamentally revised since, with some significant changes in priorities, it still cannot give a long-term indicator of discourse.

The ECIS publication, the *International Schools Journal* (*ISJ*), shows what thinkers, mainly teachers in international schools, offer as insights into their practice. Articles are invited openly, and some are commissioned by the editor on topics that are perceived to be of current interest. From its foundation in 1981 the editors often chose special editions on contemporary matters, and the editor since 2004 has been deliberately focusing on particular topics (Ellwood, pers. comm.). There are two issues each year, and unsolicited articles of interest are regularly included.

Another possible source through the period is the IB Diploma programme. This has been well explored from various angles in recent years (Hayden, 2006; Hill, 2010; Tarc, 2009; Walker, 2004), including in this volume, Wilkinson and Wilkinson (2013), Cambridge (2013), Bunnell (2013) and Allan (2013). But as the sources show, its changing nature and its relationship with its changing clientele reflect the interplay between system and context primarily at the formal curricular level, while Doherty (2009) notes that this is recontextualized at the teacher level in a variety of ways. These studies have been a rich source of material for the study of educational evolution.

Because of their closeness to the teachers and the length of the record available, I have chosen to draw data from the ECIS conference programmes and the *ISJ* articles. They clearly show changes in practice and discourse over most of the period.

Elements of the discourse since 1972

The first point to note is that all the main influences on international education today have been from sources conventionally categorized as culturally Western. Even the IB, developed in the environment of international schools (Bunnell, 2013), has been described by a former Director General as characterized by a 'Western liberal humanist culture' (Walker, 2000). This implies an atmosphere of individualism which makes the study of attitudes to identity a particularly appropriate analysis. As Walker himself has suggested, this might not be the case in another 40 years' time, when the dominant sponsor of international schools could be China!

The first source under consideration is the programme of the annual conference of the ECIS. This is compiled by a specific officer, under the supervision of the Executive Director. Their criteria are presumed relevance and interest shown in the previous year. The great bulk of presentations concern things to be done to students, without thought for their diversity.

For most of the period about half of all presentations are on behalf of commercial entities, offering services which have been generated mainly in domestic systems, for domestically perceived needs. These would themselves make an interesting study. However, teachers regularly contribute, offering perceptions that they have developed and practice in their current schools, and consequently there is an element of current classroom practice in the programme, and a teacher-to-teacher dialogue. The Administrators' Conference of the ECIS, held in April, is the location at which policy changes are more feasible, while the larger November conference is for teachers. Attendance peaked around 2005, but since then competition with the obligatory curriculum-based IB training courses for limited professional development funds and general financial stringency have substantially eroded attendance.

The *ISJ*, on the other hand, draws articles from a community which studies international education as well as one which practices it. This is likely to reflect the level of recontextualization between academics and teachers, somewhat earlier in the process than conference presentations. We may expect to see more academic analyses of practice, and also academic ideas earlier in their downward journey towards the classroom.

If we look at the two sources, we can see several strands that run through them, with varying popularity, in which students are categorized on recognizable constructs (Figure 4.1).

Analysis of results

First it is worth noting that some topics played different parts in the two levels of discourse: the more academic *ISJ* and the more pragmatic ECIS conference.

The description of students in terms of GAT is more prominent in the conference programmes, and ability as a discriminator is almost absent from the *ISJ*. It may be that GAT presentations are largely by practitioners who, in the American entrepreneurial tradition, choose to leave the classroom with a good idea and become independent and seek business, rather than debate the topic. It is clear that attention was given to the GAT, especially in the earlier years, when the majority of schools were American. Yet this declined very suddenly at the time when GAT funding was reduced in favour of the NCLB and other programmes, from 1982. Foreman-Haldimann (1982, 1998) has traced the early stages.

The *ISJ*, on the other hand, is closer to the academic origination of practice, and to theory that is still being developed. This is supported by the appearance of cross-cultural topics in the *ISJ* from about 1982, while they did not fully emerge in conference programmes until 10 years later, by which time they were less prominent in the ISJ. It appears that the case for their importance was made at one level and then they moved into practice.

	n	SEN	Lang.	ESL	Cult.	Lrn. st.	G A T	'global'
1972	---	-	-	-	-	-	-	-
	6	*0*	*1*	*0*	*1*	*0*	*0*	*0*
1977	-	-	-	-	-	-	-	-
	53	*1*	*3*	*0*	*0*	*0*	*0*	*0*
1982	19	3	0	1	3	0	2	0
	93	*7*	*0*	*1*	*0*	*0*	*0*	*0*
1987	15	0	0	0	2	1	0	1
	221	*8*	*1*	*6*	*1*	*0*	*3*	*0*
1992	15	1	2	0	5	0	0	3
	224	*3*	*1*	*6*	*5*	*1*	*5*	*0*
1997	16	0	1	2	1	0	1	1
	319	*9*	*3*	*11*	*13*	*1*	*7*	*3*
2002	18	2	2	3	0	1	0	4
	288	*3*	*2*	*11*	*12*	*1*	*3*	*3*
2007	21	0	3	3	2	1	0	6
	283	*9*	*3*	*7*	*14*	*4*	*0*	*10*
2012	25	1	1	1	1	1	0	11
	215	*7*	*8*	*10*	*10*	*3*	*1*	*9*

FIGURE 4.1: *Occurrence of themes in ISJ and ECIS conference programme*

Notes: n = size of sample;
SEN = Special Educational Needs;
Lang. = any mention of language difference;
ESL = English as a Second Language;
Cult. = Cross-cultural diversity;
Lrn.st. = Learning styles;
G A T = Gifted and Talented;
'global' = any form of 'global. . .' except 'global warming'.
ISJ results in normal type;
ECIS conference results in italic

This view is supported by the near absence of Special Educational Needs from the *ISJ*, despite its presence in the more practical conferences. Practice seems to have been adopted unquestioningly from domestic sources. This is borne out by the few articles that do appear, which invariably bemoan the lack of specialist research, and the common confusion of language and cognitive deficits. Possibly, there are so few Special Educational Needs (SEN) teachers in international schools that there is no professional community to generate original ideas, though it also seems likely that their role, in a problematic relationship with the mainstream programme, leads SEN teachers to fall back on their early training for authority, rather than to question it.

Learning styles is a theme that has emerged from the Multiple Intelligences Theory of Howard Gardner (1983), which has attracted strong allegiance. It is acceptable in the egalitarian atmosphere of the US as a way of multiplying the fields in which achievement is possible, and at the same time providing extra fields for remediation. A weakness of a 'level-playing field' approach is that it tends to give a single dimension of competition on which students can be measured, which is bound to generate losers and winners, with associated risks of showing up social or ethnic scales of merit. Both Multiple Intelligences and Learning Styles have been questioned (Reiner and Willingham, 2010), but the Harvard Project Zero which uses them has been popular in overseas schools.

Table 4.1 also shows that cross-cultural issues were recognized from early times at the level of the *ISJ*. Indeed, one of the first collected volumes of articles to be published together was that on cross-cultural issues, preceded only by ESL (Murphy, 2004). A striking change happened around 1995, when interest apparently transferred to the conference. Two factors may have contributed: the foundation by Bernadette van Houten in 1995 of a Cross-Culture Committee within ECIS, which will have nominated some speakers, and secondly the activity in the European Union following the 1992 Maastricht Treaty, giving freedom of employment within the community. This latter contributed to the internationally mobile community a new image of cultural mobility, especially outside the Anglo-Saxon community.

'Global' is a descriptor which is not applied to differentiate students, but it is an indicator of the mindset of the speaker. Like the word 'World' recently applied to schools participating in the IB, demoting the word 'International' to an initial, it offers a single step from the local arena to the universal, without the need to recognize the multiplicity of nations. Its recent dramatic flourishing, first in the *ISJ* and then in conference programmes, might simply be an indication of fashion, but it could also represent the substitution of a universalist view for a pluralist one. The tension between globalist and internationalist concepts of education is dealt with at more length by Cambridge (2013).

Conventional identity models

In the way they categorize children, these sources show a slow development of the conceptualization of identity. Space does not permit an extensive account of identity, so a short summary will be given to introduce the dimensions which the data show to be developing.

Identity is a portmanteau category in which to include the persistent habits of perception and behaviour of a person, and with which to discuss the person's social interactions in its development and performance. It is not an existent; as a metaphor it is a word that we readily apply to ourselves or to another. When the word is applied as an intrinsic and immutable property of a person, as it often is in conversation, identity is said to have an 'essential' character. This perception is not borne out by evidence.

Identity can be seen in terms of the component values of Good and Right, or of the complete imagined roles of a Good and Right person, to which the individual is committed. Bond and Lun lay out the role of education in identity construction:

[T]he socialization agenda of a nation directs parents and other educating agencies like schools to inculcate children with the Good and the Right. The Good refers to those roles towards which the human capital of a nation is oriented, so that the nation may both survive and flourish; the Right refers to that world-view deemed appropriate to guide its citizenry to realize the nation's agenda. The institutional fabric of a given nation will then channel its human capital into economic-social-political-cultural expression. (2013, p. 3)

It is often described in terms of self-identity and group-identity – one applied to personal properties, the other to properties of the person through membership of a specific group (Schaetti, 2000; Thoits and Virshup, 1997). The term 'social identity' has been applied sometimes in place of group identity, and sometimes extended to include those elements of personal identity that have been acquired by social interactions, such as the 'mirror of the self' postulated by Cooley (1902).

The account of identity development given by Erikson (1968), widely accepted in the early 1970s, suggested that it was an epigenetic task of a broadly constructivist nature, to be performed actively by the subject through a series of alternating crises and resolutions in a succession of experiences.

In sociological accounts identity was seen in terms of the role performed by a person in a social environment (Stryker, 1980), and more recently postmodernists have viewed it as constructed in the moment. Giddens has remarked that 'a person's identity is not to be found in behaviour, nor – important though it is – in the reactions of others, but in the capacity to keep a particular narrative going' (Giddens, 1991, p. 54). By contrast, psychological accounts laid more stress on the enduring internal properties which identity conferred, and a psychodynamic account such as Erikson's stressed the necessity of identity achievement (Erikson, 1968; Marcia, 1980). Harré extended this to emphasize the agency of the person in identity building (1995).

One of the most relevant variables in accounts of identity is the question of its nature – unitary or multiple. Some writers (James, 1890; Stryker, 1980; Weinreich, 2003) see it as a complex of many elements, some dissonant, being applied in sets at appropriate times and situations. More primitive and folk accounts portray identity as a single system, stressing the Latin root – 'idem': the self.

There is clearly an element of self-examination in our experience of identity. This can be looked at in terms of self-comparison with outer entities, such as social groups (Turner, 1982), or with one's inner perceptions of self derived from our perception of the views of others (Cooley, 1902; Goffman, 1959; Stryker, 1980). This in turn leads us to look at the action of identification, which, as we shall see later, can be a more fruitful way of modelling human action and judgement.

What has changed and what needs to change?

All in all, it seems reasonable to suggest that discourse in international education has changed little over the last 40 years. There are particular practices in the field, but the dimensions on which students are categorized have changed only in limited ways. Most notable is the way, explored elsewhere in this volume, in which the ideological voices have divided into pluralist internationalists and universalist globalists, which can be associated with Old World and New World views respectively. The idealist voice is still loud, at least in the Anglophone schools, but attention is still largely on curriculum as the lever for change. The data from this limited study of the discourse on the nature of student identity suggest that the major development in perception of the students is a growing awareness of the needs of the non-Anglophones, exhibited through mother tongue programmes, through ESL and through cultural support, and that this could be supported by developments in pedagogy rather than curriculum. Progress has taken decades and is faced with a fresh cohort of nationally trained teachers each year, especially given the current rate of expansion, but there is some progress in respecting different needs. 'Differentiation' could be the banner under which culturally specialized pedagogy could emerge in creative schools.

In her pioneer studies of Japanese children with experience in the US, Minoura (1992) concluded that 'to a young child there is no difference between Japan and the USA: to a young child everything is new'. It is to be expected that from total dependence in infancy to independence in adulthood there is a gradual increase in the stringency of the selection of new norms, as the edifice with which they must be consonant grows in complexity. At the receptive and uncritical stage the teacher needs principally to be recognizable as a substitute for the mother. As Garbarino and Bronfenbrenner (1976, p. 73) wrote:

> In our view, developmental movement…is based on and stimulated by attachment, the primary socialisation of the organism to "belong" to and with social agents…Ordinarily this development of attachment is initially directed toward the parents, but comes to be orientated toward other social agents as a function of the patterns of social interaction that obtain in early and middle childhood.

This calls for some cultural knowledge, obtainable from colleagues or parents of the child's community.

At later ages the child is capable of operating in more than one situated identity (Stryker, 1980), but there will be a difference in the salience of what is experienced through the second, more superficial, culture. It is a commonplace of all cultural meeting places that people using expressive language such as swearing in their second language will not appreciate fully what emotion is invested in it, nor how deeply their own parents would disapprove.

The young child is accepting, the older less so. At a certain stage the child realizes that other groups of people have different ways, and can try to reach an accommodation. Just as Leopold (1953/1971) observed his daughter learning from her bilingual parents that language codes are arbitrary, so a child exposed to more than one cultural set of values learns to be objective about norms. There may be conventional metacultural skills developed over generations in diasporic communities, but there certainly appear to be metacultural skills of acceptance developed by many individual children from a mobile upbringing. 'Tolerance' is a word that is uncomfortable for many monoculturally raised people, but it seems reasonable to suggest that after plural cultural experience alterity is more likely to be seen as a normative deviation, and less likely to be seen as a moral error.

A modern model of identity

Education includes the development of human behaviour in two ways: becoming Good At and becoming Good. These have been separated as apollonian and deontic, or normative and moral, Bond's Good and Right. Others have pointed out that we are also influenced by contra-identification with the Bad and the Wrong (Weinreich, 2003). It can be suggested that becoming 'good at' involves unquestionably useful skills, while becoming 'good' involves skills which need an external justification, as they may be contrary to the immediate personal well-being, but there is evidence that the difference between them is culturally local (Haidt and Kesebir, 2010; Shweder et al., 1990).

The proposed mechanism is effectively the human value system, whose function is to make us do what we need for survival. Schwartz and Bilsky (1987) wrote about values: 'Values are conceptions of the desirable that influence the ways people select action and evaluate events.'

The human brain has the capacity to search and recall its carefully categorized content at high speed. To do this we record and memorize what we see not as detailed patterns of tiny signals or items but as categories that we recognize: a face, a particular face, a letter, a word, a concept, a schema (Rumelhart, 1978), a script (Shanck and Abelson, 1977). Damasio (1994) has shown that in order to make conscious decisions to do the Right thing to survive, we mark remembered items with signals from the unconscious somatovisceral nervous system, the Good with a 'promote' signal and the Bad things with an 'inhibit' signal. These signals he called Somatic Markers (SMs). We know them as Emotions, which we experience as Feelings (Damasio, 2000), sometimes just inarticulate 'gut feelings' (Immordino-Yang and Damasio, 2007). Much of this is unconscious, but some of these negotiations are conscious, and we can put them into words; we call this Reasoning (Haidt, 2000). It is public and dialectical and can constitute an experience observed and evaluated by another, but Haidt (2012) argues with good evidence that it seldom changes our decisions, or those of others. Nevertheless, it is this debate which is the field in which we take account of the convictions of others, and it is at the core of what we sense as our social and moral lives.

Schools are an arena for debates of this kind, though certainly not between equals (Allan, 2013). It can be seen that on this account the unit of cultural communication and behavioural functioning is a memorized and categorized item, here referred to as a 'value' (Pearce, 2011, 2013), associated with a somatic marker of one polarity or the other. The acceptance of these units from referent others (Bruner, 1985; Keats et al., 1983) is the process of education as portrayed by Bond and by Bruner. The use of them involves conscious or unconscious self-comparison with a real or imaginary exemplar – identification. Damasio further proposes that the accumulation of these units takes place by the experience and recognition of an item, accompanied by a positive or negative SM. Since positive SMs are associated with those we like – for this is the definition of 'like' – we can expect that acceptance of items will be greatly affected by the relationship between teacher and student. Bruner's Vygotskyan reference is thereby provided with a mechanical model. The gatekeepers of our learning are thus two: consonance with previous values (Festinger, 1957) and association directly or indirectly with a positive SM.

Conclusion

The need for a process approach

Can we apply this model to the learning of the child in an international school? At a basic level all children learn very early the joys of 'getting it right'. 'Being good' is always rewarded by the important early caregiver, and so is 'being good at'. Thus, there is a fundamental drive to learn, and to show that one has learned. But how does the child already schooled in one mode of learning fare in a new system? At this point the structuralist models of development which are so easy to teach, and so attractive to use, must be replaced with particulate models. The pattern is fragmented, and faced with discontinuity of experience and of environment it is necessary to look for the processes by which development happens.

In terms of schooling it seems that acceptance of the units of learning is favoured by a positive relationship with the teacher. In a classic comment George Kelly, the pioneer of Personal Construct Theory, responded to the question 'once asked how his theory applied to the problem of a child failing to learn to read...replied "find out if the child likes the teacher"' (Ravenette, 1968). But personal liking is not an essential. As Festinger (1957) remarked, we employ the more general effect of cognitive dissonance, evaluating an observed 'value' and matching it with the existing set. We feel, through a number of SMs, a blend of dissonance or consonance, and this conditions our rejection or acceptance of the item into our value system.

In classroom terms this means that we need to differentiate our teaching, especially of items with a known emotional salience, according to our understanding of the value system of the student. If not, cultural dissonance may block the acceptance of the new value into the student's value system. In symbolic interactionist terms, the student perceives what we say in terms of their existing value system, which may not be as we see it.

Positive SMs, experienced as trust, can be gained by associating with a mother tongue teacher in a team-teaching situation, as we well know from school trips. Since values can be acquired singly as well as through a complete cultural social imaginary, 'settling in' is a gradual process. Above all, it is essential to accord respect to other cultural value systems. Anything less is a direct offence.

Differentiation itself is currently an attractive and popular principle (Allan and Tomlinson, 2000), which has appeared at the most recent ECIS conference. It offers a format within which cultural differentiation could take place, and in the future it may be the most acceptable basis on which international education can apply culturally appropriate pedagogy, provided that cultural plurality is permitted. Within the defused atmosphere of the globalist paradigm, this could be a useful umbrella under which valuable richness of pedagogy could be developed. Above all, it responds to the age-old complaint raised by Montaigne (1579/1958):

> When a teacher...undertakes to school several minds of a very different structure and capacity with the same lessons and the same measure of guidance, it is no wonder that, among a whole multitude of children, he scarcely finds two or three who derive any proper profit from his teaching.

Must we then use a different method for each student? Humans are more competent than this. The value system that we assemble progressively will necessarily have to accommodate discrepancies. There are many things in life that we can accept in one form or context, but reject in another. We meet so many complex situations and can apply so many values to any one situation that we spend most of our conscious thought trying to balance positives and negatives, or framing contentious issues in different and less offensive ways. This is a skill which we practice through story-telling and literature, where we apply judgement to imagined situations, proxies for real life. It is here that local evaluations make the difference; cultural differences in value systems are largely in the weight given to items or in the different definitions applied to their categorization, rather than in the polarity of the evaluation itself. Linville (1985) has proposed that there is greater stability in a 'complex identity', which offers a range of frames for acceptance of initially dissonant elements, and this is the situation in international schools.

In conclusion, some elements of our model can be seen in present practice. Mother Tongue (MT) programmes, as pioneered at the International School of London, offer the student an intrinsically positive linguistic and emotional locus for learning. This has been proposed (Williams, 2012) as additionally giving the child confidence which is transferrable to mainstream classes. The practice of working in co-national groups, as described by Allan (pers. comm.), allows students with limited English language to work to the best of their ability as a relief from the handicap of the English-medium class. The benefits of residential trips for uniting old and new students in a location which is novel to all are well known in international schools, as they are at Camp David or Oslo.

Summary of the present position

An examination of the discourse surrounding international school students shows a primitive portrayal of identity. Crude representations of national or 'global' identities are largely essentialist in character, and diversity of need is commonly overlooked. Learning is promoted in national ways, and likely to lead to national attitudes, sometimes in tension with parental root values.

Learning is always available through offering the child a chance to get 'the right answer', especially where a teacher has established a positive relationship. It is likely to be selectively biased towards the students of the teacher's own cultural background, unless care is taken to make 'matches' with some element of the child's value system. A current initiative at the International School of London is to use MT teachers as advisors on cultural particularities, as they are at some schools, and also formally to induct new students and their families into local school norms and practices, in a plural transition programme. The outcome is likely to be a complex understanding of the world. Selmer and Lam (2004) have remarked that an internationally mobile childhood may be the ideal background for an employee in the very company that caused that mobility. International education exposes children to a complex world, and the successful student will develop a complex understanding of it.

Assimilation remains an option in overseas national schools, perhaps the norm in an American system school in keeping with the national tradition of welcoming immigrants. It is well practised, but if it is to be the deliberate policy, it needs to be advertised as such to prospective parents from other communities.

For the present, there can still be a contribution to intercultural learning and teaching in the light of these conceptions. An immediate recasting of identity in terms of processes would highlight the importance of those with whom self-comparisons are made, in action, evaluation and development. This leads us to value more highly those with whom students can make strong identifications, such as Mother Tongue teachers. In this context, the students will find themselves better valued, and more deeply engaged with the temporary learning environment. This attachment is a prerequisite for social learning, and ensuring that each child has some attachment may be the key to better learning for a greater number.

Finally, we may note that each year an increasing number of children pass successfully through international education, in international or domestic schools. It is a characteristic of humans that we have an enormous capacity to rationalize the world in which we grow up.

Future challenges for identity theory

Two very significant advances in understanding the mechanism of behaviour are likely to alter dramatically our view of teaching and learning. First is Damasio's observation of the Somatic Marker, the means by which emotion is used to promote or inhibit a nerve pathway, and hence influence action evaluation, and the development of the moral framework (Damasio, 1994; Haidt, 2012; Hauser, 2006). It offers a mechanism for the Vygotskyan view of learning as a self-construction in a social environment. Furthermore, it links emotion with action and judgement, making any separation of factors in terms of affective *or* cognitive a category error; all judgements have an emotional component.

The second revolutionary step is the acceptance of the strength of unconscious activity, or intuition, as Haidt expresses it (Haidt, 2000, 2012). This, in turn, brings into question the authenticity of the category of cognitive action. If unconscious and conscious elements interact continuously, how can we only consider what we can verbalize, a virtual opportunity sample of purposive activity? These ideas are yet to have much impact, but in another 40 years' time they should have revolutionized our understanding of human action and its socially acquired direction.

References

Allan, M. (2013), 'Multinational, international, multicultural or intercultural? – understanding international education through discourse theory', in R. Pearce (ed), *International Education and Schools: Moving Beyond the First Forty Years*. London: Bloomsbury, pp. 149–165.

Allan, S. D. and Tomlinson, C.A. (2000), *Leadership for Differentiating Schools and Classrooms*. Alexandria, VA: ASCD.

Bates, R. (2010), 'Is global citizenship possible, and can international schools provide it?' *Journal of Research in International Education*, 11(3), 262–274.

Bernstein, B. (2000), *Pedagogy and Symbolic Control: Theory, Research, Critique* (2nd edition). Lanham, MC: Rowman and Littlefield.

Bond, M. H. and Lun, V.M.-C. (2013), 'Citizen-making: The Role of National Goals for Socializing Children'. Manuscript Submitted for Review. Hong Kong: Hong Kong Polytechnic University.

Brummitt, N. and Keeling, A. (2013), 'International schools: charting the growth',
    in R. Pearce (ed), *International Education and Schools: Moving beyond the first
    forty years?* London: Bloomsbury, pp. 25–36.
Bruner, J.S. (1985), 'Vygotsky: a historical and conceptual perspective', in J.V.
    Wertsch (ed), *Culture, Communication and Cognition: Vygotskyan Perspectives.*
    Cambridge: Cambridge University Press, 21–34.
Bunnell, T. (2013), 'International Baccalaureate and the role of the "Pioneer"
    International Schools', in R. Pearce (ed), *International Education and Schools:
    Moving Beyond the First Forty Years.* London: Bloomsbury, pp. 167–182.
Caffyn, R. (2013), 'Boundaries and boundary management in international schools;
    psychodynamics and organisational politics', in R. Pearce (ed), *International
    Education and Schools: Moving Beyond the First Forty Years.* London:
    Bloomsbury, pp. 205–221.
Cambridge, J.C. (2013), 'Dilemmas of international education: a Bernsteinian
    analysis', in R. Pearce (ed), *International Education and Schools: Moving
    Beyond the First Forty Years.* London: Bloomsbury, pp. 197–205.
Cooley, C.H. (1902), *Human Nature and the Social Order.* New York: Schocken.
Council of International Schools. http://www.cois.org/page.cfm?p=4 (Accessed
    3 March 2013).
Council of International Schools. http://www.cois.org./uploaded/documents/
    Accred/8_1_Standards/8th_Ed_Standards_(V8.1).pdf (Accessed 27 May 2013).
Damasio, A.R. (1994), *Descartes' Error: Emotion, Reason and the Human Brain.*
    New York: Putnam.
Damasio, A. (2000), *The Feeling of What Happens.* London: Vintage.
Doherty, C.A. (2009), 'The appeal of the international Baccalaureate in Australia's
    educational market: a curriculum of choice of mobile futures', *Discourse:
    Studies in the Cultural Politics of Education,* 30(1), 73–89.
Doherty, C.A. and Mu, L. (2011), 'Producing the intercultural citizen in the
    International Baccalaureate', in F. Dervin, A. Gajardo and A. Lavanchy
    (eds), *Politics of Interculturality.* Newcastle upon Tyne: Cambridge Scholars
    Publishing, pp. 173–197.
Erikson, E. (1968), 'Identity and identity diffusion', in C. Gordon and K.J. Gergen
    (eds), *The Self in Social Interaction.* New York: Wiley, pp. 197–205.
Festinger, L. (1957), *A Theory of Cognitive Dissonance.* London: Tavistock,
    Fontys. http://fontys.nl/Over-Fontys/Fontys-Lerarenopleiding-Sittard.htm
    (Accessed 2 March 2013).
Foreman-Haldimann, M. (1982), 'The gifted and talented: part 1 – an overview',
    International Schools Journal, 4, 55–72.
Foreman-Haldimann, M. (1998), 'Special learning needs in international school:
    the optimal match concept', in M. Hayden and J. Thompson (eds), *International
    Education: Principles and Practice.* London: Kogan Page, 132–145.
Garbarino, J. and Bronfenbrenner, U. (1976), 'The socialization of moral judgement
    and behaviour in cross-cultural perspective', in T. Lickona (ed), *Moral
    Development and Behaviour: Theory, Research and Social Issues.* New York:
    Holt Rinehart Winston. pp. 70–83.
Gardner, H. (1983; 1993), *Frames of Mind: The Theory of Multiple Intelligences.*
    New York: Basic Books.
George Mason University. http://fasttrain.gmu.edu/ (Accessed 2 March, 2013).

Giddens, A. (1991), *Modernity and Self-Identity*. Stanford, CA: Stanford University Press.

Goffman, E. (1959), *The Presentation of Self in Everyday Life*. New York: Doubleday-Anchor.

Haidt, J. (2012), *The Righteous Mind: Why Good People are Divided by Politics and Religion*. London: Allen Lane.

Haidt, J. (2000), 'The emotional dog and its rational tail: a social intuitionist approach to moral judgment', *Psychological Review*, 108, 814–834.

Haidt, J. and Kesebir, S. (2010), 'Morality', in S. Fiske, D. Gilbert and G. Lindzey (eds), *Handbook of Social Psychology, 5th edition*, Hoboken: Wiley, pp. 797–832.

Harré, R. (1995), 'Agentic discourse', in R. Harré and P. Stearns (eds), *Discursive Psychology in Practice*. London: Sage, pp. 120–136.

Hauser, M. (2006), *Moral Minds: How Nature Designed Our Universal Sense of Right and Wrong*. New York: Harper Collins.

Hayden, M.C. (2006), 'The international Baccalaureate and international education', in T. Pound (ed), *The International Baccalaureate Diploma Programme: An Introduction for Teachers and Managers*. Routledge: London, pp. 25–43.

Hayden, M. (2007), 'Professional development of educators: the international education context', in M. Hayden, J. Thompson and J. Levy (eds), *The Sage Handbook of Research in International Education*. London: Sage, pp. 223–232.

Hill, I. (2010), *The International Baccalaureate: Pioneering in Education. The International Schools Journal Compendium, vol. 4*. Woodbridge: John Catt International.

Immordino-Yang, M.H. and Damasio, A. (2007), 'We feel, therefore we learn: the relevance of affective and social neuroscience to education', *Mind, Brain and Education*, 1(1), 3–10.

James, W. (1890), *The Principles of Psychology*. New York: Dover.

Jones, C. (1985), 'Education in England and Wales: a national system locally administered', in B. Holmes (ed), *Equality and Freedom in Education: A Comparative Study*. London: George Allen and Unwin, pp. 24–62.

Keats, J. A., Keats, D. M., Biddle, B. J., Bank, B. J., Hauge, R., Wan-Rafaei and Valantin, S. (1983), 'Parents, friends, siblings, and adults: unfolding referent other importance data for adolescents', *International Journal of Psychology*, 18, 239–262.

Kolb, D.A. (1976), *The Learning Style Inventory: Technical Manual*. Boston, MA: McBer.

Leach, R.J. (1969), *Schools and Their Role in the Field of International Education*. Oxford: Pergamon.

Leopold, W.F. (1953/1971), 'Patterning in children's language learning', in A. Bar-Adon and W.F. Leopold (eds), *Child Language: A Book of Readings*. Englewood Cliffs, NJ: Prentice-Hall, pp. 134–141.

Linville, P. (1985), 'Self-complexity and affective extremity: don't put all of your eggs in one cognitive basket', *Journal of Social Cognition*, 3(1), 94–120.

Marcia, J. (1980), 'Identity in adolescence', in J. Adelson (ed), *Handbook of Adolescent Psychology*. New York: Wiley, pp. 159–187.

Marland, Jr., S. P., (1972), *Education of the Gifted and Talented: Report to the Congress of the United States by the U.S. Commissioner of Education and Background Papers Submitted to the U.S. Office of Education*, 2 vols.

Washington, DC: US Government Printing Office (Government Documents Y4.L 11/2: G36).

Maxwell, T. W., McConaghy, C. and Ninnes, P. (2004), 'Offering a doctoral programme internationally: tensions and congruities', *Journal of Research in International Education,* 3(1), 71–86.

Minoura, Y. (1992), 'A sensitive period for the incorporation of a cultural meaning systems: a study of Japanese children growing up in the United States', *Ethos,* 20(3), 304–339.

Montaigne, M. de (1579/1958), 'On the education of children', in *Essays,* London: Penguin.

Murphy, E. (ed) (2004), 'Culture and the international school: living, learning and communicating across cultures', *The International Schools Journal Compendium,* 2, Saxmundham, Suffolk: Peridot Press.

Pearce, R. (2011), 'When Borders overlap: composite identities in children in International Schools', *Journal of Research in International Education,* 10(2), 154–173.

Pearce. R. (2013), 'A new language for Culture, Identity and Values', *International Schools Journal,* (in press)

Ravenette, A.T. (1968), *Dimensions of Reading Difficulties.* Oxford: Pergamon Press.

Reiner, C. and Willingham, D. (2010), 'The myth of learning styles', *Change: The Magazine of Higher Learning,* 42(5), 32–35.

Rumelhart, D. (1978), 'Schemata: the building blocks of cognition', in R. Spiro and W. Brewer, (eds), *Theoretical Issues in Reading Comprehension.* Hillsdale, NJ: Erlbaum, pp. 33–58.

Savvides, N. and Faas, D. (2014), 'Does Europe matter? A comparative study of young people's identifications with Europe at a state school and a European School in England', in press.

Schaetti, B. (2000), 'Global nomad identity development: a review of the literature'. *Paper for doctoral program.* The Union Institute.

Schwartz, S.H. and Bilsky, W. (1987). 'Toward a universal psychological structure of human values', *Journal of Personality and Social Psychology,* 53(3), 550–562.

Selmer, J. and Lam, H. (2004), '"Third Culture Kids": future business expatriates', *The International Journal of Human Resource Management,* 33(4), 430–445.

Shaklee, B.D. and Baily, S. (eds) (2012), *Internationalizing Teacher Education in the United States.* Lanham, MD: Rowman and Littlefield.

Shanck, R.C. and Abelson, R.P. (1977), *Scripts, Plans, Goals and Understanding: An Enquiry into Human Knowledge Structures.* Hillsdale: Erlbaum.

Shweder, R. A., Mahapatra, M. and Miller, J.G. (1990). 'Culture and moral development', in J.W. Stigler, R.A. Shweder and G. Herdt (eds) *Cultural Psychology: Essays on Comparative Human Development.* New York: Cambridge University Press, pp. 130–204.

Snowball, L. (2007), 'Becoming more internationally-minded: international teacher certification and professional development', in M. Hayden, J. Thompson and J. Levy (eds), *The Sage Handbook of Research in International Education.* London: Sage, pp. 246–255.

Stryker, S. (1980), *Symbolic Interactionism.* Menlo Park, CA: Benjamin, Cummings publications.

Tarc, P. (2009), *Global Dreams, Enduring Tensions: International Baccalaureate in a Changing World*. New York: Peter Lang, Publishers.

Thoits, P.A. and Virshup, L.K. (1997), 'Me's and We's: forms and functions of social identities', in R.D. Ashmore and L. Jussim (eds), *Self and Identity: Fundamental Issues*. New York: Oxford University Press, pp. 106–133.

Tomlinson, C. (1999), 'Mapping a route toward differentiated instruction', *Educational Leadership*, 57(1), 12–16.

Turner, D. (1985), 'Education in the USA: freedom to be unequal', in B. Holmes (ed), *Equality and Freedom in Education: A Comparative Study*. London: George Allen and Unwin, pp. 105–134.

Turner, J.C. (1982), 'Towards a cognitive redefinition of the social group', in H. Tajfel (ed), *Social Identity and Intergroup Relations*. Cambridge: Cambridge University Press, pp. 15–40.

University of Bath. www.bath.ac.uk/ceic/ (Accessed 2 March 2013).

Walker, G. (2000), 'One-way streets of our culture', *International Schools Journal*, 19(2), 11–19.

Walker, G. (2004), *International Education and the International Baccalaureate*. Bloomington, IN: Phi Delta Kappa Educational Foundation.

Weinreich, P. (2003), 'Identity structure analysis', in P. Weinreich and W. Saunderson (eds), *Analysing Identity: Cross-Cultural, Societal and Clinical Contexts*. London: Routledge, pp. 7–76.

Wertsch, J.V. (1985), *Vygotsky and the Social Formation of Mind*. Cambridge, MA: Harvard University Press.

Wiley, D. (2001), 'Forty years of the Title VI and Fulbright-Hays international education programs: building the nation's international expertise for a global future', in P. O'Meara, H.D. Mehlinger and R.M. Newman (eds), *Changing Perspectives on International Education*. Bloomington, IN: Indiana University Press, pp. 11–29.

Wilkinson, D. and Wilkinson, V. (2013), 'The Pestalozzi influence on international education', in R. Pearce (ed), *International Education and Schools: Moving beyond the First Forty Years*. London: Bloomsbury, pp. 107–117.

Williams, C.V.R. (2012), *'International Mindedness in International Schools'*, presentation at ECIS annual conference, Nice, France, 23 November 2012.

CHAPTER FIVE

English Language Teaching: The Change in Students' Language from 'English Only' to 'Linguistically Diverse'

Maurice Carder

Introduction

Forty years ago English was expected to be the language of instruction in the majority of international schools, and there was 'accommodation' for English Language Learners (ELLs) rather than any meaningful pedagogical strategy. At that time the complex factors underlying language acquisition were only just becoming recognized by researchers, and research showing the benefits of maintaining the mother tongue, and bilingualism, was little known in universities, let alone in schools. Those who did not know English were often left to 'sink or swim' or were given well-meaning but peripheral 'support'.

Since that time huge amounts of research have taken place on language acquisition; and bilingualism, from being cast in a negative light, is now trumpeted in the popular press as staving off Alzheimer's disease and contributing to cognitive benefits into old age (Pavlenko and Jarvis, 2002). Today, we know that maintaining the mother tongue at a similar level to the Second Language, English – or any other Language of Instruction (LOI) – will benefit learners; and also that raising linguistic awareness, training staff and instituting specific programmes will benefit Second-Language Learners (SLLs). However, it is necessary to provide appropriate programmes of instruction and carefully considered assessment procedures. Recommended measures will include a carefully planned overall scheme of:

- information on factors promoting language development targeting parents and members of boards of governors;

- the selection of school leaders and teachers who are professionally trained in pedagogies which are appropriate for children from many different language backgrounds;

- a curriculum which develops equity for all learners and therefore includes a specialized focus on appropriate curriculum content for SLLs, developed through Content and Language Integrated Learning (CLIL) (Wolff, 2003), in addition to a mother tongue programme for students who do not have English as their best language.

Unfortunately, the gap between theory and practice, between what is desirable and what actually takes place in schools, can be huge. Additionally, the variety of international schools around the world and the different agencies governing them means that enabling good practice is often fraught with a complex of obstacles, which can be to the detriment of the education of the students and the well-being of the staff. In too many international schools there are still SLLs who are left to sink or swim; there are well-qualified ESL teachers who are marginalized and not empowered to lead separate departments focusing on second-language and mother tongue programme delivery; and there are too many school leaders in international schools who bring the baggage of the approach of their national system, where ELLs are principally immigrants and thus constitute a political issue, to a linguistic environment which should be socio-linguistically a level-playing field. In addition, there are the sacred cows of national education systems which cannot be touched, notably the rejection of 'tracking' or 'streaming', whereby it is deemed unacceptable for any student to be placed in a separate stream in order to develop particular skills, but which fly in the face of good practice for SLLs at certain stages of their development (see more on this issue in the section 'The best pedagogic models for SLLs').

A word on terminology will be helpful at this stage. Because of developments in research findings both in the field of linguistics, the sphere of education, and various national education systems – in their turn influenced by politics and politicians who frequently know little about the complexity of the matters involved – a broad range of terms has accumulated to refer to the students who are involved in the massive task of absorbing a new language, English, into their cognitive base so that they can proceed through their schooling, and thus their whole life, with as much success as possible. 'ESL', 'EFL', 'EAL', 'LEP', 'SLL', 'ELL', 'L2' and 'TESOL' are the best known; there are many more, including the International Baccalaureate's (IB) cumbersome 'learners who are learning in a language other than their mother tongue'. Each one of these terms carries its own 'baggage' (Carder, 2009). My preferred term is ESL – English as a Second Language – to refer to the field as this is the term that is used for the academic study of the discipline under discussion: Second-Language Acquisition (Block, 2003). A useful all-embracing term that has found currency is Culturally and Linguistically Diverse students – CLD (Scanlan and López, 2012, p. 584). Since this includes a cultural reference, is relatively neutral and does not, as far as I know, show affiliation to any national system, I shall use this term often, with occasional use of ESL students, ELLs or SLLs.

I shall also distinguish between Second Language and Foreign Language: the former refers to the learning of a language for use in the whole curriculum, in our case largely English; the latter to learning a new language as one subject in the curriculum, often French or Spanish. In the vast subject areas of sociolinguistics and language learning there has been an overlap of these two terms for ideological reasons that is not helpful for those engaged with providing instructional models. There is also a conflict between usage in North America and the UK; in the former Second and Foreign are used interchangeably, which confuses issues even more. In addition, the IB uses 'second language' to refer to any language learnt after the first language, which is unhelpful in an educational and curricular context.

LEP, Limited English Proficiency, a term which originated in the US, has an obvious negative inference (limited). Unfortunately, it is a term which must be used in the US when applying for government financial assistance.

'EAL', English as an Additional Language, is a term originating in England (in the UK education is devolved to the various constituent parts of the Kingdom), but in England there is no professional recognition of 'EAL' teachers or of 'EAL' as a subject (Carder, 2009). A summary of the inadequacies in England of provision for CLD students is given in the section below on ESL.

The other side of the bilingual coin, for it is potential bilinguals we are discussing, is the mother tongue of the students. Terminology again presents a challenge, with terms such as heritage language, native language, first language, best language, L1 and many more. In international schools students have a multitude of language repertoires, and depending on their age they may be fluent and literate in their mother tongue, or only fluent orally, or perhaps in a state of having lapsed but being willing to re-programme their literacy skills. I shall use the term mother tongue (MT) (not mother tongue language, which is a tautology). Those who wish to read a more nuanced view of the issue can refer to Carder (2013a).

The onus of developing good practice lies with school leaders, with the back-up of the agencies which provide curriculum, assessment and accreditation for international schools, especially the IB, the ECIS/CIS and the Cambridge International Examinations. The Principals Training Centre, which provides preparation for international school leadership, can also play a key role. Crawford and Krashen (2007, p. 10) state that '[p]erhaps no other area of education has been more politicized in recent years', so boards of governors appointing school leaders need to be aware of these factors when appointing school leaders.

CLD students in international schools study in a different context from those in national systems

Adorno wrote (1967, p. 10) that 'education must transform itself into sociology, that is, it must teach about the societal play of forces that operates beneath the surface of political forms'. The majority of students in European Council of International Schools (ECIS) institutions worldwide are SLLs (ESL Gazette, 2005). Thus, the common term used for such students, 'minority students', is not appropriate as they are a majority. International school students live in an 'international space', and much of their lives will be lived in an 'international' arena; their parents often work in international organizations where English is likely to be the medium. Students' friends will be international school students, and they are often viewed by those not in this milieu as being an elite; elite children, however, require just as much understanding and attention to their linguistic, emotional and related trajectories as any other children. Therefore the most relevant model for these students is one of pluralism and multiculturalism; in international schools an assimilationist model is not appropriate as there are no political pressures for assimilation, there is no nation state to assimilate to, nor political machinations about provision for immigrants. English has become a world language (Brutt-Griffler, 2002). Thus a model can be provided that promotes enrichment in each student's mother tongue while encouraging students to gain biliteracy with English through a carefully structured programme of English language development through academic content.

The status of mother tongues in international schools

The way Second-Language students' programmes are perceived is an important factor as this may impact on students' motivation. Staffing and curriculum for another language area, Foreign Languages (mostly French or Spanish), are seen in most international schools as routine and necessary. Edwards (2004, p. 143), writing about the UK, comments that 'the foreign languages taught in school enjoy high status with the dominant English-speaking group; the heritage languages associated with minority groups are regularly marginalized'. Fishman (2004, p. 417) notes, 'How long must languages and cultures be trivialized if they are learned at home, and only respected if they are acquired later when they are usually learned less well?' In Foreign Language classes students generally learn a language progressively in a carefully structured way over 5 years. Mother tongues are often ignored or peripheralized.

Shohamy (2006, p. 68) also comments:

> Immigrants realize very fast, given such propaganda and myths, that the languages they used in their home countries are of no value in the new societies and may communicate disloyalty, resulting in negative language stigmas and stereotypes about belonging and exclusion.

Edwards comments about provision for mother tongues in England (Edwards, 2004, p. 123), 'Levels of official support for community-based language teaching are more impressive in Canada and Australia than in the UK and USA.'

It is clear that international school students would be well served by a structured mother tongue programme, with a clearly outlined curriculum and pedagogical model.

The status of ESL programmes in national systems and international schools

'The ESL programme is the basis, and the primary prerequisite for Second Language Learners in a school' (Crawford and Krashen, 2007). There is not space here to give a detailed overview of the convoluted path that provision for ESL students has followed in different national systems over the years (Carder, 2008), but some extracts are necessary to show how the discipline has become politicized to such an extent that CLD students and their teachers have been the victims of managerial ignorance and political manipulation.

Helen Moore (2002, p. 112) traces the history of ESL provision in Australia, from the 1970s and 1980s to the situation in 1991 when there was a policy change and 'ESL became viewed as a sub-category of English literacy', with one government official describing ESL's previous linkages with multilingualism as 'soft' and 'wet'. ESL became a part of the subject English. Henceforth ESL courses were frequently taught by teachers with minimal or no ESL qualifications. By 1999 an ESL educator described the situation where 'ESL provision for children who need it is now very much a matter of chance' (Moore, 2002, p. 129). The decisions that led to this situation 'were developed through the network of power centered on national economic restructuring' (Moore, 2002, p. 131). ESL educators were excluded from political processes as 'they could be represented as a corrupting faction' (Moore, 2002, p. 132).

In England there was a different development as educational policy was largely decided by periodical governmental 'reports'. However, the aim was always assimilation; the intention was to help each immigrant to 'become "invisible", a truly integrated member of the school community, sharing the traditional curriculum and participating in regular classes as soon as possible' (Derrick, 1977, p. 16, cited by Leung and Franson, 2001a, p. 153). The Department of Education and Science (DES) carried out two surveys (1971, 1972) which showed the education system's wariness of segregation along racial and language lines, apparent from this extract from the Ministry of Education (1963, p. 9):

> whenever it is desired to treat immigrant children in a rather different way from our own children, for example by putting them in a special class for intensive English teaching, the parents should be briefed as fully as possible about the school's purposes; otherwise it may be cited as an example of racial discrimination. (cited by Leung and Franson, 2001a, p. 153)

In England now '[a]t present ESL is not offered as a specialist subject in initial teacher education. Indeed, no professional credential is required for ESL teaching; all teachers with a statutory teaching qualification (in any area or phase of education) may undertake ESL teaching' (Gardiner, 1996). Furthermore

> for many ESL teachers, working as an 'ESL support teacher' may carry 'a pervasive aura of impermanence and lower status' leading in many cases to ESL teachers abandoning their role and taking up mainstream classroom positions to ensure more permanent employment. To be an ESL teacher in England is seen as a negative career decision. Mainstreaming in England has arguably led, for ESL teachers, ESL students and the whole area of bilingualism in England, to a loss of curriculum status, pedagogic focus and professional identity. (Leung and Franson, 2001b, p. 211)

In a paper presented at the European Conference on Educational Research (ECER) (Mehmedbegović, 2011), containing interviews with various teachers and students, it is reported that in England

> Bright children from migrant backgrounds are routinely placed in classes for low ability pupils because bilingualism is still wrongly associated with special educational needs; trainee secondary teachers found that every one of the bilingual learners they were shadowing had been placed in low ability sets even though they outperformed pupils in higher sets. A Punjabi-speaking Year 4 girl in a rural school said: 'I don't know why I am here. I did this Maths two years ago'; newly qualified teachers often receive only one lecture on EAL during their training course and previous research has indicated that 70% of them do not feel equipped to engage

with bilingual learners; descriptions such as 'severe EAL' and 'children with bilingual problems' are not uncommon; as a result, many bilingual secondary children identify themselves as monolingual. Their experience is that their home languages are of little value in the education system. An interviewee stated: 'I have not met any headteachers with specialist knowledge in EAL.'

Canada has traced a similar path of governmental machinations and downgrading of status for ESL programmes, and of the impact of questionable decisions on such programmes (Carder, 2008, 2013b). In the US this is more complex as much is decided on a state basis and will depend on funding (Crawford, 2000). However, there are some excellent ESL teacher training programmes, perhaps the one at George Mason University being the best known.

As international schools are loosely linked systems in a globalized world they are free to follow whatever provision for CLD students they choose, within the guidelines laid down by their respective accrediting agencies and chosen curriculum providers. However, the nationality and former experience of the school leader will play a key role in such provision as they bring the familiarity, prejudices and potential career development opportunities of their own system with them. Insights into how ESL students are actually positioned are given in Allan (2002, 2003), and a useful checklist of what could be achieved in a language-aware international school can be found in Allan (2008).

Next, it will be useful to look at the requirements and recommendations of the Council of International Schools (CIS) and the IB, two of the principal agencies in the world of international schools.

Council of International Schools

The CIS has apparently taken its terminology and recommended practice for second-language students from England (which has separate educational provision from Scotland and Northern Ireland), using terms such as 'learning support'. However, as we have shown, the English model works in quite different circumstances from those which obtain in international schools and has a record of amateur programmes and language policies for non-English speakers. In a book about multilingualism in the English-speaking world (Edwards, 2004, p. 125), government policies aimed at minorities in England regularly appear grudging compared to those in Australia and Canada: 'National language policies ensure a high level of support in Canada and Australia; traditional antipathy and indifference in the UK and USA have resulted in a much lower level of support.'

In international schools, students are in a different language landscape and a different sociological context. In summary, Second-Language students have great potential for becoming fluent in the Second Language of the school to a literate level, overwhelmingly English in international schools, and also for maintaining and developing literacy in their mother tongue(s) provided that there is universal awareness of the need for carefully developed and delivered instructional programmes involving the whole community. This can provide innumerable benefits: linguistic, sociological, cognitive and affective which in turn could come to fruition by an appropriately designed model for instruction of these languages in international schools, with accreditation instruments that measure these programmes provided by the CIS.

Until about 2005 the ESL and mother tongue committee of the ECIS had regular input to the ESL section of the CIS Accreditation Guide. This policy was reversed, with no consultation. Thus, a comprehensive listing of best possible practice for ESL students was no longer written by ESL educators, and the section for ESL was described as 'learning support', appeared under 'student support services' and was relegated to the back section of the Accreditation document: 20 years of consistent professional input on ESL matters was swept away by managerial edict, reflecting the situation in Australia already described.

At the 2008 Geneva conference the chair of the board of the CIS related how the ESL and MT committee was in effect wasting its time attempting to change the profile of good SLL programmes through conferences. The only way, he said, was to do it through boards of governors: none were present at the conference, showing that the onus for influencing them lies with the CIS. Since then the CIS has upgraded the relevant wording in the 8th edition of the guide: 'Effective language support programmes shall assist learners to access the school's formal curriculum and other activities.' However, this shows the continued use of the term 'support' which puts such programmes clearly in the peripheral box, and school leaders will certainly relegate them accordingly, to the detriment of SLLs, deflecting the responsibility for mother tongue provision to parents.

A welcome initiative by the ECIS is the ITC, the International Teacher Certificate, developed and examined by the University of Cambridge. Its main aim is to 'equip teachers with the global mind-set necessary for successful teaching in the 21st century'. This certificate has five standards, one of which focuses on the 'language dimension' of teaching and learning. The intercultural aspect of education in international schools is also addressed by the standards.

The IB – focus on languages

Diploma programme

When the International Baccalaureate Organization was set up, the primary clientele was almost entirely international schools and United World Colleges.

However, predictions are that international schools will soon constitute only about 10% of IB intake, over 50% now being in the US, with inevitable consequences for the relevance of IB programmes for international school students (Carder, 2011). Over time curriculum for the student body at these schools was developed in line with the realization that increasing numbers of students had English, the language of instruction at over 90% of the schools, as a Second Language. Thus, in 1988 a working party was constituted with the brief of providing appropriate curriculum and assessment at Diploma level, the principal examination of the IB for the final 2 years of secondary schooling, for students who were working in English as their Second Language. Previously, students had to offer a language A in Group 1 and a language B in Group 2, A being their 'Mother Tongue' and B being a 'Foreign Language'. The new paradigm offered an alternative, language A2. In Group 1 language A was renamed Language A1, and in Group 2 students could offer language B, as before, or language A2, intended for the cohort of students for whom English was a Second Language. The new exam was introduced in 1996, but discontinued in 2012, when the IB reverted to language A and language B, albeit with a wider choice of language A, including less focus on literature, and for this the IB could fairly be held answerable to charges of 'second-language washing'. There is now no specific exam for SLLs to show their skills (Carder, 2006, 2007b).

Recently the IB has produced some important papers on language issues (see IB, 2008a, 2008b, 2011), but there is no requirement for schools to follow requirements and there are limited sanctions on schools for not adhering to good practice.

Middle Years Programme

The focus in this section will be on the middle years of schooling as these are crucial for SLLs.

Parallel to the development of language A2 at Diploma level, the IB had by now introduced the MYP – Middle Years Programme – for students at the age of 11–16, pre-Diploma. However, the terminology they used for languages was a throwback to the pre-A2 terminology of the Diploma: language A and language B.

Foreign Language learners typically begin the language in year 1 of the MYP (age 11) and progress to Year 5 (age 15–16), where they gain certification. MYP students are required to take a language B and follow the language B programme, which is one of the eight MYP curriculum areas.

Language B students usually have three or four lessons a week throughout their 5 years, and the assessment criteria focus on their language competence as Foreign Language speakers. Language B students do not require the language for use in school. They learn the language as one subject, of many, and the MYP provides a guide for language B which is obligatory.

SLLs, on the other hand, come to a school with varying degrees of competence in the language, usually English, which will be required for academic use in all school subjects – in social use, and in almost every aspect of their lives – thereby involving their emotional and cognitive selves. It may eventually become their best language and be used for academic advancement, leading to career choice and general usage. They can be described as 'developing-language-A students'.

The separate definition of 'Foreign Language' and 'Second Language' learners is crucial as can be seen: the former are learning a language in isolation as one subject among many in the curriculum; the latter need the language for every aspect of schooling. They cannot survive, progress or succeed without a comprehensive mastery of English (or any other LOI), especially as one of the main tenets of the IB's philosophy is cultivating 'critical thinking', implying a sophisticated knowledge of English which can be bent to the intellectual and critical needs of the maturing student.

This separate definition of Foreign and Second has become not only blurred but merged and overruled by the IB, as it states that any language learned in the MYP subsequent to a first language (mother tongue) will be defined as a second language. This provides the justification for not providing separate curriculum or assessment for ESL students in the MYP, who are encouraged to follow the language B 'Foreign Language' programme, which is, of course, wholly inappropriate as it is not focused on the 'language of the curriculum', which is so urgently needed by the ESL students, another example of 'second-language-washing'.

In fact the lack of such a programme was pointed out in the early 2000s and a working party was set up to address the needs of 'Second Language' learners, with the understanding that there were clear differences between those learning a Foreign Language as just one subject and those learning a Second Language for access to the entire curriculum. A guide was compiled (2004) titled 'Second Language Acquisition and Mother Tongue Development', language A and language B guides already having been compiled (and regularly revised). Strong advice was given by the working party involved in the compilation of the guide that it not be called 'A Practical Guide', as was proposed by IB personnel, as that would lead to ESL students being seen as 'something peripheral'. However, that is exactly what has happened. The guide is little known, does not appear prominently on IB websites alongside the language A and language B guides and has not been revised since 2004. Furthermore, at workshops for language B, to which teachers of ESL students are now addressed, workshop leaders are continually reported to have little knowledge of the needs of CLD students and ESL teachers leave wondering where they should turn for appropriate IB training. In fact those developing the second language acquisition (SLA) and mother tongue development (MTD) guide produced a whole package of materials for training, but these have not been used.

In IB documents and websites there is continual emphasis on the politically correct 'every teacher is an ESL teacher', with links to instant lessons and catch-up strategies. However, this 'chatting' strategy does little justice to the need for properly trained ESL teachers, a clearly defined programme for the language-awareness training of all content teachers, and a professionally designed language programme of curriculum and assessment for ESL students in the MYP. A source close to the IB recounted

> All schools are expected to cater for SL/MT and all teachers are expected to implement SL teaching strategies. Creating an entirely separate programme (a parallel MYP) would be an enormous undertaking which could then potentially hinder language learners' progress as they are removed from their L1 peers (perhaps creating language ghettoes). Sheltered instruction or ESL-specific subject curriculums, for example, were never on the table for the IB.

These points can be addressed one by one: 'All schools are expected to cater for SL/MT and all teachers are expected to implement SL teaching strategies.' This is naïve. We know very well that many school leaders come from national systems where SL students are marginalized and 'supported' by untrained and unqualified teachers, and these leaders are simply ignorant of the huge potential of SLLs in a well-planned programme. Teachers are largely not trained in awareness and teaching strategies, or offered facilities to undertake or continue the necessary training. The IB does not penalize schools if they do not ensure such measures are taken.

'Creating an entirely separate programme (a parallel MYP) would be an enormous undertaking.' This makes it appear that CLD students would be totally segregated, whereas it is rather a question of communicating to schools that SLLs are in a different category from language B students as they have different and more urgent linguistic needs. They need above all recognition as being in a separate category from language B students. I suspect that the IB failure is due to various factors: the status of SLLs in national systems, where they are immigrants and seen as socially marginal, and the complications (including financial) of ensuring that school leaders are aware of the issues, that all teachers are trained, and providing a relevant curriculum.

A study on MYP schools in Australia (Sniedze-Gregory, 2012, p. 1) concludes that even though 'IB policy states that students must be supported and encouraged in acquiring the language of instruction' – in itself a vague and unprofessional pedagogical recommendation – 'many Australian MYP schools are struggling to adhere to IB language policy' (Sniedze-Gregory, 2012, Abstract). In the IB Programme Standards and Practices (IBO, 2010) Standard C3:7 states: 'Teaching and learning addresses the diversity of student language needs, including those for students learning in a language(s) other than mother tongue'; this statement constitutes the entire IB-MYP ESL programme – which can simply be ignored with little fear of IB sanctions.

'Creating an entirely separate programme could then potentially hinder language learners' progress as they are removed from their native-speaking peers (perhaps creating language ghettoes).' This statement is biased as it implies that any programme for ESL students would automatically remove them from their native English-speaking peers. As will be shown below this is not how a good model works. SLLs may be given separate English language instruction as beginners, but they will be gradually integrated as their knowledge develops, continuing in content SL classes when needed, but steadily integrating as appropriate. The phrase 'language ghettoes' comes from the politically correct socio-educationalists who are fixed on not allowing any form of 'tracking/streaming' as it is seen as harming the chances of the less privileged in state schools. But this does not apply to designing an appropriately graded series of transitions for those in the middle school years in international schools who need to develop their language skills in order to be successful in the whole curriculum.

'ESL-specific subject curriculum was never on the table for the IB.' To which one can only respond: why would an educational body which claims to provide an *international* curriculum with clear implications for the language abilities of the student body *not* provide appropriate curricula for ESL students? All evidence points to the need for CLDs to have content-related instruction. Crawford and Krashen (2007, p. 44) state: 'For diverse schools, a program of communication-based ESL and sheltered subject-matter instruction, combined with native-language support by paraprofessionals, is often the best solution'; and Janzen (2008, p. 1030) in Scanlan and López (2012, pp. 601–602) writes, 'The academic uses of language as well as the meaning of individual words need to be explicitly taught for students to fulfil the genre or discourse requirements privileged in academic settings and to understand the material they encounter.' Above all a different mode of assessment is required for SLLs in the MYP, and separate training workshops for ESL teachers from those for language B.

Cambridge International Examinations

Cambridge offers routes candidates can follow from post-kindergarten stage through to university entrance. Cambridge's provision also includes support for teachers through publications, online resources, training, workshops and professional development. They offer examinations specifically in ESOL at various levels of proficiency and have centres throughout the world. Since they also offer training for teachers in ESOL they can be seen as a viable alternative to the IB-MYP, which offers no dedicated course for ESL students or specific training workshops for ESL teachers. Recently they have published a book which focuses on content language for ESL students (Chadwick, 2012).

Assessment

ESL students require specific modes of assessment. A key factor in language learning is motivation, and for Beginners in English to receive low grades from content teachers when the students are doing their utmost to work their way up the ladder of the entire school curriculum is clearly counter-productive and severely de-motivating. Cummins has written:

> The typical picture is that assessment regimens are initially mandated by the central authority with vague directions regarding the criteria for exemption of certain students or for accommodations of various kinds for students who might be unable to participate in the assessment without support, e.g. some...ELL students. (Cummins, 2000, p. 145)

This reflects the IB approach: ELLs have to follow the language B, Foreign Language, assessment criteria, whereas ESL students are best assessed by multiple measures, including classroom grades, projects and portfolios of student work. At higher levels of proficiency the amount of 'numerical assessment' can be increased and portfolio work reduced. ESL students in content classes can be given modified grades.

In the context of the MYP students should also have an equal right to certification. If SLLs leave the SL programme before Year 5 for the mainstream they will not gain certification in the language, and may score at a lower level in the medium of instruction, language A (usually English). In addition, to qualify for full certification at the end of Year 5, students must have completed study in language A. For ESL students this means their mother tongue. Most international schools do not, regrettably, offer such courses. This means that ESL students would not qualify for full certification – after working diligently at their English language skills. This peripheralizes ESL students – the students who are at the core of international schools – by denying them full certification. As Kieffer et al. (2009, in Scanlan and López, 2012, p. 597) show, 'Teachers must provide CLD students with content-specific academic language instruction to support their performance on content area assessments.'

Special educational needs

Because of the status of 'EAL' in England – reporting to SEN – British school leaders in international schools need to re-educate themselves and learn that CLD students should not be placed in special education programmes. Scanlan and López (2012, p. 584) report that 'The language assessments commonly used with CLD students are suspected to incorrectly identify language abilities (MacSwan and Rolstad, 2006), contributing to disproportionately high disability labelling (Artiles, 2003; Artiles et al., 2005).'

There may be 'grey areas' in determining students' needs, but to put regular ESL students in with SEN students is educationally a profoundly negative experience for potentially high-flying bilingual ESL students and simply shows the ignorance of those devising school structures.

The best pedagogic models for SLLs

There is now consensus, backed up by research, on the best programme for CLD students to develop their language proficiency in a Second Language to a level where they can compete with native English speaking peers. Thus it is no longer possible for curriculum providers, accreditation agencies, school leaders or educators to prevaricate about there being a lack of agreement on the most suitable programmes for SLLs, or continue to state that how exactly a Second Language can be taught and learned is subject to debate. There is also the issue of research versus practice: 'the huge gap between research/theory and practice' is a statement often encountered in the area of Second-Language Acquisition. Quite simply, much of the research has not been applied to the classroom.

The best programme is conceived as having three or four strands, and has been conceptualized by several professionals. Much of the theoretical work has been combined by a practising ESL teacher into a model which can be applied in international schools (Carder, 2007a). At the Early Childhood level (ages 3–6) it emphasizes the importance of SLLs remaining with their native-speaking peers. In Primary, ages 6–11 or 12,

> ESL children should be taught in small grade-level groups of no more than eight students. Children are usually divided into groups such as Beginners, Intermediates and Advanced, if there are enough students to warrant this; if the number of ESL students is small, then a simple division between Beginners and all others can work. All ESL classes should meet for a minimum of 45 minutes, and children should be withdrawn from the mainstream at a time when the class is engaged in an English language activity, never from an activity that is not so language-dependent, such as art and music, often the only subjects in which beginning English speakers can express themselves freely. Beginners and Intermediates should meet for a minimum of five times a week, and the Advanced group the same, though four times a week is often deemed adequate for these students. Carder, 2007a, p. 40)

Concerning withdrawal or inclusion for SLLs at this level, the following section makes the case:

> One of the recent educational ideas sure to stir controversy on several continents is that of inclusion. Of course, it is true that withdrawal should

be avoided in very young children, where all teaching must be deeply contextualized and nothing is gained by the teaching of separate skills. Whatever the origins of this counter-intuitive arrangement, no record has yet been compiled of ESL beginners taught by their ESL teacher hovering nearby while the mainstream teacher conducts her class. The arrangement is simply not targeted enough to suit the particular and immediate needs of beginning ESL students. Withdrawal, for beginners over the age of six, is essential if children are to learn survival English at the beginning of their stay in the school, when the fundamentals of the language are developed and the way is prepared for higher levels of language learning. (Carder, 2007a, pp. 43–44)

For students in the Middle School a carefully graduated programme of withdrawal leading to integration should be instituted. Beginners will need the best of ESL teachers, someone trained and experienced, to cope with the multiple demands of steadily building up language skills and confidence in 11- to 15-year-olds. Thereafter intermediate CLD students will continue to be withdrawn from certain more academic subjects (ideally English and Humanities/Social Sciences), while their ESL teachers provide them with the content language and writing skills necessary for 'mainstream subjects'. Such a programme is given in detail in Carder (2007a, pp. 46–61). Enough has been written above about the problems of ELLs in MYP courses for educators to lobby the IB to institute a better alternative consisting of a professional package of ESL instruction, curriculum and assessment.

At Diploma level students can choose their ideal English IB course from the language B and language A options. Students whose level of English is minimal will proceed to the lowest level of English B, and better students be placed accordingly on a language B to language A progression. They also take their mother tongue as a language A if possible, though some students who have not kept up literacy in their mother tongue may be placed in language B (see Carder, 2007a, pp. 97–117 for setting up a mother tongue programme).

Much of the theoretical background for the model given above is based on the work of Thomas and Collier, Cummins and Krashen. Thomas and Collier (1997, 2002) developed the 'Prism Model' which is a triangle (intended to be three-dimensional – thus the prism definition) with separate labels on the three sides describing language learned in their mother tongue (L1) and second language (L2) in the academic, cognitive and linguistic domains (Carder, 2007a, p. 35). The central area of the prism represents the social and cultural processes that students go through in their daily lives. Cummins has been a giant in the field of appropriate pedagogy for SLLs both at the theoretical and practical levels. An overview of his work can be found in Baker and Hornberger (2001). He did much to turn around negative views of bilingualism to show how bilingualism, well nurtured in good programmes, can lead to cognitive and academic benefits for SLLs.

However, this can only be done by building on SLLs' former knowledge learnt in their mother tongue and by building constructively on their English language skills when they have passed a certain threshold of knowledge. Useful and applicable strategies can be found in Schecter and Cummins (2003) and Mertin (2013).

Krashen (Crawford and Krashen, 2007) has not only introduced many theories about second-language acquisition but also been a tireless activist in promulgating his ideas. He has shown how the silent period experienced by beginners should be respected; the importance of reading for SLLs in making rapid gains in learning a language; the difference between language learning and language acquisition; but above all how the major factors preventing the institution of good second-language programmes are politically motivated, and how the focus should always be on what we know rather than what we are led to believe by the press and politicians. The references in the 2007 book contain a summary of a lifetime's work.

Finally, Scanlan and López (2012, p. 583) have produced a study that shows how various researchers have developed a 'tripartite theoretical model that emphasizes (1) cultivating language proficiency, (2) providing access to high-quality curriculum, and (3) promoting sociocultural integration'. They reviewed 79 articles from peer-reviewed journals from 2000 to 2010 which showed congruence in supporting this model. Their focus is on how the school leadership bears the onus for setting the direction in the school 'by articulating a shared vision, modifying organizational structures to support a culture and practices that reflect this vision, and building the capacity of the school to enact this vision by fostering professional growth' (Scanlan and López, 2012, p. 584). They argue that the best fundamental measure for success for school leaders is the academic success of traditionally marginalized students, going on to point out that CLD students have less access to high-quality teachers, instructional time and materials, appropriate assessments and adequate educational facilities, and how ELLs are significantly less likely than other students to score at or above a basic level of achievement in reading and math. The language assessments commonly used with these students are suspected of incorrectly assessing language abilities, contributing to disproportionately high disability labelling. Moreover, the deficit model dominates the discourse on English learners; that is, language is a liability. Constructions of English learners as deficient speak to the marginalization of English learners.

Crucially, these authors give research evidence for establishing an ESL programme in those schools where bilingual models are not possible because of the large number of mother tongues among the student population, which is exactly the case in international schools.

> When promoting bilingualism is not feasible, the best alternative for school leaders is promoting English proficiency while still affirming bilingualism. Monolingual approaches include sheltered instruction, structured English

immersion, and English as a Second Language (ESL) strategies (Gandara et al., 2003; Ovando, 2003; Slavin and Cheung, 2005). Often this includes specific time devoted to English language development, which is most effective when it is developmentally tailored to the specific students. Regardless of the model supporting language acquisition employed, linguistically responsive teaching is sine qua non. (Scanlan and López, 2012, p. 594)

Many schools have developed ESL programmes but now find these under threat. Scanlan and López (2012, p. 591) give research evidence for the importance of 'school leaders crafting service delivery systems that ensure access to high-quality curriculum' (Brisk, 2006; Haas and Gort, 2009; Lee and Luykx, 2005). They add, 'CLD students typically experience inequitable access to appropriately trained teachers who receive adequate professional development to meet their needs as well as inequitable access to quality teaching and learning environments in terms of curriculum, instructional time, and appropriate assessments' (Gandara et al., 2003, in Scanlan and López, 2012, p. 610). Since they show that there is clearly a shortage of teachers who are appropriately trained in the skills necessary to adequately teach all students, there is even more need for schools to have a professional ESL department which will serve as the hub of an international school's knowledge base for all matters relating to Second-Language Acquisition, mother tongue instruction, bilingualism and relevant teacher training.

Scanlan and López conclude that

the goal of crafting effective and inclusive service delivery for CLD students is widely espoused yet infrequently attained. Though work always will remain to strengthen the knowledge base for reaching this goal, *school leaders cannot claim that empirical research is ambiguous about the means toward this end* [my emphasis]. The way is clear: Cultivate language proficiency, provide access to high-quality teaching and learning, and promote the sociocultural integration of all students. (2012, pp. 615–616)

Conclusions

The world has changed significantly in the last 40 years. Globalization has become pervasive, with inevitable advantages and disadvantages; it has been described as an 'epoch-making postmodern paradigm shift which in its way is as far-reaching as the change from a mediaeval agricultural economy to modern industrial society' (Küng, 1998). Electronic communications and computers have changed the way we work. However, language remains the basis of all we do and think, and learning a language remains a lengthy process: learning one for academic study is even more demanding. At a meeting convened by the IB in Cardiff some years ago, Edna Murphy described the increase in SLLs in school demographics as a 'Copernican shift' to which we should respond. Fortunately we now know much more about the numerous factors surrounding language, and in an international school the responsibility for applying this knowledge to good practice lies with school leaders and curriculum and accreditation agencies. Strong management is needed by leaders who are not only capable of analysis but can also take appropriate decisions and implement them, a skill which can only be achieved after thorough training and long experience. The middle years of schooling are a vital area for ELLs, and having a viable programme of instruction including CLIL and sheltered instruction, relevant assessment and reward for these students needs to be robustly instituted if CLD students are not to be 'denied or relegated' and restricted from achieving their true potential. Researchers will continue to contest aspects of methodology, and the CIS and the IB will continue to prevaricate and obfuscate about providing good ESL programmes; meanwhile generations of CLD students will suffer the consequences of being treated like second-class citizens, losing fluency and literacy in their mother tongue, and not being given pro-active teaching in content-area subjects. It is often said that our world views run so deep that they can very rarely be transformed by rational argument, but this has to be vigorously contested in international schools in order for SLLs to achieve their true potential: international schools need strong ESL and mother tongue departments to act as centres of expertise, robustly supported by accreditation bodies, with a defined ESL curriculum and guide written by the IB. It is paradoxical that it is the SLL children of the international community which created the need for international schools who are suffering because of the inability of international educational bodies to provide relevant models.

References

Adorno, T. (1967), 'Education after Auschwitz'. http://www.deschoolingclassroom.tkh-generator.net/wp-content/uploads/2009/12/adorno-education_after_auschwitz.pdf

Allan, M. (2002), 'Cultural Borderlands: a case study of cultural dissonance in an international school', *Journal of Research in International Education*, 2, 83.

Allan, M. (2003), 'Frontier crossings: cultural dissonance, intercultural learning and the multicultural personality', *Journal of Research in International Education*, 2, 83.

Allan, M. (2008), 'An internationalism audit', appendix 1, pages 133–137, in E. Gallagher (ed) *Equal Rights to the Curriculum: Many Languages, One Message*. Clevedon: Multilingual Matters, pp. 133–137.

Artiles, A. (2003), 'Special education's changing identity: paradoxes and dilemmas in views of culture and space', *Harvard Educational Review*, 73, 164–202.

Artiles, A., Rueda, R., Salazar, J.J. and Higareda, I. (2005), 'Within-group diversity in minority disproportionate representation: English language learners in urban school districts', *Exceptional Children*, 71, 283–300.

Baker, C. and Hornberger, N.H. (eds), (2001), *An Introductory Reader to the Writings of Jim Cummins*. Clevedon: Multilingual Matters.

Block, D. (2003), *The Social Turn in Second Language Acquisition*. Edinburgh: Edinburgh University Press.

Brisk, M.E. (2006), *Bilingual Education: From Compensatory to Quality Schooling*. Mahwah, NJ: Lawrence Erlbaum.

Brutt-Griffler, J. (2002), *World English: A Study of Its Development*. Clevedon: Multilingual Matters.

Cambridge International Examinations. http://www.cie.org.uk/

Carder, M. (2006), 'Bilingualism in International Baccalaureate Programmes, with particular reference to International Schools', *Journal of Research in International Education*, 5, 1.

Carder, M. (2007a), *Bilingualism in International Schools: A Model for Enriching Language Education*. Clevedon: Multilingual Matters.

Carder, M. (2007b), 'The IB and languages', *International Schools Journal*, 27(1), 76–79.

Carder, M. (2008), 'The development of English as a second language (ESL) provision in Australia, Canada, the USA and England, with conclusions for second language models in international schools', *Journal of Research in International Education*, 7(2), 208–231.

Carder, M. (2009), '"ESL" or "EAL"?: programme or "support"? The baggage that comes with names', *International Schools Journal*, 29(1), 18–25.

Carder, M. (2011), 'ESL in International Schools in the IBMYP: the elephant under the table', *International Schools Journal*, 31(1), 50–58.

Carder, M. (2013a), 'International school students: developing their bilingual potential', in C. Abello-Contesse, P.M. Chandler, M.D. López-Jiménez and R. Chacón-Beltrán (eds), *Bilingual and Multilingual Education in the 21st Century: Building on Experience*. Bristol: Multilingual Matters, in press.

Carder, M. (2013b), 'Managerial impact on programmes for second language learners in international schools'. www.mauricecarder.net

Chadwick, T. (2012), *Language Awareness in Teaching: A Toolkit for Content and Language Teachers*. Cambridge: Cambridge University Press.

CIS (Council of International Schools). www.cois.org

Crawford, J. (2000), *At War with Diversity*. Clevedon: Multilingual Matters Ltd.

Crawford, J. and Krashen, S. (2007), *English Learners in American Classrooms*. New York: Scholastic.

Cummins, J. (2000), *Language, Power and Pedagogy*. Clevedon: Multilingual Matters.

Derrick, J. (1977), *Language Needs of Minority Group Children*. Slough: NFER.

DES. (1971), 'The education of immigrants', *Education Survey 13*, Department of Education and Science. London: HMSO.

DES. (1972), 'The continuing needs of immigrants', *Education Survey 14*, Department of Education and Science. London: HMSO.

ECIS (European Council of International Schools). www.ecis.org

Edwards, V. (2004), *Multilingualism in the English-speaking World*. Oxford: Blackwell Publishing.

ESL Gazette, August 2005 (publication details could not be traced).

Fishman, J.A. (2004), 'Language maintenance, language shift, and reversing language shift', in T.K. Bhatia and W.C. Ritchie (eds), *The Handbook of Bilingualism*. Malden, MA: Blackwell Publishing, pp. 406–436.

Gandara, P., Rumberger, R., Maxwell-Jolly, J. and Callahan, R. (2003), 'English learners in California schools: unequal resources, unequal outcomes', *Educational Policy Analysis Archives*, 11(36), 1–54.

Gardiner, J. (1996), 'Recruits braced for the basics', *Times Educational Supplement*, 27 October.

Haas, E. and Gort, M. (2009), 'Demanding more: legal standards and best practices for English language learners', *Bilingual Research Journal*, 32, 115–135.

International Baccalaureate Organization (IBO). www.ibo.org – to access all IB publications below.

International Baccalaureate Organization (IBO). (2008a), *Guidelines for Developing a School Language Policy*. Cardiff: International Baccalaureate Organization.

International Baccalaureate Organization (IBO). (2008b), *Learning in a Language Other Than Mother Tongue in IB Programmes*. Cardiff: International Baccalaureate Organization.

International Baccalaureate Organization (IBO). (2010), *Programme Standards and Practices*. Cardiff: International Baccalaureate Organization.

International Baccalaureate Organization (IBO). (2011), *Language and Learning in IB Programmes*. Cardiff: International Baccalaureate Organization.

International Teachers Certificate. http://www.internationalteachercertificate.com/why.asp

Janzen, J. (2008), 'Teaching English language learners in the content areas', *Review of Educational Research*, 78, 1010–1038.

Kieffer, M., Lesaux, N., Rivera, M. and Francis, D. (2009), 'Accommodations for English language learners taking large-scale assessments: a meta-analysis on effectiveness and validity', *Review of Educational Research*, 79, 1168–1201.

Küng, H. (1998), *A Global Ethic for Global Politics and Economics*. Oxford: Oxford University Press.

Lee, O. and Luykx, A. (2005), 'Dilemmas in scaling up innovations in elementary science instruction with nonmainstream students', *American Educational Research Journal*, 42, 411–438.

Leung, C. and Franson, C. (2001a), 'England: ESL in the early days', in B. Mohan, C. Leung, and C. Davison (eds), *English as a Second Language in the Mainstream: Teaching, Learning and Identity*. Harlow: Longman Pearson, pp. 153–164.

Leung, C. and Franson, C. (2001b), 'Curriculum identity and professional development: system-wide questions', in B. Mohan, C. Leung and C. Davison (eds), *English as a Second Language in the Mainstream: Teaching, Learning and Identity*. Harlow: Longman Pearson, pp. 199–214.

MacSwan, J. and Rolstad, K. (2006), 'How language proficiency tests mislead us about ability: implications for English language learner placement in special education', *Teachers College Record*, 108, 2304–2328.

Mehmedbegović, D. (2011), 'Reflecting on the provision for equipping the school workforce in England for a multilingual school population: research conducted with experts', *Paper Presented at The European Conference on Educational Research*, annual meeting of European Educational Research Association, Freie

Universität, Berlin, 12–16 September. Summarised at http://www.ioe.ac.uk/newsEvents/56528.html

Mertin, P. (2013), *Breaking through the Language Barrier: Effective Strategies for Teaching English as a Second Language (ESL) Students in Mainstream Classes.* Woodbridge: John Catt Educational.

Ministry of Education. (1963), *English for Immigrants.* London: HMSO.

Moore, H. (2002), 'Who will guard the guardians themselves?', in J.W. Tollefson (ed), *Language Policies in Education.* New York: Lawrence Erlbaum Associates, pp. 111–136.

Ovando, C. (2003), 'Bilingual education in the United States: historical development and current issues', *Bilingual Research Journal,* 27, 1–25.

Pavlenko, A. and Jarvis S.(2002), 'Bidirectional transfer', *Applied Linguistics,* 23(2), 190–214.

Scanlan, M and F.López (2012), '¡Vamos! How school leaders promote equity and excellence for bilingual students', *Educational Administration Quarterly* 48, 583.

Schecter, S.R. and Cummins, J. (eds) (2003), *Multilingual Education in Practice.* Portsmouth, NH: Heinemann.

Shohamy, E. (2006), *Language Policy: Hidden Agendas and New Approaches.* London: Routledge.

Slavin, R.E. and Cheung, A. (2005), 'A synthesis of research on language of reading instruction for English language learners', *Review of Educational Research,* 75, 247–284.

Sniedze-Gregory, S. (2012), 'To what extent are language rights upheld in Australian IB MYP schools?', *Research project for M.Ed.,* Flinders University, Adelaide, Australia.

The Principals Training Centre. http://www.theptc.org/

Thomas, W.P. and Collier, V.P.(1997), *School Effectiveness for Language Minority Students.* Washington, DC: National Clearinghouse for English Language Acquisition. www.ncela.gwu.edu/ncbepubs/resource/effectiveness/index.html

Thomas, W.P. and Collier, V.P. (2002), *A National Study of School Effectiveness for Language Minority Students' Long-Term Academic Achievement.* Santa Cruz, CA: Center for Research on Education, Diversity and Excellence, University of California-Santa Cruz. http://www.crede.ucsc.edu

Wolff, D. (2003), 'Content and language integrated learning: a framework for the development of learner autonomy', in D. Little, J. Ridley and E. Ushioda (eds), *Learner Autonomy in the Foreign Language Classroom.* Dublin: Authentik, pp. 211–222.

CHAPTER SIX

The Pestalozzi Influence on International Education

David Wilkinson and Veronica Wilkinson

Quoting Plato, Kurt Hahn wrote: 'He who wishes to serve his country must have not only the power to think, but the will to act.' It is now over 50 years since Hahn inspired many of the founders of both the United World Colleges movement and the International Baccalaureate (IB), yet Hahn was himself inspired by the educational philosophy of Johann Pestalozzi (Smith, 2012). This chapter will examine the influence of Pestalozzi's thinking on the foundation and development of the IB. In doing so, it will ask whether young people who have completed the Diploma are prepared to make a positive difference in a world that has become more interconnected, yet is one in which the gulf between the rich and the poor grows ever wider. Extending Kurt Hahn's comment, are they prepared to go beyond the service of country to the service of humanity? This question will be examined in the light of the growing demand for objectivity in testing and, with it, the control of teachers by educational authorities and examination boards over the past 50 years: this has become a universal phenomenon.

As we shall see, crucial to Pestalozzi's belief in education are the nature of the relationship between teacher and pupil and the central place of values as the platform upon which an education must be built. The two are not, however, independent of one another according to Pestalozzi; only when the teacher is free to build up a unique relationship with each individual pupil is it possible that strong values could develop through the medium of formal education. Pestalozzi stated that this is essential because the need for humans to be part of society is fundamental to an individual's well-being; yet the nature of society rests on the collective willingness of individuals to place the good of the whole beyond their own needs (Bruhlmeier, 2010, p. 18).

Pestalozzi's educational philosophy and the foundation of the IB

Johann Pestalozzi lived and worked in the latter part of the eighteenth and the early years of the nineteenth centuries. Swiss by nationality, at a time when Switzerland was not the wealthy country that it has become, he spent much of his time giving education to underprivileged and orphaned boys. He is perhaps best remembered for his holistic belief in the education of 'Head, Heart and Hands' and that education should not only enable one, as an adult, to function in society but must also develop to the full each person's unique potential. An optimist in his belief about human nature, he had the conviction that it is in the nature of the faculties that all humans possess that drives each person to use them. 'The eye wants to see, the ear to hear, the foot wants to walk and the hand to grasp. And, equally, the heart wants to believe and love, the mind wants to think' (Bruhlmeier, 2010, p. 20). What is central, however, to Pestalozzi's educational philosophy was his certainty that the faculties of head and hand are of value only if guided by those of the heart. Only the development of the heart, he wrote, 'can enable us to reach our true goal of humanity' (Bruhlmeier, 2010, p. 18). It will be useful, therefore, to examine what Pestalozzi meant by the 'education of the heart'.

Education, he believed, must raise the quality of a person's life; essential to this are the basic moral feelings of love, trust and thankfulness. These are the qualities of the heart that must be developed. In combination with the intellect and physical strength, they give a person the determination that one's actions should have a positive effect. These qualities are, however, an essential part of the nature of human beings; we possess a nature, something innate in each of us, that is unchanging regardless of external influences. In fact, Hofstede states that 'personality...is inherited as well as learned' and thus shares this view (1991, p. 6). Education is not therefore a matter of putting things into a person; it is a matter of developing that which is already within the person and the manner in which this is done is crucial to the development of the whole person.

Pestalozzi believed that the central relationship between teacher and pupil must not be constrained by externally dictated factors if this process is to enable the student to reach his full potential. This view is strongly supported by Vygotsky, who stressed the importance of teacher–student communication in his socio-educational cultural theory (1978). This has been further developed by Daniels, who described the process of teaching and learning as 'much more than face-to-face interaction or the simple transmission of prescribed knowledge and skills' (Daniels, 2001, p. 2). As we shall see, in the present context the demands on teachers of a prescriptive curriculum represent one such constraint and increasing competition for places at universities throughout the world adds a further limitation.

A question of values – international and national

The belief that the whole person should be educated was evident in the founding of the IB in 1968. Not only should students acquire knowledge and skills – the head and the hands – in the formal curriculum, they should also acquire a set of values – the heart. This is not, however, the sole concern of international education; indeed it is a universal concern. What then distinguishes the values implicit in an international education, if any, that sets it apart in this respect from a national education?

Wilson et al. (1967, p. 405) suggest ten useful ways for introducing moral education into schools and hence effecting changes in student values in a national school system. These include:

1   The pupil's need for a secure framework in terms of group identity.

2   His need for a personal identity in terms of feeling confident, successful, useful and wanted.

3   The importance of close personal contact with adults.

4   His ability to develop moral concepts, and to communicate linguistically.

5   The relevance of rule-governed activities and contracts.

6   The importance of parent-figures and of a firm and clearly defined authority.

7   The need to channel or institutionalize aggression.

8   The merits of co-operation as against competition.

9   The need to enable the pupil to objectify his own feelings.

10 The importance of getting the pupil to participate, and to make the educational situation come alive.

It is interesting to note that nowhere do they suggest that pupils learn to be flexible, to attempt to understand others' cultures and moral rules. It was, from the outset, the belief of the founders of the IB that knowledge and skills should have a global perspective and that the values that would distinguish an international education should include what Hill describes as 'empathy for the feelings, needs and lives of others in different countries' (2002, p. 27). It is, clearly articulated in the IB mission statement, 'that other people, with their differences, can also be right' that sets the values underpinning an international education apart from a national one (ibo. org). Nor, as we shall see, is this simply a lapse into relativistic thinking with respect to value judgements. If the graduates of an international education are to make an impact beyond their own national societies, it is surely this value that must be a driving force. Indeed, in identifying the universals of international education, Hayden and Thompson stress cultural diversity amongst the student body and teachers as exemplars of international mindedness (1996, p. 55).

There are dangers however in attempting to establish a set of values that cut across cultural assumptions. Hofstede noted that values are seldom recognized as being culturally relative and, thus, 'cross-cultural learning situations are rife with premature judgments' (Hofstede, 1986, p. 305). His research on differences in work-related values across 50 countries concluded that four characteristics were apparent: individualism versus collectivism, power distance, uncertainty avoidance and masculinity versus femininity. He then demonstrated how each of these characteristics is depicted in the student–student and teacher–student interactions (Hofstede, 1986, pp. 306–320).

Challenges to the education of the heart: The Theory of Knowledge course as an example of the drive for greater objectivity

Pestalozzi had a clear standpoint with respect to the belief that 'standardization and hierarchical management of the educational process can improve the quality of education.' (Bruhlmeier, 2010, p. 21) Teachers, he believed, must be free to encourage those activities that pupils want to tackle. At the same time, teachers should be happy to carry out activities suggested by the pupils themselves and not necessarily dictated by the syllabus. The teacher must also be responsive to the present needs of children rather than over-emphasizing future needs. Pestalozzi argued that a concentration on the outcome of education as a means to furthering one's future is not the basis for engagement in constructive learning (Bruhlmeier, 2010, p. 23). What, therefore, has been the impact on the teacher's freedom for action caused by the drive for greater objectivity in educational testing and the greater control on the curriculum? Has this been avoided in the IB, or has the organization followed the trend of all national systems of education?

The increasing control of teachers by educational authorities and the development of quality control checks that have led to the production of educational materials intended to help students attain standards that can be objectively tested deflect attention from what, in Pestalozzi's view, is crucial to the development of the full potential of the individual. The development of the Theory of Knowledge course over the course of the past 40 years provides an interesting case study of the way in which the demand for greater reliability has affected the nature of the course. In particular, what has been the impact on the freedom for individual interpretation by teachers of the means by which its objectives can be best attained?

The founders of the IB saw this course as central to the intellectual heart of the Diploma. It was seen to be a means by which the barriers between discrete subjects could be broken down, giving students an understanding of the unity of knowledge and of the different ways in which humanity has sought to make sense of the world. In the early days, teachers were given considerable freedom in designing their own course and were allowed to leave out sections of the syllabus that were not appropriate to their location. The guiding principle was that the Theory of Knowledge course should not become a seventh subject. Peterson, one of the driving forces behind the course, was faced with a dilemma: should it be assessed and, if so, in what manner could this be done without imposing a structure that would remove the teachers' freedom? Peterson's previous experience of un-assessed general studies programmes in the UK led him to believe that the Theory of Knowledge course should be assessed. The solution was, in his words, 'to give it a weighting which affected the points scored for the diploma as a whole, but not those of any individual subject' (Peterson, 1987, p. 179). However, this still left unsolved the issue of control of standards. At the same time, many experienced Theory of Knowledge teachers strongly opposed any form of external examination. The decision was essentially a compromise; a common examination was to be set that was internally graded and externally moderated.

As the popularity of the IB Diploma has grown, the number of schools has risen dramatically; the Diploma course has become increasingly more structured, the criteria for assessment more clearly described and the essay is now externally examined, leaving only a minority portion of the grades to be awarded internally.

This perceived need for reliability has removed much of the freedom from the teacher that was originally a source of inspiration and very much in line with Pestalozzi's belief in the need for the teacher to have the autonomy to develop a unique relationship with the student. The very success of the IB Diploma programme has meant that one of its most innovative components has become much more a mainstream programme. Has the need for greater reliability undermined the validity of the course? At the outset, it was clearly intended to extract from each student his or her unique way of seeing the connections between their subjects in order to understand the wholeness of the academic programme.

However, the development of the academic programme is only one aspect of the education that the IB provides; it is also clear, as is evident in the mission statement, about the values that it seeks to impart to young people. We will ask, therefore, whether increasing control of the academic programme through the detailing of intellectual objectives and the increasing demand for reliability and objectivity in assessment has an inevitable impact on the values that are central to its philosophy. If we follow Pestalozzi's beliefs, then because this will restrict the freedom of the classroom teacher, the growth of the relationship between teacher and pupil that is essential for the development of a strong set of values will be limited.

As noted previously, in its mission statement, the IB states that its programmes 'encourage students...(to) understand that other people, with their differences, can also be right' (ibo.org). This is crucial as an outcome that is essential if young people who have completed the IB Diploma programme are to make a positive difference in a globally interconnected world. Yet, 'if we remain merely at the stage of celebrating diversity, we are ultimately promoting fragmentation, separation and despair' (Wilber, 2000, in Skelton, 2002, p. 44). How, therefore, can an education develop both Hahn's 'love of country' and its own culture together with respect for the diversity of cultures that love of humanity requires: to transcend the parochial, not only in feeling, but also with a clear intellectual objectivity? This is at the heart of the matter; is it possible to separate the intellect from the values upon which the intellect operates?

Taking on the challenges to the education of the heart

The International Primary Curriculum has taken on this challenge. Skelton, one of the founders of this programme, believes that 'it is important to encourage notions of "independence" and "interdependence"...that these concepts are only likely to have the real power for change...if they are preceded by the knowledge and understanding that we are also very similar' (2002, p. 45). The belief that there is a shared core of humanity comes through strongly in the writings of Pestalozzi. For him, hereditary powers are secondary to 'those general human faculties, which allow the individual to recognize the truth, make rational judgments, feel love that comes from the heart...that is to enjoy full humanity' (Bruhlmeier, 2010, p. 20). That there are emotions common to all cultures has been much more recently demonstrated by Evans, who shows that all people share six basic emotions: joy, distress, anger, fear, surprise and disgust (Skelton, 2002, p. 45). The need to draw upon these inherent emotions is recognized by the founders of the International Primary Curriculum, who have set the aim of 'helping children to discover their own national and cultural identity and to learn to live with those whose national and cultural identities are different' (Skelton, 2002, p. 44).

The recognition of commonly shared emotions and of basic values is important to an education that seeks to be international in nature. But in what manner can this recognition be translated into effective practice? Has the IB in its Diploma programme succeeded in this respect? At the outset, in working on the international curriculum through the summer of 1962, Peterson had an interesting view on one aspect of this. He quoted T.H. Huxley: 'The man who is all morality and intellect, although he may be good and even great is, after all, only half a man. There is beauty in the moral world, but there is also a beauty of the world of Art' (1987, p. 194). In the text of his Nobel Prize acceptance speech (Solzhenitsyn, 1970), Solzhenitsyn wrote that art takes the individual beyond the limitations of his own experience to experience what it means to be fully human. It is not surprising then that aesthetic experience was to be an important part of the Diploma programme. One of us, DW, worked directly for Peterson from 1979 to 1980 and knew from conversations with him how he had struggled with where to include the aesthetic experience, as a compulsory part of the six-subject core, or as part of the co-curricular programme. The demands of university entrance proved to be the deciding factor, much to his disappointment, and the experience of art or music became an option as the sixth subject. The dead hand of university entrance requirements, even in those early days, lay heavily upon the educational experience that the Diploma offered.

Challenges to the education of the heart: The role of the teacher

But what has happened to the freedom of the teacher to develop the whole person? The founders of the IB were keenly aware of the need to ensure that the teacher was not to be simply an instructor. 'It is noteworthy that the curriculum development aspect was the province of the teacher' (Hill, 2010, p. 48). This is very much in the spirit of Pestalozzi's thinking as he was passionate about the need for the teacher to be a role model, free to develop each individual without the constraints, if we put this in a modern context, of being so controlled by the tick lists of specific goals demanded by much of modern national education. So, has the IB succeeded in maintaining the freedom of the teacher?

The continuing encouragement by the IB to teachers to become involved in curriculum development and as examiners is a strength: as is that for the development by schools of courses that enable them to make greater use of their particular locality, environment or culture. However, as both a curriculum and an examination system, the temptation to teach to the examination, though not required or encouraged by the IB, is strong.

The clear move towards greater reliability has inevitably reduced the freedom for individual action on the part of the IB classroom teacher, most evidently at the Diploma level, where pressure from parents and students alike to ensure that the Diploma provides a highly competitive qualification for entry to even the most selective universities is evident. However, where that external set of conditions is absent to a large degree, in the Middle Years and Primary Years programme, the innovative strength of the IB is clearly evident.

Can the IB make a difference?
Evidence from research

There has been surprisingly little attempt to assess the impact on its graduates of the IB Diploma programme with respect to its power to change values, in particular to those concerning cross-cultural attitudes. One such study was completed in 2006 by Veronica Wilkinson (2006). This study combined qualitative and quantitative methods of data collection. A questionnaire was administered twice to 556 students at the start of their IB Diploma programme and 15 months later as they were completing the course of studies. The statements were directed towards each of the outcomes expressed in the IB mission statement. The students who completed the questionnaires came from eight schools, both boarding and non-boarding. At the same time, qualitative data was collected in 12 case studies of students attending one of the United World Colleges. Each was interviewed on many occasions during the time that they were studying the IB Diploma programme.

The statistical findings indicated some shifts in attitude, as might be expected; the responses to statements indicating that the students had become more knowledgeable young people showed a significant positive change across all the students surveyed. However, with respect to the question of greatest relevance to whether studying the IB Diploma had a significant impact on 'the heart', the findings were more diverse. The IB mission statement outcome to which these statements were related was that concerning 'other people with their differences'. In this case, the only important change was amongst students who had experienced a residential situation as they studied the IB programme.

The responses to the questionnaires were informed by the interviews of the case-study students. These provided an insight into why their attitudes to students from other nationalities and cultures had significantly changed.

Tashfin, from Bangladesh, on returning from the long vacation midway through the course:

> I've changed so much; I often ask myself how I changed so much! Encounters with people from all over the world made me learn a lot of things and respect them and not jump to a conclusion without analysis. The IB has made me hard-working, the TOK classes made me question things that I would not otherwise have questioned.

As the course came to an end, 'I can now face the challenges of religion – it's fragile. I'm filtering the parts of my religious teaching which don't go with my conscience. I'm getting rid of those things.'

Alaina, from the United States, on coming to the end of the course:

> My fundamental values haven't changed, they are set in stone. Now, however, I look at more sides of a problem and I understand where people

are coming from. I don't understand everything but I consider that they might be thinking in this way because of that.

Imke, from Germany, again on coming to the end of the course:

> Perhaps I have changed in a way that I am braver. I am an individual, not hiding in a superficial crowd any more. TOK had a big influence, it gave me big thoughts about life, truth, at home we never talk about these things.

Kathryn, from Canada, as the course came to an end:

> I've changed so much! I am more confused: before I didn't think so much, now I'm more critical of the things I see. I had a naïve idealism when I came, I have lost some but not in a negative way, because it's more practical. I think about things on a small scale now, not the big problems of the world. I seem to have drifted away from being part of Canadian culture, now I feel part of not belonging. From the outside I can see things more clearly.

Students were also asked to rate the relative impact of the various components of the course on their values, particularly in respect of their attitudes to other cultures and nationalities: the factors that may significantly impact their willingness to make a difference beyond their own community as they enter the world of work. The findings indicate that they had experienced an education that was very much in the spirit of Pestalozzi. The open relationship between themselves and their teachers was rated as highly influential: more specifically, the encouragement to question and to seek their own paths to understanding. The core of the IB Diploma, particularly through the Theory of Knowledge course and the Extended essay, provided the opportunity for this relationship to develop beyond that which was possible through the more structured courses of the Higher and Standard level courses. The CAS programme allowed for an even more open relationship as it was directed through experiential learning to gaining experience outside the confines of the school. The interesting point is that, despite the increased control of the Theory of Knowledge programme that has been discussed, it is evident from students' comments that teachers of the programme have been able to retain considerable freedom for action in their own classes.

Some concluding thoughts

Pestalozzi believed that the relationship between a teacher and his or her students must lie at the core of the educational experience if the heart is to be fully educated. The education of the heart, in Pestalozzi's philosophy, is the development of a set of values, a moral code, without which a person's knowledge and skills lack a guiding principle (Bruhlmeier, 2010, p. 41). It was evident at the establishment of the IB that its founders shared this belief and the present mission statement sets values as a key part of its objectives. We argue strongly that this is vital if an IB education is to have such an impact on the young people who have experienced it that they will become active and positive in the service of humanity in an inevitable globally interconnected world, in whatever capacity they will spend their adult lives.

This chapter has asked whether the drive for greater reliability in educational testing has undermined the freedom of the teacher to develop the relationship with students that Pestalozzi believed was essential in order to properly educate the heart. It has also asked whether the fact that the considerable increase in competition for places in further education over the past 30 years has had the effect of focusing education on outcomes, rather than on the immediate. Again, Pestalozzi regarded this as a serious impediment to the development of the necessary relationship between teacher and student for the education of the heart to be effective. The driving force behind Pestalozzi's belief was that each individual is born with unique qualities which include an innate goodwill that can only be fully developed through the example of a role model; once entering formal education, this becomes the teacher. Yet this places upon the IB teacher a moral responsibility and it requires of every international schoolteacher a cross-cultural understanding that is quite often simply assumed.

The evidence, both from the structure of the IB and its mission statement, together with the comments from students who were close to completing the course, suggests that the programme is successful in providing teachers with the independence that they need to meet its objectives. What is encouraging is that in the structure of the core components of the Diploma Programme model, the CAS programme, the Extended Essay and the Theory of Knowledge course allow and promote the independence of the teacher in guiding students. Their objectives demand that students think 'out of the box' and that they put into practical effect what they have learned in the formal setting of the six academic subjects. Recent initiatives such as the World Studies Extended Essay provide a fine example of this, requiring students to investigate at an immediate and local level the manifestations of a global issue.

Is this, however, a sufficient condition for achieving the ambitious goal of educating young people so that they will make a positive difference towards a better understanding between the fractured components of our globalized world? There is, of course, no definitive answer to this question. The scanty evidence suggests that, though not a sufficient condition, the freedom of the teacher to act independently, beyond the constraints imposed by curriculum objectives and the requirement of examination success, is certainly necessary. What is clear is that an education driven by standardization and conformity, one that emphasizes the power to think and act in a way that meets the demands of society as it is, does not fit a young person with the will to change society.

Pestalozzi believed that there are basic human values that underlie their manifestation in different cultural contexts. In international education, therefore, the freedom of the teacher to act as a role model assumes a belief held by teachers in such shared basic human values of what is right and what is wrong and the importance of a core of strong ethical values that transcend national and cultural boundaries. Education must be personalized, every school and every classroom should be different. Only the teacher is capable of making it so. Our experience of international education over many years has made us optimists in this respect; there are many such practicing teachers in international schools throughout the world. Without them, international education would be quite simply a promise unfulfilled.

References

Bruhlmeier, A. (2010), *Head, Heart and Hand; Education in the Spirit of Pestalozzi* (translated by M.Mitchell.) London: Sophia Books.

Daniels, H. (2001), *Vygotsky and Pedagogy*. Falmer: Routledge.

Hayden, M.C. and Thompson, J.J. (1996), 'Potential difference: the driving force for international education', *International Schools Journal*, 16(1), 46–57.

Hill, I. (2010), *The International Baccalaureate: Pioneering in Education. 4.* Saxmundham: John Catt.

Hill, I. (2002), 'The history of international education: an international baccalaureate perspective', in M. Hayden, J. Thompson and G. Walker (eds), *International Education in Practice*. London: Kogan Page, pp. 18–29.

Hofstede, G. (1986), 'Cultural differences in teaching and learning', *International Journal of Intercultural Relations,* 10, 301–320.

Hofstede, G. (1991), *Cultures and Organisations: Software of the Mind.* Maidenhead: MacGraw-Hill.

Skelton, M. (2002), 'Defining "International" in an international curriculum', in M. Hayden, J. Thompson and G. Walker (eds), *International Education in Practice*. London: Kogan Page, pp. 39–45.

Smith, M.K. (2012), www.infed.org/thinkers/et-hahn.htm (Accessed 31 December 2012).

Solzhenitsyn, A. (1970), *Nobel Acceptance Speech*. Translated by F.D. Reeve http://www.columbia.edu/cu/augustine/arch/solzhenitsyn/nobel-lit1970.htm (Accessed 13 January 2013).

Vygotsky, L.S. (1978), *Mind in Society: The Development of Higher Psychological Processes*. M. Cole, V. John-Steiner and E. Souberman (eds) Cambridge, MA: Harvard University Press.

Wilber, K. (2000), *A Theory of Everything*. Boston: Shambala Press.

Wilkinson, V. (2006), *A Study of the Factors Affecting the Development of Attitudes of Students Following the International Baccalaureate Programme,* PhD Thesis, University of Bath.

Wilson, J., Williams, N. and Sugarman, B. (1967), *Introduction to Moral Education*. Middlesex: Penguin.

International Education and Global Engagement: Education for a Better World?

Boyd Roberts

Introduction

International education was born out of globalization and it might be thought that it would be at the forefront of engaging with a global world. But I shall be arguing that the concerns, preoccupations and vocabulary of 'international' education may be impeding the full embracing of engagement with a global world and its myriad challenges. I shall be taking international education here to be education associated with self-identifying international schools; their organizations, such as the European Council of International Schools (ECIS); and international curricula (International Baccalaureate (IB) programmes, Cambridge International Examinations (CIE), International Primary Curriculum (IPC)), and schools offering these. But no attempt is being made to be comprehensive, and the emphasis is on the IB, and particularly the IB Diploma (IBDP).

Emerging Internationalism

Although there were glimmers before, international education essentially began in the twentieth century, particularly after the Second World War. The emergence of 'international schools' educating the children of an internationally mobile population concerned with diplomacy and business the challenge of finding a suitable curriculum. The launch of the ... 1968, made available a curriculum and examination hatched by ...ndful of educators in leading international schools and initiated the ...rrent phase of international education. The immediate imperative, to devise a single curriculum and qualification to replace an array of national qualifications, was more pragmatic than educational. But the individuals and schools engaged in the design and early adoption of the IBDP shared aspects of ideology which influenced the nature and delivery of the IB curriculum. Significant among these were a passion for understanding other cultures, not only as intrinsically desirable, but also to promote a culture of peace and to ensure that the horrors of the Second World War could not be repeated. Alec Peterson, the first director general of the IB Organization (IBO), reminds us 'how desperately concerned internationally minded people in the forties and early fifties were with the prevention of a fourth Franco-German war' (Peterson, 1987, p. 3). Sutcliffe (2004) describes the importance of war experience and idealism for Europe among the founders of Atlantic College, many of whom played key roles in the emergence and early years of the IBO.

Although in the 1960s we were already living in what we would later come to appreciate as a *global* world, the focus in international schools was definitely *international*. Jeremy Bentham coined the word in the 1780s to describe increasing transactions between the growing number of nation states. Recognizing that there are differences between people associated with state boundaries is an essential feature of any understanding of the world as a whole. Similarly, it is important to know about relationships between countries, beneficial and disastrous – trade, aid, colonization, empire building, war, conflict and the building of peace.

Within international schools, the international was ever-present: the student body drawn from different countries and cultures, with different mother tongues, and the fact that many students were nationals of other countries and were therefore living their lives in a different country – in itself a potentially profound international experience. So a distinctive feature of international education was its concern with matters international.

Whatever the passions and concerns of the founders, my recollection is that the early documents of IB focused on curriculum and assessment rather than lofty ideals. This was of course well before the fashion for mission statements and the like. When pressed, Peterson gave a brief aim of the IB Diploma as 'to develop to their fullest extent the powers of each individual to understand, to modify and to enjoy his or her environment, both inner and outer, in its physical, social, moral, aesthetic, and spiritual aspects' (Peterson, 1987, p. 33). There is no mention of anything overtly international here, although he notes that

an international education which, being liberal and general, goes well beyond information and includes an appreciation of the art of other cultures and a discussion of the basis of morality in other cultures, is inevitably involved in the development of attitudes...Its intention is not simply to help the next generation to know better their enemies or rivals, but to understand and cooperate better with their fellow human beings across frontiers. (Peterson, 1987, pp. 194–195)

Touches of internationalism appeared in IB curriculum documents which also ensured that students were drawing examples widely from around the world in the 'study of man' (Group 4 – humanities), studying two languages and literature from a variety of cultures, enabling students, in the words of early General Guides, to encounter 'ways of thought different from their own'.

But internationalism was also embedded in the schools and their shared values and perspectives. In my experience, from 1977 onwards, many of the schools implementing the IB around that time were headed by strong-minded visionaries and shared an 'internationalist' ethos, shaped to varying extents by personal war-time experience, passions and commitment. With such shared values formal statements from IBO were less important.

The situation is now different. Schools are not embracing the IB because they are internationalist, but because, in some cases, they wish to become internationalist. But many – and I would guess most – schools now adopting IB are more concerned with the general qualities of the curriculum and its international acceptability rather than its concern with international understanding or a better world.

Shared values and ethos can no longer be taken for granted. So how has international education in more recent years articulated its understanding of its own interaction and engagement with an increasingly global world?

Levels of concern – a short digression

'International' continues to be a useful term to describe the relations between the parcels of land and political organizations that we call countries. But, Tate (2012) notes its limitations:

> We work in 'international' education, teach in 'international' schools and talk about 'internationalism', the relations between nations – which is an inadequate term for the complexity of what we are trying to do to prepare young people for a rapidly changing and culturally diverse world. (Tate, 2012, p. 214)

Of more recent provenance, 'global' is used to describe the increasing number of issues and interactions that cut across political and geographical borders and affect people and planet as a whole. As Hicks succinctly puts it, 'international refers to the "parts" and "global" to the whole' (Hicks, 2007b, p. 28).

The 'international' and the 'intercultural' (which international is sometimes taken to subsume) continue to be an important concern of international education. Here languages, literatures, history and cultures of different regions and an awareness of 'the other' play their part. But the world is now confronted by many urgent and important issues which are truly global, and affect us all. Obvious examples include loss of biodiversity, climate change and poverty. In considering the world at large, this global level, too, needs to be embraced.

International mindedness in international education

The term that has attained greatest currency in describing international education's engagement with the wider world is *international mindedness*. With a long usage historically (Hill, 2012), it has relatively recently become the preferred term for organizations such as IB and the IPC, and in the ECIS International Teacher Certificate (ITC, 2013).

IPC – an 'internationally-minded, thematic curriculum for 3–11 year olds' (IPC, 2013) – developed an understanding of the term 'international mindedness' at an early stage (Skelton et al., 2002). This statement has evolved relatively little over the years, and in its latest version IPC considers an international perspective (seemingly a synonym for international mindedness) is based upon:

- A knowledge and understanding of one's own national culture. International is both inter and national.

- An awareness and understanding of

  ○ the independence of and the interdependence between peoples

  ○ the independence of and interdependence between countries

  ○ the essential similarities between the peoples and countries of the world.

- A developing ability to be at ease with others who are different from ourselves (IPC, 2013).

The ECIS ITC sets out both personal and professional characteristics of an 'internationally minded teacher', including appreciation and awareness of different cultures and outlooks, and 'a recognition of the importance of developing global citizens' (ITC, 2013).

CIE (2012) also uses the term in relation to its suite of Global Perspectives courses, but does not elaborate upon its meaning. Other initiatives related to international mindedness include Ellwood and Davis's (2009) professional development manual for international schools and the work on assessment of international mindedness by Harwood and the Centre for Evaluation and Monitoring (CEM) at Durham University, UK. Harwood and Bailey (2012) recognize that what is to be assessed must be defined and consider international mindedness to be 'a person's capacity to transcend the limits of a worldview informed by a single experience of nationality, creed, culture or philosophy and recognise in the richness of diversity a multiplicity of ways of engaging with the world' (Harwood and Bailey, 2012, p. 79).

The ITC descriptor of 'internationally minded' mentions problems of a globalized world and refers to global citizenship, itself a term with varied usage. But the other expositions here do not explicitly refer to global issues, although Harwood and Bailey's (2012) elaboration gives considerable prominence to these.

International mindedness in the IB

IB's use of the term is attributed to Ian Hill (2000), then its deputy director general. The debate about whether international education was inextricably associated with 'international schools' had been brought to a close (notably in Hayden and Thompson (1995) and Murphy (2000)), and Hill argued that the key question was whether a school exemplified 'international mindedness'. Writing more recently in a personal capacity, he comments that 'international mindedness is the key concept associated with an international education. Stated another way, it can be said that the product of a successful international education is international mindedness' (Hill, 2012, p. 246).

IB has taken this line, and since 2000 the term has become a key part of its work to develop a continuum giving coherence to its three independently devised programmes. Drennen (2002) describes early work on this 'within an overarching concept of developing international-mindedness' (Drennen, 2002, p. 56).

Davy (2005), addressing an IB audience, noted that '"international mindedness" remains a challenging concept to define and bring alive in our schools'. In the absence of its own explanation of what was meant by international mindedness, IB endorsed Davy's paper for use in IBO-approved workshops. She considered that a curriculum embodying international mindedness should include the conceptual frames of:

- the role of culture in our lives and the lives of others

- the interdependence of natural and human systems on our planet

- the role of peace education and conflict resolution in our world

- environmental awareness and sustainability

- citizenship and service as an expression of individual responsibility. (Davy, 2005, p. 2)

This clearly addresses global levels of concern.

IB's own work reached its latest expression in one of its central documents, the Learner Profile Booklet, which states: 'The aim of all IB programmes is to develop internationally minded people who, recognizing their common humanity and shared guardianship of the planet help to create a better and more peaceful world' (IB, 2008a, p. 5).

IB attaches key importance to the Learner Profile as 'the IB mission statement translated into a set of learning outcomes for the twenty-first century' (IB, 2013a); 'an embodiment of what the IB means by "international-mindedness"' (IB, 2008a, p. 1); 'a map of a lifelong journey in pursuit of international-mindedness' (IB, 2008a, p. 2), and, most recently, as describing 'the attributes and outcomes of education for international-mindedness' (IB, 2012a, p. 1).

The full Learner Profile (IB, 2008a) is an admirable document, although it is now frequently used, by schools and the IB itself, as a list of ten attributes:

- inquirers
- knowledgeable
- thinkers
- communicators
- principled
- open-minded
- caring
- risk-takers
- balanced
- reflective

The Learner Profile has been significant in shifting attention to the desired outcome of education – or learner – away from the teaching activities or knowledge to be assimilated. But this list cannot be considered to explain international mindedness.[1]

In fairness, the full Learner Profile elaborates each of the terms and it is here that the 'flavour' of IB's understanding of international mindedness is better discerned. Knowledgeable, for instance, is explained as '[t]hey explore concepts, ideas and issues that have local and global significance' (IB, 2008a, p. 5), incidentally, the profile's only mention of the term 'global'.

IB promotes the use of the truncated version, and it must be a concern that people focus on this rather than the full profile. And while it may be that international mindedness can permeate all areas of the curriculum, it seems unhelpful to equate a view of a 'learner' with an understanding of international mindedness. More generally, Wells (2011) highlights the profile's lack of underpinning with theoretical development or practical implementation. (See Bullock (2011) for a theoretical underpinning.)

Fostering international mindedness and awareness of world or global issues are requirements in IB's standards for authorization processes (International Baccalaureate, 2010), which contains no further articulation of international mindedness.

Hill quotes a 2009 internal IB document's definition of international mindedness as 'an openness to and curiosity about the world and people of other cultures, and a striving towards a profound level of understanding of the complexity and diversity of human interactions' (Hill, 2012, p. 256). This is a more direct definition than that provided by the Learner Profile, but is still vague, omits any overt reference to environment and, of course, is not available to schools.

It must be concluded that IB's articulation of its key concept of international mindedness is sketchy, leaving a great deal to interpretation within the organization and in schools.

The emergence of the 'global dimension' in mainstream education

The long and distinguished history of education concerned with global issues and concerns, variously described by terms such as global education, development education, education for international understanding or world studies, is outlined by Burnouf (2004), Hicks (2003, 2007a, 2008) and Marshall (2007). But it is relatively recently, from the late 1980s onwards, that the global dimension, taken here to include these various manifestations, has left the margins of interest groups and become prominent in mainstream national education in countries including the UK, Australia and the US.

Among the publications facilitating this transfer in the UK were Pike and Selby's (1988) *Global Learner, Global Classroom* and Oxfam's *Curriculum for Global Citizenship* (1997), which has been subsequently updated (Oxfam, 2006). Oxfam's publication initially appeared when citizenship education was a central issue in the UK, and it helped to establish the term 'global citizen' in mainstream education (Hicks, 2008). Influential in a number of countries, it defined a 'global citizen' as someone who:

- is aware of the wider world and has a sense of their own role as a world citizen,

- respects and values diversity,

- has an understanding of how the world works economically, politically, socially, culturally, technologically and environmentally,

- is outraged by social injustice,

- is willing to act to make the world a more equitable and sustainable place,

- participates in and contributes to the community at a range of levels from the local to the global (Oxfam, 1997, p. 1).

In England, *Putting the world into world-class education* (DfES, 2004) recognized the reality of a global economy and workforce, in which the government wished the country and its citizens to be able to operate effectively. But the importance of what was termed the 'global dimension' was also stressed.

We live in one world. What we do affects others, and what others do affects us, as never before. To recognise that we are all members of a world community and that we all have responsibilities to each other is not romantic rhetoric, but modern economic and social reality. (DfES, 2004, p. 5)

Two distinct concerns are addressed in this document, mirrored in similar publications from other countries (e.g. Boix Mansilla and Jackson, 2011; Curriculum Corporation, 2002), namely to develop students who

- can operate effectively and competitively and

- recognize and act upon their responsibilities

in a global world. The first concern is economic and vocational. Tarc (2009) points out a distinction in French between *citoyenneté* – formal legal citizenship – and *civisme* – or civic community membership. It is the latter, expressed at levels from the local to the global, that would best describe the second element above.

The 2004 DfES document sets out eight key concepts of the global dimension:

- global citizenship

- conflict resolution

- diversity

- human rights

- interdependence

- social justice

- sustainable development

- values and perceptions

DfES (2005) drew on the experience of development education and provided further guidance to schools on how to address the key concepts, while the

Department for International Development (DfID) began funding a key website for teachers – *Global Dimension.*

A similar focus on the global dimension in mainstream education emerged in Australia at about the same time:

> Twenty-first century Australians are members of a global community, connected to the whole world by ties of culture, economics, politics and shared environmental concerns. Enabling young people to participate in shaping a better shared future for the world is at the heart of global education. (Curriculum Corporation, 2002, p. 1)

This and associated publications distilled and disseminated thinking and practice in global education, within a context of citizenship and civics education.

The successor publication, Education Services Australia (2008), identified five learning emphases in global education, notably similar to the topics and issues of the DfES documents:

- interdependence and globalization
- identity and cultural diversity
- social justice and human rights
- peace building and conflict resolution
- sustainable futures

There is a considerable tradition of global education in the US, with notable contributions including Hanvey (1976), Merryfield (1991, 2002, 2008, 2009) and Tye (1991, 1999). Addressing global and intercultural issues has been a significant concern for many years of some social studies teachers in particular, but it is relatively recently that global education entered the educational mainstream in the US. A project of the Council of Chief State School Officers (CCSSO) and the Asia Society identified the components of 'global competence' – defined as 'the capacity and disposition to understand and act on issues of global significance' (EdSteps, 2011).

The key publication arising from this work sets out four key competencies of globally competent students, who

1 Investigate the world beyond their immediate environment, framing significant problems and conducting well-crafted and age-appropriate research.

2 Recognize perspectives, others' and their own, articulating and explaining such perspectives thoughtfully and respectfully.

3 Communicate ideas effectively with diverse audiences, bridging geographic, linguistic, ideological and cultural barriers.

4   Take action to improve conditions, viewing themselves as players in the world and participating reflectively (Boix Mansilla and Jackson, 2011, p. 11).

Above the national level, UNESCO's (1974) recommendation on what it called 'international education' encompassed references to issues now considered as global, including disease and famine, population growth, natural resources and environmental pollution, and can still inform educational thinking. Its later report *Learning: the Treasure Within* considers education in our global context. It makes some striking and prescient comments, for instance:

> The truth is that all-out economic growth can no longer be viewed as the ideal way of reconciling material progress with equity, respect for the human condition and respect for the natural assets that we have a duty to hand on in good condition to future generations.

> We have by no means grasped all the implications of this as regards both the ends and means of sustainable development and new forms of international co-operation. This issue will constitute one of the major intellectual and political challenges of the next century. (Delors, 1996, p. 13)

The North-South Centre of the Council of Europe has also been prominent in advancing the case for addressing global concerns in school education. Its 1997 Global Education Charter called for policy-makers and school authorities to give institutional support to global education in schools. This is incorporated in its valuable and more recent Global Education Guidelines (North-South Centre of the Council of Europe, 2008).

One aspect of global education becoming more prominent in recent years is education for sustainable development. As lead organization for the UN's Decade of Education for Sustainable Development (2005–2014), UNESCO has developed many publications pitched at practitioners in schools (e.g. UNESCO, 2012, 2013). Similar documents have also been produced by a number of countries, such as Sweden (Brunner and Urenje, 2012) and Wales (DCELLS, 2008; DELLS, 2006), and by NGOs (e.g. Hicks, 2012).

Emergence of the global in international education

For a number of years individuals in international education have made the case for addressing global issues in schools (e.g. Jenkins, 1998; Thomas, 1998), echoed by occasional keynote speakers at IB and ECIS conferences. But until relatively recently the most significant deliberations about how education should address and respond to global issues were taking place outside the sphere of international education. Why should this be so? International education has had its own level of concern with languages, cultures, international understanding and promotion of peace. Global concerns have emerged slowly, gradually and, sometimes at the time, imperceptibly: there is nothing comparable to the Second World War as an event which focused minds on peace and conflict. International education has its own conferences, curricula and qualifications, and its own publications, fields of research and preoccupations. Perhaps this focus on matters international – and the associated 'international' vocabulary – has made international education less attuned to the emergence and influence of global education elsewhere. Understandably, working outside a single national context, it has also been little concerned with citizenship education. So work by NGOs, international and national bodies on global dimensions and citizenship in education took place mostly in parallel to thinking in international education. It is an unfortunate irony that while our students are expected to know about other cultures and outlooks, many in international education were unaware of developments in other areas of education of direct relevance to our work.

The UK chapter of the Alliance for International Education convened a seminar in September 2010, _Education for a better world_, bringing together prominent international education organizations with those in development and global education based in the UK. This introduction between the parallel worlds of global and international education has resulted in other interactions subsequently (e.g. Think Global, 2011).

In alerting international education to changes in the wider world, the publication in 2002 of Jean-François Rischard's _High Noon: 20 global problems, 20 years to solve them_ was significant (2002). Addressed to a general audience, it was widely read in international education circles, where it prompted a general call to action and stimulated a number of valuable initiatives. Rischard had put forward a proposal for 'global issues networks' of experts as a counter to the more bureaucratic arrangements of existing nation-states and international agencies. Clayton Lewis, then director of the International School of Luxembourg, argued that international schools formed such a flexible international network and could be used to engage students to take action on global problems. In 2003 he convened a conference for students from six European international schools, who reported on projects involving research and action on one of Rischard's 20 issues (Global Issues Network, 2013; International School of Luxembourg, 2004). This idea struck a chord in international schools worldwide and has given rise to _Global Issues Network_, with regional conferences along similar lines complemented by electronic communication.

Meanwhile, in 2006, the National Association of Independent Schools (NAIS) in the US launched _Challenge 20:20_. US schools are paired with schools in other countries and students work together on an Internet-based project on one of Rischard's 20 problems. A number of international schools have taken part, and continue to do so. And in 2007, ECIS, which had been addressed by Rischard at one of its conferences, organized a substantial pre-conference institute on global issues.

The IB was also stimulated by Rischard's book to develop its first major initiative for all ages, specifically relating to global issues. The IB community (initially triennial) theme, launched in 2007, invited IB schools to focus on six global issues, under Rischard's heading *Sharing our Humanity*, over a period of 3 years. Presentations were given at IB conferences, and a dedicated public website with free posting enabled schools to interact and share activities relating to the theme. The website linked to resources drawn from different countries and in IB's working languages. A regular column on global issues was introduced in the IB magazine, *IB World*. The Global Campaign for Education's 'World's Biggest Lesson' in 2003, in which schools around the world taught the same lesson at the same time, stimulated the formulation of similar IB global lessons, available to all.

The community theme was a voluntary project with relatively low perceived impact on schools. On its conclusion a broader continuing focus on global issues was adopted. The theme website was reformulated as *Global Engage* (IB, 2013d), global lessons continue and responsibility for enhancing the global dimension within IB programmes became part of the remit of a regular post.

While the community theme was in operation, in 2009 IB published *Educating for global citizenship* (Roberts, 2009), and later that year and in 2010 *Global Issues Organizers* for the Middle Years Programme appeared (Lelievre et al., 2009a, 2009b, 2010, 2010a, 2010b). These were published commercially rather than as core publications distributed to all IB schools.

IB's Primary and Middle Years programmes, formulated more recently than the Diploma, have incorporated environmental issues from the outset, and some IBDP syllabuses have had a clear and strong focus on global issues, notably Geography and Environmental Systems and Societies, although studied by relatively few candidates. A requirement for all Diploma students to have 'engaged with issues of global importance' (IB, 2008b, p. 6) was first introduced in Creativity, Action and Service (CAS), although with little guidance for schools on how this might be achieved.

The position within the IBDP might have been very different. In the early 1990s there was considerable concern about the omission of global issues from the IB diploma programme, headed by prominent individuals within the IB community, such as head of the United World College of the Atlantic Colin Jenkins (1992a, 1992b) and Swedish government representative Bengt Thelin (1992). The IB director general at the time, Roger Peel, talked of a 'required focus on global issues, either as a separate unit at the core of an expanded hexagon, or via an expanded form of TOK (*Theory of Knowledge*)' (Peel, 1992, p. 7). But no change to requirements ensued, partly because of inconclusive reactions from IB school heads. IB subsequently became immersed in assimilating an externally developed Primary Years Programme, and in what Tarc (2009) terms its 'corporatization' and 'branding' phases. Regrettable indeed. It was the failure of the IBDP adequately to address global issues that was one of the stimuli for the development of the International Global Citizen's Award, launched in 2006 (http://www.globalcitizensaward. org/). But after a substantial hiatus, there is now clear and welcome movement on global issues within IB, with specific initiatives and publication of general guidance. Although currently retaining the term international mindedness to describe interactions with the world at large, IB is also using the term 'global engagement' which embraces content and process and implies commitment and associated action (Harrison, 2012, pers. comm.).

A recent central publication, *What Is an IB education?* distinguishes between international and global levels, and talks of 'international mindedness in a global context' (IB, 2012a, p. 6). It makes specific reference to global engagement, explained as follows:

> Global engagement represents a commitment to address humanity's greatest challenges in the classroom and beyond. IB students and teachers are encouraged to explore global and local issues, including developmentally appropriate aspects of the environment, development, conflicts, rights and cooperation and governance. Globally engaged people critically consider power and privilege, and recognize that they hold the earth and its resources in trust for future generations.

> An IB education aims to develop the awareness, perspectives and commitments necessary for global engagement. The IB aspires to empower people to be active learners who are committed to service with the community. (IB, 2012a, p. 7)

Global engagement is now being encouraged in IB's professional development workshops and supporting documents are being produced (IB, 2012a).

From this year, Diploma students may submit an extended essay (a Diploma core requirement) in World Studies, researching an issue of contemporary global significance with an interdisciplinary approach. (Incidentally, the Extended Essay Guide (2012b) refers to global 'consciousness', 'sensitivity', 'understanding' and 'global self', adding (yet) more terms to IB's vocabulary of international/global terminology.)

A new Global Politics course in the Diploma is being launched, with, significantly, the option to undertake an assessed 'engagement activity' (IB, 2013c). Recent Global Engagement briefs provide IB's fullest and clearest core guidance relevant to all programmes (IB, 2012c, 2012d, 2012e, 2012f, 2012g). Specific reference to engagement at the global level will also be made in various other publications emerging during the course of 2013 (Harrison, 2012, pers. comm.).

IB has made considerable strides in a short time, although it is still possible for DP students and schools to pay little attention to global issues.

And in international education curricula bodies in general, including IB, the articulation of an approach to a 'global dimension' and its relationship with international perspectives need elaboration. In the best of national documents there is a clear framework giving direction to ways in which global and international elements and perspectives, including education for sustainable living, can be addressed within the curriculum, with guidance on appropriate pedagogy.

The International Schools Association (ISA) is a small membership organization that has a record of innovation and oversaw the emergence of the Middle Years Programme subsequently adopted by IB. Its *Education for Peace – a curriculum framework K-12* (ISA Global Issues Network, 2013) is broader than its title suggests and carries forward work undertaken by the International Education System Pilot Project (see Thomas, 1998). *Education for Sustainability – a curriculum framework K-12* (ISA, 2013) elaborates two of the thematic areas of *Education for Peace* – environment and development. To the best of my knowledge, these two documents represent the most thorough attempts within international education to develop a coherent approach to addressing key global issues across all areas of the curriculum at all school levels. How much they impact on practice is unknown.

International mindedness – a term whose time is up

International mindedness seems an inadequate term to embody international education's concern for the wider world. First, as Haywood (2007) and Gunesch (2007) note, it is not properly defined. Whatever its general qualities, IB's Learner Profile is not a satisfactory articulation of the term.[2] Hill defines education for international-mindedness as

> the study of issues which have application beyond national borders and to which competencies such as critical thinking and collaboration are applied in order to shape attitudes, leading to action which will be conducive to intercultural understanding, peaceful coexistence and sustainable development for the future of the human race. (Hill, 2012, p. 259)

This illustrates the difficulty and complexity of attempting to define such a term in one considered sentence.

Second, and unsurprisingly, the term is being used and interpreted variously and loosely (Cause, 2009b; Doherty and Mu, 2011). A search of international school websites mentioning international mindedness reveals this clearly. In some schools it embraces global issues, while in others the focus is very much on intercultural understanding – sometimes at the level of flags, fashion, foods and festivals – or what Skelton has called 'international mindedness lite' (Skelton, 2007, p. 380, 388). I have heard or read of international mindedness described as or equated with critical thinking, 'a call to dialogue' or 'a growing sense of the other'. Doherty and Mu conclude that teachers in IB schools develop their own understandings of the term that are 'diffuse and contradictory' (Doherty and Mu, 2011, p. 197). At best, understandings can be partial.

Thirdly, 'mindedness' itself encourages vague and lax usage. It is a word rarely used in normal parlance and has a somewhat tepid quality – an inclination, a predisposition. Lewis (2005) considers it 'too passive' and 'fuzzy'. It does not seem consistent with an approach that encourages a deliberate and whole-hearted study of issues, nor of taking action to address them.

Fourth is the use of the term international. Cause (2009a) has argued that 'international mindedness' can embrace the intercultural and the global. But we would then need a new word for things that do concern interactions between nations. While there are some issues where the categorization is marginal, both terms and levels of concern seem complementary and necessary. Using 'international' as our preferred term to describe interactions with the world at large encourages either loose usage or consideration at the international level only, without embracing global concerns.

Hill (2000) talked of internationally minded schools to escape the ultimately unproductive discussion of what constituted an international school. If we follow Hill and consider 'the product of a successful international education is international mindedness' (Hill, 2012, p. 246), we are in danger of attempting to define one loosely defined term by reference to another without a clear definition. Potentially, years of arid discussion beckon.

The limited amount of research on international mindedness in international education suggests that simply offering an IB programme has little impact on global mindedness of students (Keller, 2010). Gigliotti-Labay (2010) in a US study found that while teachers and administrators had an understanding of international mindedness, most IB schools were implementing it in a superficial way. Her data suggested that teachers and administrators were not entirely clear how to implement international mindedness, that it was weakly conceptualized by IB and that there was little accountability of schools for its implementation.

Moreover, Skelton (2007) has argued that international mindedness has had 'an unbearable weight put on it' (Skelton, 2007, p. 380). Is there another way forward?

Ways forward: Education for a better world

We have noted two approaches or purposes in educating students for a global world. The first is concerned with economic advantage, and the second encourages young people to develop as responsible members of a global civic community, recognizing that they affect and are impacted upon by global issues. We may also wish to educate students about the global world, simply as part of their general education.

These approaches differ not only in purpose but also in content and pedagogy and so benefit from separate consideration. Among its other shortcomings international mindedness may sometimes appear to combine all three approaches above. Our interactions with a global world are too important and complex to be handily summarized under any single term and we can too readily become submerged in the 'big terminology debate' (Marshall, 2007). Instead I would like to focus on how we can work more effectively on this second approach.

IB's strapline 'education for a better world' may prove helpful. Although it may elicit an ill-defined and unjustified warm glow in anyone thinking they are associated with it simply by working in an IB school, it suggests a potentially productive and focused, but highly challenging, way forward. But education for a better world cannot simply be asserted. It must be thought through carefully and delivered so that outcomes can be properly evaluated.

IB's mission and Learner Profile have demonstrated that written phrases can have impact on practice, even when largely aspirations and exhortations. *What Is an IB education?* (IB, 2012a) is a very welcome advance but does not obviate the need for further guidance to schools. Education for a better world will be more effective if it is thoroughly underpinned by thinking and pedagogy within a full and considered organizing and guiding framework. I offer a few starting suggestions.

Drawing on the conceptual thinking of Hanvey (1976), Pike and Selby (1988, 1999, 2000) and particularly Hicks (2007b, 2013), our approach to education for a better world needs to encompass four dimensions:

The issues dimension: addressing issues in broad areas, perhaps following IB's recent categorization – the environment, development, conflicts, rights and co-operation and governance (IB, 2012); maybe adding diversity

The spatial dimension: considering each issue at all levels, from the local to the global, and the interactions between levels

The temporal dimension: considering past and present, and particularly looking to the future

The process and pedagogical dimension: participatory and cooperative learning that looks at issues from different perspectives, and emphasizes ethical considerations.

Education for a better world – clearly transformative education – also requires us to undertake this with a sense of hope, fulfilled, where appropriate, through engagement and action. It needs thorough articulation of how we recognize 'good' and 'better' with tough-minded ways of evaluating when bolstering the good or changing things for the better has happened through education. We cannot duck out of this by arguing that making things better will (only) happen at some future point when students have left school. There should be a critical and hard-headed focus on how students and schools can act for a better world here and now, as well as envisaging and preparing students for future life in a future world. When action is inappropriate now, we may be contributing to priming development of attitudes and values, and of background knowledge, that may lead students to effect change in the future, or accept or resist change led by others – notably in the political field.

Finding time to consider all the issues above may be unrealistic. The range could be narrowed by focusing on a constellation of issues directly related to the everyday lives of young people in international education, readily susceptible to consideration at local to global levels. Forty per cent of IB schools are in the US, the world's richest nation, and nearly 60% are in countries of the G8 (IB, 2013b). Schools offering international education in other countries mostly cater to the better off. We should perhaps accept that, at least for the present, our basic work in international education is largely with comparatively privileged students and that with this group there is much work to be done, which we have the opportunity and responsibility to undertake. Barbara Stocking, chief executive of leading development NGO Oxfam, recently noted in a *Guardian* interview that 'it's not just the poor places that need to be changed, but our habits...It's hard to get across the message that it's us lot, who are actually using all the global goods, who need to change. Not poor people' (quoted in Renton, 2013). Walker, talking about challenges in global education, asks, 'How can we prepare young people for the inevitable relative loss of material wealth to become the first generation in modern history that is "worse off" than its parents?' (Walker, 2012, p. 15). Consideration could therefore focus on:

- A human population of 8 billion and growing
- Standards of living and differential use of finite resources by people leading different lifestyles around the world
- Meeting the needs and wants of a growing population, and aspirations of emergent middle classes in countries such as Brazil, India and China
- Resulting pressures on habitats and species
- Issues of fairness and equity
- The backstories of the production of what young people in international schools use, for example working conditions of producers and environmental impact
- Food and water
- Waste
- Climate change

Conceiving of a better world is an ethical activity. Walker (2012) has highlighted the disappointing – and concerning – finding in a recent IB student survey that students considered 'principled' to be the least important of the ten IB Learner Profile attributes (and how many IB teachers too?). Development of an ethical sense is a real challenge to educators and can be little more than identified here. But we can note that awareness of an issue does not necessarily lead to caring about that issue. It is this capacity to care that needs to be nurtured and modelled. This calls for more than critical study of issues. And, where possible and appropriate, caring about something should lead to action, itself another capacity that needs to be developed and supported.

A particular pedagogy is needed in education for a better world. Starting with everyday lives and stimulated by students' situations and interests it includes critical enquiry, research, reflection, participatory and co-operative learning and, when possible, considered resulting action. There need be no undue concern about ensuring all issues are addressed as it is the quality of engagement that is essential. This type of pedagogy is distinct from that associated with transmission of knowledge and skills and passing exams. The teacher works alongside the student as accompanying mentor, recognizing that in working together on education for a better world, they are, in some ways, co-equals. (Roberts (2009) considers such pedagogy at some length.) This poses challenges for educators in exam-oriented courses.

So how can we be better at education for a better world? There is an increasing amount of guidance for individual schools and teachers available from NGOs, national education authorities and practitioners (see links on IB's Global Engage website, IB (2013d)). A participatory, investigative approach, with attention to ethical development and reflection is time-consuming. Hard choices will need to be made, calling into question our role as teachers and schools in relation to the next generation. Vested interests will need to be faced down and we cannot be neutral. Addressing education for a better world is a choice. Not doing so is equally a choice. UNESCO's recommendation on international education (UNESCO, 1974) included developing teachers' 'commitment to the ethics of human rights and to the aim of changing society' – which education for a better world will demand.

Education for a better world and the IB Diploma

The IB's Diploma programme is its longest established, taught by nearly 70% of IB schools, and for half of IB schools it is the only IB programme offered (IB, 2013b). Within IB it seems the obvious place to seek to have greatest impact on schools, although the most challenging.

There should be a change in curriculum as Rischard (2007) advocated for all IB programmes, with education for a better world permeating all subject areas and teaching, reflected in changes in assessment. (All down-to-earth teachers at the upper secondary level teach towards assessment). In this regard, new types of assessment in IB's Global Politics course and the projects in CIE's

Global Perspectives at IGCSE and AS level and within its Pre-U are interesting and welcome. Curriculum change has a long lead time, and the pedagogy and approach for education for a better world do not sit comfortably with teaching for acquisition of subject-based knowledge and skills for higher education. A separate dedicated component may also be required.

In the meantime, some smaller-scale changes could be made through which the IBDP could better address education for a better world. This would reinforce and exemplify to schools IB's commitment to this aim.

1   Small changes in assessment.

   Include questions in languages oral examinations requiring candidates to consider what they understand by 'a better world' and what actions can be taken to this end, with assessment on the quality of the language only.

   Add short additional elements to written papers, for example 'Is the current distribution of wealth (or is poverty) acceptable?' (Economics); 'Is wasting food at home an ethical issue?' (Biology or Geography). These would carry no marks, but failure to attempt them seriously might lose a mark.

2   Revise Creativity, Action and Service.

   Replace the service component with 'action for a better world', either for all, or by offering this as an alternative. Action for a better world would include but not be restricted to what is currently considered 'service' (see Roberts, 2011). Action must be informed, and provision made for acquisition of appropriate knowledge.

3   Modify language requirements.

   One-third of the Diploma programme is taken up with their study. Yet some students start the programme proficient in several languages. Reintroducing a linguistic competence test for such students would enable them to substitute another subject for a second language. This gives students more opportunities to study subjects like geography, global politics or environmental systems and societies.

4   Change the emphasis in the Theory of Knowledge course to highlight the application of ethics to everyday situations.

5   Bunnell has argued elsewhere in this volume for the recognition of 'pioneer' schools (2013). I would like to suggest something similar in relation to addressing seriously education for a better world. Some schools are content with the *status quo* while others are frustrated at not being able to educate for a better world more thoroughly within the current IBDP curriculum. A group of schools could opt to implement some of the changes above, in which education for a better world is given greater emphasis.

But are we being too timid? If the IBDP were to be devised today by similarly visionary educators, the outcome would, I venture, be rather different. Perhaps, it is time to side-step the tinkering with a nearly 50-year-old model designed for the internationally mobile in a different world and offer interested schools a complete alternative new version – IBDP 201x – putting education for a better world at its heart. IB's track record and reputation should enable it to retain university acceptance and schools wishing to continue with IB 1968 could do so – at least for the time being.

Educating earthlings

Sometimes it is helpful to have simple aids for focus or recollection. Traditional basic learning has been summed up as the three Rs: reading, (w)riting and (a)rithmetic. In a similar vein, education for a better world can be called the three Es for earthlings (see also Roberts, 2012):

Ecologacy – living on earth in a way that recognizes people and planet – the environment, including other species

Ethicacy – the ability to make sound, ethical judgements

Efficacy – the ability to take effective action.

Ecologacy (my term) embraces 'eco' (from the Greek for home) and '-log-' or study of, with the suffix '-acy' indicating a quality or capacity, and mirroring literacy. Ecologacy is therefore a capacity to live well on the planet, shaped by knowledge and understanding. 'Home' in this context embraces all fellow inhabitants of the planet, human and non-human, and the environment in general, including its physical aspects. Ecologacy therefore embraces sustainability, although it goes further. It also encompasses intercultural competence and understanding. Ecologcacy has a broader meaning than ecological literacy, or ecoliteracy, coined by Orr (1991), and is distinct from 'ecolacy' (Hardin, 1981), defined as having a working understanding of the complexity of the world and the long-term consequences of interactions.

Ethicacy is about 'doing ethics' – being able to make well-considered and well-intentioned decisions in everyday life. It is certainly not indoctrination. It also means recognizing that other people taking a different line may also be right – at least in their own terms.

Efficacy appropriates an existing word for slightly different purposes. Here it means having an ability to get things done, to work effectively in the real world with other people – a commitment to an outcome and determination and resolution to see things through. Efficacy is a necessary counterpart to ethicacy. It is the capacity to translate good intentions into good actions and outcomes. Ethicacy and efficacy are less concerned with what we know, but with what we do, and why and how we do it.

These are not new skills or attributes, like proficiency with information technology. Rather they are a timely refocus for the twenty-first century on essential timeless human capacities.

A challenge

International curriculum bodies undertake all of the functions often carried out by different bodies in national systems. They authorize schools, determine curricula, provide professional development and, for older students, undertake assessment and provide certification and qualifications. Taken together these provide enormously powerful ways to shape education in schools. They also operate outside specific national concerns and the influence of short-term expediency of elected politicians. They can draw the best from the world, including the expertise and vision of excellent classroom teachers, and, significantly, make it available to the world. They have unique opportunities and potential to move beyond the vague talk of international mindedness and, without in any way belittling what they are already doing, to develop better, more robust and more transformative education for a better world – if they have the vision, will and guts to do so.

Notes

1 WWF-UK drew on IB's primary student profile, forerunner of the learner profile, to develop 'Characteristics of effective learners'. It added two terms to embrace elements it considered received insufficient attention in the IB profile: global and civically engaged (WWF-UK, 2004, p. 20; WWF-UK, 2011, p. 12).
2 The Learner Profile was under review by IB at the time of writing.

References

Boix Mansilla, V. and Jackson, A. (2011), *Educating for Global Competence: Preparing Our Youth to Engage the World*. New York and Washington: Asia Society and Council of Chief State School Officers. http://www.edsteps.org/CCSSO/SampleWorks/EducatingforGlobalCompetence.pdf

Brunner, W. and Urenje, S. (2012), *The Parts and The Whole: A Holistic Approach to Environmental and Sustainability Education*. Visby: Swedish International Centre of Education for Sustainable Development.

Bullock, K. (2011), 'International Baccalaureate learner profile: Literature review', International Baccalaureate. http://www.ibo.org/research/resources/documents/LPLitReview_final.pdf (Accessed 7 March 2013).

Bunnell, T. (2013), 'International Baccalaureate and the role of the "pioneer" International Schools', in R. Pearce (ed), *International Education and Schools: Moving beyond the first 40 years*. London: Bloomsbury, pp. 167–182.

Burnouf, L. (2004), 'Global awareness and perspectives in global education', *Canadian Social Studies* 38, 3. http://www.educ.ualberta.ca/css/Css_38_3/ARburnouf_global_awareness_perspectives.htm (Accessed 15 January 2013).

Cambridge International Examinations. (2012), Developing an international outlook with Global Perspectives http://www.cie.org.uk/news/announcements/detail?announcement_id=48152 (Accessed 1 February 2013).

Cause, L. (2009a), 'Fostering inclusive and ethical intercultural relations: The International Baccalaureate, international-mindedness and the IB learner profile', Paper delivered at the International Conference on Migration, Citizenship and Intercultural Relations, 19–20 November 2009, Deakin University: Australia. http://www.deakin.edu.au/arts-ed/ccg/events/pdf/mpn%20 008.pdf (Accessed 19 January 2013).

Cause, L. (2009b), International mindedness and 'social control'. *Asian Social Science,* 5(9), 32–46. http://journal.ccsenet.org/index.php/ass/article/view/3728/3329 (Accessed 23 January 2013).

Council of Europe. (1997), *Global Education Charter.* http://www.coe.int/t/dg4/nscentre/ge/GE-Guidelines/GEgs-app2.pdf

Curriculum Corporation. (2002), *Global Perspectives: A Statement on Global Education for Australian Schools.* Carlton, Australia: Curriculum Corporation. http://www.asiaeducation.edu.au/verve/_resources/global_perspectives_statement_2005_web.pdf

Davy, I. (2005), Promoting international mindedness in our schools. http://math-hl-ws-acs-123.wikispaces.com/file/view/Promoting+International+Mindedness.pdf (Accessed 2 January 2013).

Delors, J. (1996), *Learning: The Treasure Within. Report to UNESCO of the International Commission on Education for the Twenty-first Century.* Paris: UNESCO. http://www.unesco.org/delors/delors_e.pdf (Accessed 10 January 2013).

Department for Children, Education, Lifelong Learning and Skills (DCELLS) Wales. (2008), *Education for Sustainable Development and Global Citizenship A Common Understanding for Schools.* Cardiff: DCELLS. http://wales.gov.uk/docs/dcells/publications/081204commonunderstschoolsen.pdf (Accessed 21 January 2013).

Department for Education, Lifelong Learning and Skills (Wales). (2006), *Education for Sustainable Development and Global Citizenship – A Strategy for Action.* Cardiff: DELLS http://wales.gov.uk/docrepos/40382/4038232/403821/683829/esdgcG192-e.pdf?lang=en (Accessed 21 January 2013).

Department for Education and Skills (DfES). (2004), *Putting the World into World Class Education.* London: DfES. http://dera.ioe.ac.uk/5201/1/Putting%20The%20World%20Into%20World-Class%20Education.pdf (Accessed 13 January 2013).

Department for Education and Skills (DfES). (2005), *Developing the Global Dimension in the School Curriculum.* London: DfES. https://www.education.gov.uk/publications/standard/publicationdetail/page1/DFES-1409-2005 (Accessed 14 January 2013).

Doherty, C.A. and Mu, L. (2011), 'Producing the intercultural citizen in the International Baccalaureate', in F. Dervin, A. Gajardo, and A. Lavanchy (eds), *Politics of Interculturality.* Newcastle upon Tyne: Cambridge Scholars Publishing, pp. 173–197.

Drennen, H. (2002), 'Criteria for curriculum continuity in international education', in M. Hayden, J. Thompson, and G. Walker (eds), *International Education in Practice.* London. Kogan Page, pp. 55–67.

EdSteps. (2011), Global Competence in Action. http://www.edsteps.org/CCSSO/SampleWorks/gcpdf.pdf (Accessed 29 January 2013).

Education Services Australia. (2008), *Global Perspectives: A Framework for Global Education in Australian Schools*. Carlton: Australia. Education Services Australia. http://www.globaleducation.edu.au/verve/_resources/GPS_web.pdf

Ellwood, C. and Davis, M. (2009), *International Mindedness: A Professional Development Handbook for International Schools*. London: Optimus Education.

Gigliotti-Labay, J. (2010), 'Fulfilling its mission? The promotion of international mindedness in IB DP Programmes', Ed.D. diss., University of Houston. In *Dissertations & Theses: The Humanities and Social Sciences Collection* [database on-line]. http://www.proquest.com (publication number AAT 3438266 (Accessed 25 July 2011).

Global Dimension. http://globaldimension.org.uk/

Global Issues Network. (2013), http://www.global-issues-network.org/ (Accessed 15 January 2013).

Gunesch, K. (2007) 'International education's internationalism: Inspirations from cosmopolitanism', in M. Hayden, J. Levy and J. Thompson (eds), *The Sage Handbook of Research in International Education*. London: Sage, pp. 90–100.

Hanvey, R.G. (1976), An Attainable Global Perspective http://www.globaled.org/an_att_glob_persp_04_11_29.pdf (Accessed 15 January 2013).

Hardin, G. (1981), 'An ecolate view of the human predicament', *Alternatives: Global, Local, Political*, 7(2), 242–262.

Harwood, R. and Bailey, K. (2012), 'Defining and evaluating international-mindedness in a school context', *International Schools Journal*, 31(2), 77–86.

Hayden, M. and Thompson, J. (1995), 'International schools and international education: A relationship reviewed', *Oxford Review of Education*, 21(3), 327–345.

Haywood, T. (2007), 'A simple typology of international-mindedness and its implications for education', in M. Hayden, J. Levy and J. Thompson (eds), *The Sage Handbook of Research in International Education*. London: Sage, pp. 79–89.

Hicks, D. (2003), 'Thirty years of global education: A reminder of key principles and precedents', *Educational Review*, 55, 265–275.

Hicks, D. (2007a), 'Responding to the world', in D. Hicks and C. Holden (eds), *Teaching the Global Dimension*. Abingdon: Routledge, pp. 3–13.

Hicks, D. (2007b), 'Principles and precedents', in D. Hicks and C. Holden (eds), *Teaching the Global Dimension*. Abingdon: Routledge, pp. 14–30.

Hicks, D. (2008), 'Ways of seeing: The origins of global education in the UK'. http://www.teaching4abetterworld.co.uk/docs/download2.pdf (Accessed 2 January 2013).

Hicks, D. (2012) *Sustainable Schools, Sustainable Futures*. Godalming: WWF-UK. http://www.teaching4abetterworld.co.uk/docs/download18.pdf (Accessed 2 January 2013).

Hicks, D. (2013), 'A futures perspective'. http://www.teaching4abetterworld.co.uk/futures.html (Accessed 30 January 2013).

Hill, I. (2000), 'Internationally minded schools', *International Schools Journal*, 20(1), 24–37.

Hill, I. (2012), 'Evolution of international mindedness', *Journal of Research in International Education*, 11(3), 245–261.

International Baccalaureate. (2008a), *IB Learner Profile Booklet*. Cardiff: International Baccalaureate.

International Baccalaureate. (2008b), *Creativity, Action, Service Guide*. Cardiff: International Baccalaureate.

International Baccalaureate. (2010), *Programme Standards and Practices*. Cardiff, UK: International Baccalaureate. http://www.ibo.org/documentlibrary/ programmestandards/documents/programme_standards_practices_2011.pdf

International Baccalaureate. (2012a), *What is an IB Education?* Cardiff: International Baccalaureate Organization (UK) Ltd.

International Baccalaureate Organization. (2012b), Diploma Programme Extended Essay Guide. (Originally published 2007, updated August 2012) Cardiff: International Baccalaureate Organization.

International Baccalaureate Organization. (2012c), Global Engagement: Teaching and Learning about Rights.

International Baccalaureate Organization. (2012d), Global Engagement: Teaching and Learning about Conflict. Creating a More Peaceful World.

International Baccalaureate Organization. (2012e), Global Engagement: Teaching and Learning about Cooperation and Governance.

International Baccalaureate Organization. (2012f), Global Engagement: Teaching and Learning about Development.

International Baccalaureate Organization. (2012g), Global Engagement: Teaching and Learning about the Environment.

International Baccalaureate. (2013a), IB Learner Profile. http://www.ibo.org/ programmes/profile/ (Accessed 15 January 2013).

International Baccalaureate. (2013b), IB World School statistics. http://www.ibo.org/ facts/schoolstats/progcombinationsbyregion.cfm (Accessed 23 January 2013).

http://www.ibo.org/facts/schoolstats/progsbycountry.cfm (Accessed]http://www.ibo. org/facts/schoolstats/progsbycountry.cfm (Accessed 26 January 2013).

International Baccalaureate. (2013c), Global politics. http://www.ibo.org/diploma/ curriculum/group3/GlobalPolitics.cfm (Accessed 29 January 2013).

International Baccalaureate. (2013d), Global Engage website. http://globalengage. ibo.org/

International Primary Curriculum (IPC). (2013), IPC website http://www. greatlearning.com/ipc/ (Accessed 11 January 2013).

International Schools Association. (2013), Education for Sustainability – a Curriculum Framework K-12. http://www.isaschools.org/images/ISA/education_ for_sustainability.pdf (Accessed 22 January 2013).

International Schools Association Global Issues Network. (2013), *Education for Peace - A Curriculum Framework K – 12*. http://www.isaschools.org/images/ISA/ education_for_peace.pdf (Accessed 4 January 2013).

International School of Luxembourg. (2004), High Noon and the Global Issues Network. The Partnership, Issue 17, October 2004. http://www.islux.lu/assets/ pdf/Partnership-Issue-17-October-2004.pdf (Accessed 14 January 2013).

International Teacher Certificate. http://www.internationalteachercertificate.com/ internationallyminded.asp (Accessed 2 January 2013).

Jenkins, C. (1992a), 'Our country, our planet' (book review)', *Contact, the Journal of the International Baccalaureate Schools,* 3(3), 52.

Jenkins, C. (1992b), 'Letter to the editor', *Contact, the Journal of the International Baccalaureate Schools,* 3(3), 54.

Jenkins, C. (1998), 'Global issues: A necessary component of a balanced curriculum for the twenty-first century', in M. Hayden and J. Thompson (eds), *International Education: Principles and Practice*. London: Kogan Page, pp. 92–102.

Keller, M. (2010), 'Global Mindedness and Internationalism: The Effect of the International Baccalaureate Program on School Wide Attitudes of Students', Ed.D. diss., Union University. In *Dissertations & Theses: The Humanities and Social Sciences Collection*. http://www.proquest.com (publication number AAT 3443003) (Accessed 25 July 2011).

Lelievre, B. and East, M. (2009a), *Global Issues Project Organizer 1*. Oxford: Oxford University Press.

Lelievre, B. and East, M. (2009b), *Global Issues Project Organizer 2*. Oxford: Oxford University Press.

Lelievre, B. and East, M. (2010), *Global Issues Project Organizer 3*. Oxford: Oxford University Press.

Lelievre, B., East, M., Knight, A. and Kunkel.T. (2010a), *Global Issues Project Organizer 4*. Oxford: Oxford University Press.

Lelievre, B., East, M., Knight, A. and Kunkel.T. (2010b), *Global Issues Project Organizer 5*. Oxford: Oxford University Press.

Lewis, C. (2005), 'What must a school do to be globally responsible?' *International Schools Journal*, 24(2), 17–23.

Marshall, H. (2007), 'Global education terminology debate: Exploring some of the issues', in M. Hayden, J. Levy, and J. Thompson (eds), *The Sage Handbook of Research in International Education*. London: Sage Publications Ltd. pp. 38–50.

Merryfield, M. (1991), 'Preparing American Social Studies teachers to teach with a global perspective: A status report', *The Journal of Teacher Education*, 42(1), 11–20.

Merryfield, M. (2002), 'Rethinking our framework for understanding the world', *Theory and Research in Social Education*, 30(1), 148–152.

Merryfield, M. (2008), 'The challenge of globalization: Preparing teachers for a global age', *Teacher Education & Practice*, 21(4), 434–437.

Merryfield, M. (2009), 'Moving the center of global education', in T. Kirkwood-Tucker (ed), *Leadership and Vision in Global Education: The Globalization of Curriculum and Pedagogy in Teacher Education and Schools*. New York: Peter Lang, pp. 215–239.

Murphy, E. (2000), 'Questions for the new millennium', *International Schools Journal*, 19(2), 5–10.

North-South Centre of the Council of Europe. (1997), *Global Education Charter*. Appendix 2 of North-South Centre of the Council of Europe (2008). http://www.coe.int/t/dg4/nscentre/ge/GE-Guidelines/GEguidelines-web.pdf (Accessed 21 January 2013).

North-South Centre of the Council of Europe. (2008) *Global Education Guidelines*. Lisbon. North-South Centre of the Council of Europe. http://www.coe.int/t/dg4/nscentre/ge/GE-Guidelines/GEguidelines-web.pdf (Accessed 21 January 2013).

Orr, D.W. (1991), *Ecological Literacy: Education and the Transition to a Postmodern World*. Albany, NY: State University of New York Press.

Oxfam Development Education Programme. (1997), A Curriculum for Global Citizenship. Oxford: Oxfam.

Oxfam Development Education Programme. (2006), Education for Global Citizenship – A Guide for Schools. Oxford: Oxfam GB. http://www.oxfam.

org.uk/~/media/Files/Education/Global%20Citizenship/education_for_global_
citizenship_a_guide_for_schools.ashx

Peel, R. (1992), 'Challenges to the IB curriculum', *Contact, the Journal of the International Baccalaureate Schools,* 3(1), 6–7.

Peterson, A.D.C. (1987), (Second edition 2003) *Schools across Frontiers: The Story of the International Baccalaureate and the United World Colleges.* La Salle, IL: Open Court.

Pike, G. and Selby, D. (1988), *Global Teacher, Global Learner.* London: Hodder and Stoughton.

Pike, G. and Selby, D. (1999), *In the Global Classroom 1.* Toronto: Pippin Publishing.

Pike, G. and Selby, D. (2000), *In the Global Classroom 2.* Toronto: Pippin Publishing.

Renton, A. (2013), 'Barbara Stocking: 'Poverty is about power and politics', *The Guardian.* Wednesday 16 January 2013. http://www.guardian.co.uk/global-development/2013/jan/16/barbara-stocking-oxfam-ideals?INTCMP=SRCH

Rischard, J.F. (2002), *High Noon: 20 Global Problems, 20 Years to Solve them.* New York: Basic Books.

Rischard, J.F. (2007), Presentation at Global Issues Network conference, Beijing, April 2007.

Roberts, B. (2009), *Educating for Global Citizenship – A Practical Guide for Schools.* Cardiff: International Baccalaureate.

Roberts, B. (2011), 'Engaging with the community', in G. Walker (ed), *The Changing Face of International Education.* Cardiff: International Baccalaureate, pp. 86–102.

Roberts, B. (2012), 'Back to basics – the three Es of education', *International Schools Magazine,* 14(3), 45–46.

Skelton, M., Wigford, A., Harper, P. and Reeves, G. (2002), 'Beyond Food, Festivals and Flags', *Educational Leadership* 60(2), 52–55. http://www.ascd.org/ASCD/pdf/journals/ed_lead/el200210_skelton.pdf (Accessed 17 January 2013).

Skelton, M. (2007), 'International-Mindedness and the Brain: The difficulties of "becoming"', in M. Hayden, J. Levy and J Thompson (eds), *The Sage Handbook of Research in International Education.* London: Sage, pp. 379–384.

Sutcliffe, D. (2004), *International education: mirage or oasis?* (Peterson lecture, May 2001). International Baccalaureate Organization. http://www.ibo.org/council/peterson/sutcliffe/documents/sutcliffe_lecture.pdf (Accessed 7 March 2013).

Tarc, P. (2009), 'What is the "International" in the International Baccalaureate: Three structuring tensions of the early years (1962–1973)', *Journal of Research in International Education,* 8(3), 235–261.

Tate, N. (2012), 'Challenges and pitfalls facing international education in a post-international world', *Journal of Research in International Education,* 11, 205–217.

Thelin, B. (1992), 'We need an education for global survival', *Contact, the Journal of the International Baccalaureate Schools,* 3(1), 70–72.

Think Global. (2011), *Cultivating a Global Outlook for the Global Economy.* London: Think Global. http://clients.squareeye.net/uploads/dea/documents/Cultivalting%20a%20global%20outlook2.pdf (Accessed 28 January 2013).

Thomas, P. (1998), 'Education for peace: The cornerstone of international education', in M. Hayden and J. Thompson (eds), *International Education: Principles and Practice*. London: Kogan Page, pp. 103–118.

Tye, K. (ed) (1991), *ASCD Yearbook 1991: Global Education: From Thought to Action*. Alexandria, VA: Association for Supervision and Curriculum Development.

Tye, K. (1999), *Global Education: A Worldwide Movement*. Orange, CA: Interdependence Press.

UNESCO. (1974), Recommendation concerning education for international understanding, co-operation and peace and education relating to human rights and fundamental freedoms. http://www.unesco.org/education/nfsunesco/pdf/Peace_e.pdf (Accessed 29 January 2013).

UNESCO. (2012), *Education for Sustainable Development Sourcebook*. Paris: UNESCO. http://unesdoc.unesco.org/images/0021/002163/216383e.pdf

UNESCO. (2013), Key publications on Education for Sustainable Development and Climate Change Education. http://www.unesco.org/new/en/education/themes/leading-the-international-agenda/education-for-sustainable-development/publications/

Walker, G. (2012), 'Tea and oysters: Metaphors for a global education', *International Schools Journal*, 31(2), 8–17.

Wells, J. (2011), 'International education, values and attitudes: A critical analysis of the International Baccalaureate (IB) Learner Profile', *Journal of Research in International Education*, 10, 174–188.

WWF-UK. (2004), *Pathways: A Development Framework for School Sustainability*. Godalming, UK: WWF-UK www.eauc.org.uk/sorted/files/wwf_pathways_1.pdf (Accessed 17 January 2013).

WWF-UK. (2011), *Pathways: To Education for Sustainable Development*. Godalming: WWF-UK http://assets.wwf.org.uk/downloads/pathways4.pdf (Accessed 17 January 2013).

PART THREE
The New Critique

CHAPTER EIGHT

Understanding International Education Through Discourse Theory: Multinational, International, Multicultural or Intercultural?

Michael Allan

Introduction

Much of the writing in the field of international schools and international education has been directed towards defining what it actually is, and establishing a category for this field and its study which is both inclusive and exclusive. Indeed the editor of this volume issues a caveat to try to mitigate the confusion of superficially indistinguishable terminology. In asking how this etymological quest seems to be paramount in the literature we might pose two questions. First what is the reason for this, and second what is its effect? Possible motives might be to establish that international education has a distinct pedagogy; for marketing purposes in exploring a 'niche' market; to pursue an ideological belief in the virtue of internationalism as a force for peace; to establish a specific school of thought for academic career purposes; as a form of taxonomy, confusing knowledge of a concept with the definition of a word; or to further commercial and economic ends, to hazard a few reasons.

However, words not only have meanings, they have power, the power to change states of affairs and the power to bring about action, among many others. Thus, in exploring the effect of these multiple interpretations of international education, we move into the realm of discourse and power. Using this juxtaposition, this chapter discusses whether the first 40 years of the development of international schools can be better understood using the tools of discourse analysis.

The first section outlines the theoretical underpinning of discourse analysis. This is then applied to the 'macro' discourses surrounding international schools and to the 'micro' discourse in the following section. The conclusion suggests some implications for the understanding of international schools that result from this analysis.

Discourse theory

Discourse theory is also a ubiquitous term and is used in many different disciplines. Its cross-disciplinary potential has already been demonstrated by numerous combined approaches, and discourse analysis as an interpretive tool within qualitative methodology in many areas is also well documented. Discourse theory can incorporate various contexts and further analyse the relative effects of each on the particular situation. This also has benefits in terms of transferability. If phenomena in a case study are situated within various wider discourses, then it is easier for other researchers to transfer conclusions to a different situation, as the effect of macro-discourses will have been incorporated, and other researchers can situate their case relatively within the same discourses (Allan, 2007). It is one of the intentions of this chapter to demonstrate how this eclecticism permits a cross-disciplinary and coherent approach to understanding the complexity of the educational process in international education on many levels. However, it has also produced a multiplicity of terminology, terms such as discourse, narrative, genre, script, code, and so on, each perhaps being defined in a way designed to suit the discursive position of the theorist. Following this tradition, I propose to use the term discourse in two senses; at the macro-level (common/countable noun) as a singular view of social reality, in which corresponding evaluative contexts and implicit values are conveyed through language and other means of expression and communication. At the micro-level, the term discourse (mass/uncountable noun) is used to encompass individuals' communication of their particular interpretation of specific events, situations, concepts and attitudes, as well as subject positions and their different levels of authority.

Discourse at the macro-level can be seen as a way in which society manifests itself, and thereby becomes a means of studying a certain society at a certain period, but some theorists would go further and say that it has the political power to shape society and influence events and empower some groups at the expense of others. At the micro-level, discourse can be seen as a way in which groups and individuals express their world view, and, via their place in it, also construct their social identity. Personal interactions at this level, including all the multiple natures of language, can also be seen in terms of discourse; and the construction of the self in the form of narrative is a widely held perspective in social psychology (Allan, 2007). The way in which discourse forms a conjunction of power and knowledge was propounded most notably in the writings of Michel Foucault. From Foucault comes the idea of discourse as a regulated way of speaking that defines and produces objects of knowledge, thereby governing the way topics are talked about and practices conducted (Foucault, 1970). For Foucault 'truth' did not mean objective or intrinsic facts about the nature of people, rather that in constructing ideas that are ascribed the status of 'truths', they become 'normalizing' in the way they shape and constitute people's lives. He asserts the inseparability of power and knowledge in showing how the 'truths' of traditional notions of knowledge positioned one form of knowledge in ascendancy over another. Discourse thus embodies meaning and social relationships and it serves to empower its users and marginalize others from the debate by determining the frame of reference within which their standpoint may be judged (Allan, 2007). The discourses then not only refer to objects of discussion, they become them: 'Discourses...do not identify objects, they constitute them and in the practice of doing so conceal their own invention' (Foucault, 1971). In this paradigm, knowledge does not reflect the power relations between different groups of society, but embodies them. Power and knowledge are inseparable and mutually reinforcing, and are made manifest in discourse. 'Discourses are therefore about what is said and thought, but also who can speak, when and with what authority...The possibilities for meaning and interpretation are pre-empted through the social and institutional position from which a discourse comes' (Ball, 1990, p. 17).

An example of how discourse has been used in the formation of educational policy is the response of neo-liberals to the economic crises in Western economies, in an attack on Keynesian socialistic policies (and, by association, the public sector) aided by the fall of Communism at the end of the 1980s, and a search for alternative market devices to solve social problems. The response of the 'New Right', together with the media, to this 'crisis of capitalism' in Western countries in the late 1970s was to create a discourse of a 'crisis in education' in which notions like standards, literacy and heritage were mobilized against the 'isms' of education such as progressivism, comprehensivism, egalitarianism, multiculturalism and pluralism. Their professional interpretations of educational policy were replaced in the new discourse by 'truth', 'rationality', 'parental choice', 'the market', 'efficiency' and 'management' (Ball, 1990, p. 18). This discourse constitutes civil society on the basis of property rather than citizenship and implies a shift from child-centred education and the transmission of cultural values to the idea of human capital and the market value of education.

At the macro-level, the post-modernist view of discourse is that texts are subject to multiple and conflicting interpretations and language becomes a barrier to truth in that objective knowledge cannot exist (Tomlinson, 1995). Policy-making then becomes an area of competition among the discourses of competing interest groups and conflicts over meaning and interpretation. Outcomes are determined by the dominant discourse; or as Fulcher says, policy is seen as a 'struggle between contenders of competing objectives, where language – or more specifically discourse – is used tactically' (Fulcher, 1989, p. 7). In the arena of multicultural education, discourse theorists have been criticized by critical multiculturalists like McLaren (1997) and Macedo (1994) for not engaging with economic and political forces, including, of course, the coercive exercise of power, leading to 'weak theories of social constructivism that fail to locate agency in the larger social totality of advanced capital flows' (McLaren, 1997, p. ix).

Indeed other aspects of post-structuralism, the political and the economic, also have a determining role to play in the formation of educational policy. Whether these influences can be incorporated into an all-embracing discursive conflict theory is considered later. There may also be evidence of a new social 'grand narrative' (Whitty, 1997, p. 121), perhaps of 'corporatism' (Kennedy, 1995), or a neo-Marxist explanation of merely a shift in emphasis or battlefield, from national class struggles to that of global capitalism and underprivileged minorities. These questions will be considered in the examination of educational policy-making in the international arena in the following section.

Macro-discourses – 'multinational' and 'international'

This section will concentrate particularly on the interaction between the current discourse of globalization and ideology-driven policy-making in international education, looking particularly at ideas of international education, how far they are compatible with the context of the market-driven global economy and the multinational commerce which has led to the growth in the numbers of international schools. Changes in the nature of post-industrial capitalist societies have inevitably led to a re-examination of the nature and role of education. Education was no longer seen as an instrument to train workers for an industrial society and a means of transmitting the accompanying national cultural values inherent in this, but the values of the marketplace were applied to education and it was held that schools too should be cost-effective, satisfy the demands of stakeholders and include the concept of assessment of outcomes as an indicator of success. A need was seen for a return to market forces to ensure cost-efficiency, and the role of education as a micro-economic tool in improving competitiveness was emphasized (OECD, 1979, 1989). Human capital was identified as a key component of economic growth and this was seen as the justification for aligning education policy and economic policy and for the state assuming control. This discourse of the 'New Right' became manifest in education throughout the English-speaking world during the 1980s. In the US this shift has been identified in the 1984 document 'The Nation at Risk' (Cibulka, 1995); in the UK it has been traced to the White Paper *Better Schools* of 1985, or even *The Black Papers* of Cox and Boyson in 1975 (Kennedy, 1995) and is seen in the 'corporate federalism' of the 1982 and 1987 Hawke Labour governments (O'Neill, 1995) and 'back-to-basics' movement in Australia (Carter, 1995), and in the educational reforms of the Labour Government in New Zealand from 1987 (Peters, 1995). What all of these have in common is the identification of a crisis in education, to which the answer is seen to be greater centralized control in order to raise standards and to make education more directly relevant to the needs of industry, involving the removal of the influence of educational administrators at local level, and a move towards a market-driven model at school level. Can we also see evidence of this discourse in the growth of international schools and development of an international curriculum?

In Europe, the 1989 report of the European Round Table (ERT) 'Education and European Competence' identified the causes of high unemployment as 'caused by inappropriate or outdated education'. It identified the situation today as not related to the requirements of nationhood or basic industrial needs, but those of a unifying Europe with a free labour market and transferability and compatibility of skills. 'The concept of strong nationalism has been taken over by Europeanism. *Diversity and separate identity should be overcome* and exchanged for educational systems which are mutually strengthening and supportive' (ERT, 1989, p. 18, italics added). This question of international transferability and comparability was highlighted as being the major single problem area. Here the post-industrialist discourse of education has become 'international'.

In the Netherlands, this was translated into policy in the documents 'Broadening Horizons' (Minister O & W, 1988) and in 'Internationally Oriented Education in the Netherlands (IGO)' (Europees Platform, 1996) which states that 'among other things, internationally oriented education in the Netherlands intends to meet the needs and wishes of the Dutch and international business community and their employees' (Europees Platform, 1996, p. 7). 'Globalisation expands boundaries, broadening our horizons and making our world smaller…Pupils who come into contact with the international and intercultural community at a young age through internationalisation at school have a broader perspective and better chances on the international job market' (European Platform, 2013). As a result of this discourse, international schools were established throughout the Netherlands, funded jointly by the Dutch Ministry of Education and trusts administered by groups of local companies, mainly multinational corporations, who see education for 'children from differing countries and cultures' as essential for 'Holland developing into one of Europe's major centres of international business' (SBIO, 1996). There are now 20 such schools in the Netherlands which could be seen as examples of the corporatist alliance between government and business, addressing in particular the importance of international schools in the economic growth derived from multinational companies. In 2006 the UK government provided funds so that every Local Authority in England could have 'at least one centre offering sixth-formers the chance to do the IB' (Shepherd, 2009). State-funded international schools are also found in Scandinavia, Spain and China; and worldwide, more than 50% of IB students are in state-funded schools (IB, 2013).

As well as English-medium education, the wide recognition of the International Baccalaureate (IB) Diploma as a university entrance requirement and the status given by CIS accreditation are the factors which are important in the transferability required by the employees of multinational corporations and diplomats whose children attend these schools (Hayden and Thompson, 1995; Matthews, 1989), as well as establishing a high-status Western-style education for local elites. The importance given to these elements in promoting an explicitly Western education could be said to represent the 'market-driven' (Matthews, 1989), or 'pragmatic' (Cambridge, 1998), discourse of international school philosophy, that of 'multinationalism'. Paris, as an example, distinguishes between 'Globalisation (which) occurs when there are impositions of ideas involving a dominant-recessive relationship. (and) Internationalisation (which) occurs when there is a sharing of ideas, where ideas are utilized, agree upon and mutually accepted' (Paris, 2003 p. 235). Taylor et al. (1997), in analysing educational policy from the point of view of social justice, suggest that globalization policies are affecting the cultural field within which educational policy operates, diminishing the cultural and political autonomy of minority linguistic cultures. They define internationalism as a multilateral relationship, whereas globalization focuses on the supranational. Cambridge and Thompson summarize the debate thus:

> The globalist approach to international education is influenced by and contributes to the global diffusion of the values of free market economics…The internationalist approach to the practice of international education is founded upon international relations, with aspirations for the promotion of peace and understanding between nations. (Cambridge and Thompson, 2004, p. 173)

The discourse of market-driven globalization or 'multinationalism' will directly impinge on policy in international schools, and may conflict with the discourse of 'internationalism' which could be said to be at the heart of most international school philosophy and which is discussed later.

However, globalization as such is not a new phenomenon, after all in 1848 Marx and Engels noted: 'In place of the old local and national seclusion and self-sufficiency, we have intercourse in every direction, universal interdependence of nations. And as in material, so also in intellectual production. The intellectual creations of individual nations become common property' (Marx and Engels, 1848). In 1944 the interdependence of national economies was recognized at the Bretton Woods Conference in New Hampshire, where the ideas of John Maynard Keynes were incorporated into a series of international agreements which laid the foundations of today's global economy. Rapid technological change in the Western economies reduced the dependence on labour as the principal factor of production, and this had far-reaching consequences in the formation of post-industrial society. The opening up of world markets and international transfer of capital led also to a threat from far eastern economies to the West's domination of the manufacturing markets.

This accompanied a re-examination of sociological and economic models and eventually led to what has been recognized as a post-structuralist idea of globalization. This is defined by Corson as education being set firmly within capitalist social relations, 'the most assimilatory cultural forces that the world has ever seen' (Corson, 1998, p. 3). It is the marketplace view of the world where bonds are economic and not cultural or social, resulting in a tendency to project a respect for sameness rather than the diversity which exists.

The discourse expressed so strongly by Corson and other critical realists is echoed by most writers on international schools, who see globalization as the *bête noire*, despite the fact that it is the *raison d'être* for most international schools. Hill (2006) chronicles this, quoting Smith (2003), for example, that globalization is guilty of 'eroding senses of national identity to unprecedented losses of indigenous languages and cultures under the homogenising pressures of global capital'. The main objection to globalization seems to be that it is inherently a manifestation of Western culture and as such is synonymous with Westernization.

This notion of the globalization of society as being all-pervading Westernization has been questioned by commentators who see convergence of cultural characteristics as an inevitable feature of modernization. In addition to economic modernization, Yang (1988) identified a socio-cultural modernization reflected in the expansion of education as well as in occupational diversification, secularization, urbanization and mass communication. This discourse of convergence is based on the hidden premiss that 'modernity' is a paradigm that is universal in its manifestation and that as countries become wealthier, the higher proportion of 'post-materialists' would 'make people similar and render our current enchantment with cross-cultural differences in behaviour an archaeological curiosity – a historical digression' (Smith and Bond, 1993, p. 211). This discourse would use the seemingly irrefutable desirability of modernity to marginalize those in developing countries who would wish to maintain a cultural pride by distinguishing their culture from that of the West. Their argument is dismissed by the assertion that modernization is not to be confused with Westernization, but is new to all societies, Western and non-Western. However, Yang's (1988) and Hofstede's (1994) research both show a strong correlation between the norms and values of modernity and those of Western culture. The incorporation of international education in this discourse was recognized by Leach (1994) 'The early rationale for the mass expansion of Western-style schooling in non-Western countries…can be found in the economic theory of human capital and the sociological theory of modernization' (Leach, 1994, p. 218). Rizvi argues that the Organization of Economic Co-operation and Development (OECD) gives an example of this in that its suggestions regarding international education are located 'in a largely celebratory fashion, within a neo-liberal imaginary of global processes, and do not adequately engage with their complex dynamics and unequal circumstances' (2007, p. 391). He goes on to propose a more critical concept 'internationalization' which seeks to develop a range of 'epistemic virtues' in an attempt to differentiate between a philosophy of international education based on epistemological tenets and mere discourse.

The move towards a distinct ideology for international education has been institutionalized by the International Baccalaureate Organization (IBO or IB), whose mission statement adopted in 1996 states that 'strong emphasis is based on the ideals of international understanding and responsible citizenship, to the end that IB students may become critical and compassionate thinkers, lifelong learners and informed participants in local and world affairs, conscious of the shared humanity that binds all people together while respecting the variety of cultures and attitudes that makes for the richness of life' (IBO, Education for Life, 1998). The IB provides the curricular documents, methodologies and assessment techniques by which the international curriculum can be defined in international schools. Are these ideals of internationalism expressed by the IB a real basis for a multicultural education or a marketing tool in the 'franchising' operation of the IB in establishing a globally recognized product on the lines of Nike or McDonalds, the 'International MacCalaureate'? Kevin Bartlett defines a 'deeper internationalism…that more profound empathy with other cultures and concern with international issues which would characterize a global concern' (Bartlett, 1993, p. 36), and also 'celebrates cultural diversity and promotes an international-minded outlook' (Cambridge and Thompson, 2004, p. 173).

This is another, and to some extent, conflicting discourse, which stresses intercultural learning, and has been termed 'ideological' (Matthews, 1989), and is expressed in the mission statements or philosophies of international schools and organizations (Allan, 2002). The IBO mission statement adopted in 1996 states:

strong emphasis is based on the ideals of international understanding and responsible citizenship, to the end that IB students may become critical and compassionate thinkers, lifelong learners and informed participants in local and world affairs, conscious of the shared humanity that binds all people together while respecting the variety of cultures and attitudes that makes for the richness of life. (IBO, 1998)

There is, indeed, a great deal of evidence that the purpose, or way forward, for international schools is being considered within the juxtaposition of these two discourses, 'market-driven' multinationalism and ideological 'internationalism' (Cambridge, 2002; Cambridge and Thompson, 2004; Jones, 1998).

However, in terms of Foucauldian discourse theory, leaders in international education seem to be struggling to define, and claim ownership of, a discourse that will maintain them in a position of leadership, for example international understanding, global citizenship and cultural literacy, and not establish an international/multicultural pedagogical approach that is liberated from national discourses and cultural specificity of education. In the 'idealistic' discourse, the discursive enemy to an internationalist ideology is global capitalism, and its assumption of market value as being the only value worth seriously considering. While rhetorically lauding the ideological vision of internationalism, in reality they do not seem to mount a real challenge to the market-driven discourse that governs most schools.

The debate as to whether 'Modernization' is 'Westernization' is an excellent example of the way a dominant discourse monopolizes the perspective and marginalizes other points of view, in that both concepts are essentially Western. It situates the argument within a Western discourse and demeans ('de-means') other terms of reference. Critical multiculturalism is stronger in its condemnation. 'In parading before people the virtues of diversity, liberal multiculturalists have displaced the contextual specificity of difference, recycling colonialism under the guise of democracy' (McLaren, 1997, p. ix). In 'liberal' or 'relativist' multiculturalism, the discourse is still how to make the educational process accessible to non-Anglophone, or non-white, students. It does not recognize the cultural specificity of its educational philosophy, or takes as granted that it is the superior model, removing this hidden assumption from discussion or criticism. This process is akin to the apocryphal sociological 'test' for racism: 'Are zebras black with white stripes or white with black stripes?' It is the question that is racist; zebras, of course, have both black stripes and white stripes.

This is evidence of how discourse in the field of international education cannot be separated from wider ones. The dual, at times seemingly contradictory, facets of global post-modernism are that on the one hand human diversity is being recognized; on the other hand people's real socio-cultural identities have little value in the marketplace. Roland Barthes

(2000) described the way the 'bourgeoisie' in post-war Europe manipulated the discourse so that it appears to be the objective 'reality' against, or with reference to, which everything else must be defined, thereby avoiding any possibility that it itself can be defined and perhaps criticized. We can see a parallel to the reproduction and self-perpetuation of Western capitalism, where anything 'exotic' is demeaned so that it can be characterized as being only skin-deep and trivial, thus enabling human nature to be emphasized as universal, reinforcing Western humanism (an atheist form of Christianity), rather than exploring the real differences among cultures. This parallel could be extended further to so-called 'international' schools and their dominant Western values, curricula and pedagogy.

Neo-Marxists see the global economy as an International Dependence model, either of dualistic development describing the chronic co-existence of rich and poor, both in nations on a global scale, and between rich elites and the poor majority in national populations, or in terms of neo-colonial dependence (Todaro, 1993). Certain groups within developing countries who enjoy high incomes, social status and political power constitute a small elite ruling class whose principal interest is to perpetuate the international capitalist system of inequality and conformity by which they are rewarded. Rather than international interdependence, the dominant countries expand through self-impulsion while the dependent countries can only expand as a reflection of this. The education offered by international schools seen in this light can only serve to perpetuate the dualism.

Ball, in trying to recognize the forces of change without losing sight of structural models completely, identifies the three ideas discussed here which may be used in policy analysis: political struggles between interest groups; correspondence between education and the economy; and the role of discourses, the idea that discursive practices maintain power relations. It would be neat to be able to summarize this section by saying that policy in international schools is the result of conflict between contenders of the competing discourses of internationalism as serving the needs of a culturally diverse student body in 'multiculturalism' and internationalism as serving the interests of the economic stakeholders in 'multinationalism'. However, this would not give due credit to the economic explanations of policy-making inherent in corporatism, nor to the political conflicts in the global economy represented in neo-Marxism and other theories of knowledge in policy-making.

The challenge for international education seems to be to reconcile two seemingly opposing aspects of post-modern global society: global integration and national fragmentation, or 'ethnic tribalism'. In doing so it must incorporate the demands of the stakeholders, which are found in the discourse of 'multinationalism', and of the cultural minorities, which are held to be of such value in the discourse of 'internationalism'. The perspective presented here suggests that an examination of policy at macro-level can be successfully achieved by using discourse analysis as a coherent methodology. The idea that at the micro-level individual school culture can be seen as a conflict of discourses within the school (Allan, 2003), each a product to some extent of the national discourses of involved parties, and encompassed by these global discourses of multinationalism and internationalism is examined in the next section.

Micro-discourse – 'multicultural' and 'intercultural'

George Walker (2007) has recognized the change at macro-level in the social environment surrounding international education at the beginning of the twenty-first century in response to globalization. Hitherto, international education has been largely concerned with the relationship between groups contained within different geographical boundaries, whereas the modern multicultural nature of national school classrooms means that 'conflicts *between* nations give way to culturally-based conflicts *within* nations' (Walker, 2007, p. 405). Does this mean that the need for 'intercultural' education will now take precedence over 'international' education? Within the philosophy and the culture of international schools this could be seen as an identification of two differing discourses.

In this section, the micro-level of discourse found in international school cultures will be considered, and although they might be thought to be free from the exigencies of what is euphemistically termed 'integration' in national multicultural schools, it must be remembered that macro-discourses and the external environment may be regarded as the source of many of the values and beliefs that coalesce to form the culture of the school. Matthews suggests that the uniqueness of international education is found not in the curriculum and in associated activities but in the diversity of the student population, effect of residence and education outside national cultures, the type of teacher found in international schools and the adjustment of the teacher to the special needs of a mobile, transient, highly motivated multilingual population. It is the professional background and experience of teachers that 'yield the educational values that provide the potential and development of a common culture' (Bush, 1995 p. 137). The majority of teachers in IB schools are native English speakers from the UK, the US, Canada and Australia. Matthews classifies international school teachers into three groups – long-term international teachers, expatriate wives and transients – and gives an average of eight nationalities per school. (Matthews, 1989). This he says gives a multiplicity of didactic approaches; however, they are all within the Western tradition. Allan (2002, 2003) explains how this often combines with a predominant Anglophone student body to produce a mono-cultural school environment. Hayden and Thompson quote an international student saying she had not experienced an international education but rather 'a Western education, because everything I was taught was delivered in a Western point of view since all the teachers were from the west' (Hayden and Thompson, 1996, p. 51).

International schools then face the same inter-cultural dissonance as national schools and in this respect the use of language takes on even more importance. Post-structuralist views of language see the person as being constructed through the language, language cannot be separated from its culture and a national culture is defined in its language (Allan, 2011). English is the language of instruction in the majority of international schools. In this environment, the predominant language reinforces the predominant culture, English-speaking. The result can be that an international education can be a homogenizing induction into Western global culture, creating a cultural hegemony which accompanies the Western-dominated global economy – rather than the encouraging of diversity which is espoused in intercultural learning.

This has been termed linguistic imperialism by critical multiculturalists (Corson, 1998; Giroux, 1992; McLaren, 1997) in education, who combine Foucauldian ideas of discourse and power, Vygotksyan perspectives on learning and the critical pedagogy of Paulo Freire, in examining the position of discourses of underprivileged groups in schools. This standpoint became apparent in the examination of treatment and performance of cultural minorities in Western education systems, which are characterized as consisting of modernist discourses where 'the dualistic way of seeing reinforced a rationalistic, patriarchal, expansionist, social and political order, welded to the desire of power and conquest' (Kincheloe and Steinberg, 1997, p. 36). Critical multiculturalism attacks the privilege and bias afforded by Eurocentric (white, middle-class and patriarchal) discourses in schools and de-constructs learning, enabling the power structure implicit in the relative positions of different discourses to be exposed and attacked (McLaren, 1997). As these are not always congruent, dissonance among discourses must result, though not necessarily to the extent that they can be described as conflict. A school may not be 'a cultural arena where ideological, discursive and social forces collide in an ever-unfolding drama of dominance and resistance' (Kumaravadivelu, 1999, p. 475), but we might only have to substitute 'international' for 'regular' to agree with Corson that parents 'want the best of both worlds for their children's education: they certainly want admission to the mainstream and high-status culture of literacy that is the chief output of regular education, but they also want schools to recognise "their own things" – their own cultural values, language varieties, traditions, and interests' (Corson, 1998, p. 203).

Nevertheless, such post-modernist ideas of the inherent inequalities found in culturally diverse or multicultural schools are often ignored or even dismissed by commentators in the area of international schools.

Multicultural education is anchored in state systems of education and seeks to respond to the needs of migrant children, generally representing a lower socio-economic section of the community. International education is historically linked to the international school movement catering principally for the children of diplomats, UN personnel, and employees of international companies as they move around the world; for this reason, international education has often been described as elitist. (Hill, 2007)

Hill does, however, go on to urge for much more interaction in research and practice between multicultural and international education.

In a seminal work on the application of discourse analysis in multicultural educational contexts, Van Dijk (1981) showed how students bring to the classroom a culturally specific set of linguistic and cognitive processes. Thus, they may neglect information which does not fit in with their knowledge, opinions and attitudes, or will pay extra attention to the information which is part of their actual interest and topics. The same holds for the more specific contextual goals, tasks and wishes of language users. These may determine that the same discourse will be assigned different importance in different contexts, at different times, by the same learners or by different learners. Despite this, most studies of the use of language in classrooms have examined the structural idea of language rather than as a living expression of human culture or the hermeneutical context in which it is sent and received. Great attention is given to the nature of teacher–student interaction, but analysed mainly from a structural linguistic or pragmatic sense. If the nature of classroom discourse has been found to be so critical in mono-cultural situations, then it must be even more so in cross-cultural situations. Intercultural education means exploring the nature of language and culture rather than the mechanics of one. Ideas and tasks are presented in a way compatible with the child's frame of cultural reference, or at least other explanations and the equal validity of each are made plain. Pupils then have the possibility and responsibility to address this from their own cultural way of understanding; in doing so they also develop meta-linguistic and meta-cognitive understanding (Allan, 2011). Critical multiculturalists see mono-cultural (monological) discourse as a manifestation of cultural hegemony, enculturation being presented as the only avenue to academic success, with political and economic intentions and results. In order to learn something new the child must abandon or contradict basic cultural constructs from which communication and behavioural norms are derived.

Classroom discourse also includes the hidden rules of behaviour or 'scripts' (Edwards, 1997) which vary considerably among cultures, and among schools. 'Discourse rules for participation in classrooms are not only complex, but vary a great deal across classrooms and across activities within the same classroom' (Donahue, 1994, p. 229). Hymes found that many children rapidly acculturate to the classroom's norms of 'when to speak, when not, and as to what to talk about, with whom, when, where and in what manner' (Hymes, 1971, p. 277), but children who fail to conform to the norms for participating in talk are often at risk for being devalued by both teachers and classmates. Wells and Chang-Wells (1992) showed how teachers base the assessment of pupils on an examination of the communicative competence they display in structured group discussions about texts which they have read. Morine-Dersheimer (1985) showed that teachers' predictions on literacy acquisition were based on four categories of classroom discourse: participating in class discussion, talking out of turn, listening attentively and using non-standard English.

Mono-discursive pedagogy is one of the issues international education must address in catering equitably to the needs of culturally diverse student populations. English-language learners, learning a language orally, *in situ*, will learn first (and maybe only) the forms that are most common in the prevalent discourse. This may, or may not, allow them to formulate critical reflections on the other or their own culture, as it is not feasible in the *language* of that *discourse*. Giroux defines true multicultural pedagogy, or 'border pedagogy':

> As a pedagogical process intent on challenging existing bodies of knowledge and creating new ones, border pedagogy offers the opportunity for students to engage the multiple references that constitute different cultural codes, experiences and languages. This means educating students to read both these codes historically and critically while simultaneously learning the limits of such codes, including the ones they use to construct their own narratives and histories. (Giroux, 1992, p. 29)

Conclusion

This chapter has attempted to show how the development of international education can be understood by the discourse(s) through which it is manifest. It seems, from this brief review of discourses involving international schools, that there has been an effort to distance this area from the ideas of multinationalism and multiculturalism by trying to establish a separate discourse of internationalism and interculturalism. We can refer back to the questions posed in the introduction to consider why this might be. Whether any fundamental difference arises from the meaning of these terms, or just the perspective from which they are perceived, belongs in the realm of post-structuralist discourse theory of Derrida and company. However, the difference between an educational discourse and an educational philosophy is that the former does not necessarily have any epistemological basis. This in itself is somewhat of an indictment of international education in failing to develop a coherent multicultural pedagogical philosophy in a seemingly ideal situation, autonomy from nationalist policy and curriculum constraints. Developments in multicultural education in national school systems do not seem to have been acknowledged and there has been very little research into how an education free from cultural bias and equally accessible to all linguistic and cultural groups can be delivered. Until this happens, 'international education' will remain a discourse rather than an educational philosophy.

References

Allan, M.J. (2002), 'Cultural borderlands', *International Schools Journal,* XXI(2), 42–53.

Allan, M.J. (2003), 'Frontier crossings: Cultural dissonance, intercultural learning and the multicultural personality', *Journal for Research in International Education,* 1(2), 83–110.

Allan, M.J. (2007), 'Voices from abroad: A contextual approach to educational research and cultural diversity', in M. Hayden, J.J. Thompson and J. Levy (eds), *A Handbook of Research in International Education*. London: Sage Publications, pp. 426–440.

Allan, M.J. (2011), 'Thought, word and deed: The roles of cognition, language and culture in teaching and learning international schools'. *IB Position Paper,* International Baccalaureate: Geneva. http://blogs.ibo.org/positionpapers/files/2011/05/IB-position-paper1.pdf

Ball, S.J. (1990), *Politics and Policy-Making in Education*. London: Routledge.

Barthes, (2000), *Mythologies*. London: Vintage.

Bartlett, K. (1993), 'Internationalism: Getting beneath the surface. Part 1: Internationalism? It's about thinking!', *International Schools Journal,* 26, 35–38.

Bush, T. (1995), *Theories of Educational Management*, London: Paul Chapman Publishing Ltd.

Cambridge, J.C. (1998), 'Investigating national and organizational cultures in the context of the International School', in M.C. Hayden and J.J. Thompson (eds), *International Education: Principles and Practice*. London: Kogan Page, pp. 197–211.

Cambridge, J.C. (2002), 'Global product branding and international education', *Journal of Research in International Education,* 1(2), 227–243.

Cambridge, J.C. and Thompson, J.J. (2004), 'Internationalism and globalisation as contexts for international education', *Compare,* 34(2), 157–171.

Carter, D. (1995), 'Curriculum reform and the Neo-corporalist state in Australia', in D.S.G. Carter and M.H. O'Neill (eds), *International Perspectives on Educational Reform and Policy Implementation*. London: The Falmer Press, pp. 31–43.

Cibulka, J. (1995) 'The evolution of educational policy reform in the United States: Policy ideals or *Realpolitik*', in D.S.G. Carter and M.H. O'Neill (eds), *International Perspectives on Educational Reform and Policy Implementation*. London: The Falmer Press, pp. 15–30.

Corson, D. (1998), *Changing Education for Diversity*. Buckingham: Open University Press.

Donahue, M. (1994), 'Differences in classroom discourse styles of students with learning disabilities', in D. Ripich and M. Creaghead (eds), *School Discourse*. San Diego, CA: Singular Press, pp. 229–260.

Edwards, D. (1997), *Discourse and Cognition*. London: Sage Publications.

ERT (1989), Education and European Competence, European Round Table.

Europees Platform (1996), *International Georiénteerd Onderwijs [Internationally Oriented Education in the Netherlands]*, Stichting Europees Platform voor het Nederlandse Onderwijs: The Hague.

European Platform (2013), http://www.europeesplatform.nl/sfmcgi?3326&cat=64 (Accessed 5 February 2013).

Foucault, M. (1970), *The Order of Things*. London: Tavistock.

Foucault, M. (1971), 'Orders of discourse', *Social Science Information*, 10, 7–30.

Fulcher, G.(1989), *Disabling Policies? A Comparative Approach to Educational Policy and Disability*. London: The Falmer Press.

Giroux, H.A. (1992), *Border Crossings: Cultural Workers and the Politics of Education*. New York: Routledge.

Hayden, M.C. and Thompson, J.J. (1995), 'Perceptions of international education: A preliminary study', *International Review of Education*, 41(5), 389–404.

Hayden, M.C. and Thompson, J.J. (1996), 'Potential difference: The driving force for international education', *International Schools Journal*, XVI(1), 46–57.

Hill, I. (2006), 'Do International Baccalaureate programs internationalise or globalise?', *International Education Journal*, 7(1), 98–108.

Hill, I. (2007), 'Multicultural and international education: Never the twain shall meet?', *International Review of Education*, 53(3), 245–264.

Hofstede, G. (1994), *Cultures and Organizations: Intercultural Cooperation and Its Importance for Survival*. London: HarperCollins Business.

Hymes, D. (1971), 'On communicative competence', in J.B. Pride and J. Holmes (eds), *1972, Sociolinguistics*, Selected Readings. Harmondsworth: Penguin, pp. 269–293.

IBO (1998) Education for Life, International Baccalaureate Organization: Geneva.

International Baccalaureate (2013), http://ww.ibo.org/who/slidec.cfm (Accessed 5 February 2013).

Jones, P. (1998), 'Globalisation and internationalism: Democratic prospects for world education', *Comparative Education*, 34(2), 143–155.

Kennedy, K.J., (1995), 'An analysis of the policy contents of recent curriculum reform efforts in Australia, Great Britain and the United States', in D.S.G. Carter and M.H. O'Neill (eds), *International Perspectives on Educational Reform and Policy Implementation*. London: The Falmer Press, pp. 53–71.

Kincheloe, J.L. and Steinberg, R.S. (1997), *Changing Multiculturalism*. Buckingham: Open University Press.

Kumaravadivelu, B. (1999), 'Critical classroom discourse analysis', *TESOL Quarterly*, 33(3), 453–484.

Leach, F. (1994), 'Expatriates as agents of cross-cultural transmission', *Compare*, 24(3), 217–231.

Macedo, D. (1994), *Literacies of Power: What Americans Are Not Allowed to Know*. Boulder, CO: Westview Press.

Marx, K. and Engels, F. (1848), *Manifesto of the Communist Party*, http://marx.eserver.org/communist.manifesto/cm1.txt (Accessed 5 February 2013).

Matthews, M. (1989), 'The scale of international education', *International Schools Journal*, 17, 7–17.

McLaren, P.J. (1997), 'Introduction', in J.L. Kincheloe and S.R. Steinberg (eds), *Changing Multicultural Education*. Buckingham: Open University Press, pp. viii–x.

Minister O & W (1988), *Inernationaliseren in onderwijs*, Europees Platform. http://www.europeesplatform.nl/sf.mcgi?3326&_sfhl=Broadening Horizons (Accessed 5 February 2013).

Morine-Dersheimer, G. (1985), *Talking, Listening and Learning in Elementary School Classrooms*. New York: Longman.

OECD (1979), *Future Educational Policies in the Changing Social and Economic Context*. Paris: OECD.

OECD (1989), *Education and Economy in a Changing Society*. Paris: OECD.

O'Neill, M. (1995), 'Introduction', in D.S.G. Carter and M.H. O'Neill (eds), *International Perspectives on Educational Reform and Policy Implementation*. London: The Falmer Press, pp. 1–14.

Paris, P. (2003), 'The International Baccalaureate: A case study on why students choose to do the IB', *International Educational Journal*, 3(2), 232–243.

Peters, M. (1995), 'Educational reform and the politics of the curriculum in New Zealand', in D.S.G. Carter and M.H. O'Neill (eds), *International Perspectives on Educational Reform and Policy Implementation*. London: The Falmer Press, pp. 45–52.

Rizvi, F (2007), 'Internationalization of curriculum: A critical perspective', in M. Hayden, J. Levy and J. Thompson (eds), *The Sage Handbook of International Education*. London: Sage Publications, pp. 390–440.

SBIO (1996), *Firm Foundations for the Future: International Education in the South of the Netherlands*. Eindhoven: Stichting voor het Bevordering van Internationaal Onderwijs.

Shepherd, J (2009), Leap from Cardiff to Amsterdam for Baccalaureate, *The Guardian*: UK http://www.guardian.co.uk/education/2009/feb/10/international-baccalaureate-moved-amsterdam (Accessed 5 February 2013).

Smith, D. (2003), 'Curriculum and teaching face globalization', in W. Pinar (ed), *International Handbook of Curriculum Research*. New York: Lawrence Erlbaum Associates, pp. 35–51.

Smith, P.B. and Harris Bond, M. (1993), *Social Psychology across Cultures*. Hertfordshire: Harvester Wheatsheaf.

Taylor, S., Rizvi, F., Lingard, B. and Henry, M. (1997), *Educational Policy and the Politics of Change*. London: Routledge.

Todaro, M. (1993), *Economic Development in the Third World*. New York: Longman.

Tomlinson, J., (1995), 'Teachers and values', *International Schools Journal*, XIV(2), 8–22.

Van Dijk, T. (1981), 'Discourse studies and education', *Applied Linguistics* 2, 1–26.

Walker, G. (2007), 'Challenges from a new world', in M. Hayden, J.J. Thompson and J. Levy (eds), *A Handbook of Research in International Education*. London: Sage Publications, pp. 404–411.

Wells, G. and Chang-Wells, G.L. (1992), *Constructing Knowledge Together: Classrooms as Centers of Inquiry and Literacy*. Portsmouth, NH: Heinemann.

Whitty, G. (1997), 'Education policy and the sociology of education', *International Studies in Sociology of Education*, 7(2), 121–135.

Yang, K.S. (1988), 'Will societal modernization eventually eliminate cross-cultural psychological differences?', in M.H. Bond (ed), *The Cross-Cultural Challenge to Social Psychology*. Newbury Park, CA: Sage Publications, pp. 67–85.

CHAPTER NINE

The International Baccalaureate and the Role of the 'Pioneer' International Schools

Tristan Bunnell

The historical context

The growth of international schools

The field in 1972

The context of this book is the founding of the International School of London (ISL) in 1972. ISL had joined a very diverse grouping of schools, described by Mayer (1968, p. 155) as having 'sprung up independently' and being 'a law unto themselves', although an element of structure had begun to appear. June 1972 had seen the European Council of International Schools (ECIS) accredit the first school (Antwerp International School), whilst the long-established body of international schools in Japan had established a regional association in 1972, in the form of the Japanese Council of Overseas Schools (JCOS). One of the first local (Allen, 2002) associations appeared in 1974 when the Rome International Schools Association (RISA) was established. Interestingly, some of the key theoretical concepts connected with international schools (e.g. 'Third Culture Kids': Useem and Downie, 1976) had yet to fully appear in 1972.

We actually know much about the extent of the field as it existed 40 years ago. Robert Leach (1969, p. 162) had listed 372 international schools worldwide, of which 76 were in Asia (including just 15 in the Middle East), educating approximately 80,000 children. Martin Mayer (1968, p. 154) had surveyed the field for almost 3 years between 1964 and mid-1967, and referred to identifying about 250 'struggling and confused schools' educating 75,000 children. Both these reports revealed a relatively small body of international schools, largely American in origin and seemingly operating in a largely isolated and parochial environment. It seems ironic to note that even 40 years later it was being commented that 'it may well be that International Schools exist mainly in a sort of bubble' (Bates, 2011 p. 7).

The only noticeably significant areas of activity at the end of the 1960s were in Geneva, Rome, Paris and Vienna, while there were no international schools in China and just two in Hong Kong, one in Thailand and another one in Malaysia. This listing included a number of schools that would now not normally be included and so it might now be considered an over-estimation, although Robert Leach himself said (p.152) that it constituted 'probably a third of those which actually do exist'. Many of the schools identified by Leach (1969) have 'encapsulated missions' (Sylvester, 1998), catering specifically for overseas students of one particular culture. The network of French overseas schools is the largest. As Leach (1969, p. 144) confirmed that only about three-fifths were English-speaking schools, we can deduce that ISL was probably one of 300 to 400 international schools worldwide (depending upon the definition) when it appeared in 1972, alongside Maru-a-Pula School in Botswana, Bandung International School in Indonesia and Ambrit International School in Rome.

Sylvester (2002a, p. 91) has suggested that there is a need to 'examine critically the current mythology of international education that sees the field simply as a direct outcome of two world wars or a by-product of the second age of globalization that followed'. The developmental history of international schooling can be linked to peak periods of globalization activity. A useful framework is that contrived in the 1920s by the Russian economist Nikolai Kondratiev (1892–1938). Beginning about 1800 this model would pinpoint that international schooling is currently associated with 'K5', the fifth 'long wave' of globalization, each spanning approximately 50 years, with the current one beginning in the late 1990s. St. Andrew's Scots School began during the 'K1' wave in Buenos Aires in 1838 to satisfy the needs of Scottish settlers, and seems one of the earliest examples of a 'market-driven' (Matthews, 1989) school. The very first international school proper has been identified by Sylvester (2002b) as the Spring Grove International College, which emerged in west London in 1866, during the peak of the 'K2' wave of free-trade globalization. One of the school's backers was the free-trade advocate Richard Cobden. The first formally 'ideology-oriented' international schools emerged in Yokohama and Geneva in 1924, at the peak of the 'K3' wave as giant firms emerged and there was a concentration of finance and banking. It was during the peak of the 'K4' wave of the early 1960s that the ECIS organization appeared, as transnational corporations began to grow and develop.

The current field

What this analysis means, of course, is that any numbers are always vague estimations, but they give a useful context for arguing that any international school which appeared 40 years ago should be considered as historically and educationally important. Leach (1969, p. 144) had admitted that '[p]robably no more difficult task may be set before the educationalist than to attempt a delineation of international schools in this world'. However, the body of international schools has undeniably grown enormously over the last couple of decades and the growth has seemingly become easier to map. The current statistics, as revealed by *ISC Research* and discussed by Anne Keeling and Nick Brummitt in this book, are startling when compared to the studies by Mayer (1968) and Leach (1969), revealing perhaps the manner in which international education in its international schooling context has become 'another franchised commodity to be sold in ever-expanding markets' (Wylie, 2011, p. 31). The *ISC Research* database in November 2012 showed that 7 cities had over 90 international schools apiece. The United Arab Emirates (UAE) in October 2012 had the most schools – 370, almost exactly equal to the worldwide sum estimated by Leach in 1969. Although the exact number of schools is impossible to quantify (Hayden and Thompson, 2008, p. 17), and the broad definition offered by *ISC Research* does not in the main include schools in English-speaking nations such as England, or the US or Australia, it is very clear that huge growth has occurred over the past decade in particular.

Although most international schools are obviously relatively 'new', a significant number have reached, like ISL, the 40th anniversary mark. Indeed, the year 2012 saw a significant number hit the 50th anniversary mark (e.g. International School of Dusseldorf, Copenhagen International School), and China's largest international school, Shanghai American School, even celebrated its 100th anniversary in 2012. Another school named 'ISL', the International School of Lusaka, will celebrate its 50th anniversary in 2013, as will the International School of Helsinki.

The growth of the International Baccalaureate

The International Baccalaureate over five decades

The universe of international schools now appears fundamentally different from that which ISL had entered in 1972. Both the *scale* (over 6,000 schools) and *nature* (mainly for-profit and catering for local elites) of international schooling has changed quite radically. The scale and nature of the International Baccalaureate (IB) world has also fundamentally changed over this same time period. This chapter highlights the role of the 'pioneer' international schools in the growth and development of the programmes of the IB. ISL was undeniably an IB 'pioneer' and it was always intended the school would adopt the IB. Several commentators at the time (e.g. Ronsheim, 1970; Terwilliger, 1972) were sceptical about how 'international' these schools really were but it has since been asserted that the adoption of the IB programmes 'has for many schools become the most obvious outward manifestation of their international schools status' (Wilkinson, 2002, p. 189). This was seemingly true of ISL. The school was formally authorized to offer the IB Diploma Programme (IBDP) in January 1977, becoming the 57th school in the world, and it stands today as the second longest-established IB school in England. St. Clare's, Oxford, was authorized as the 41st school in the world the previous year, although North Manchester High School for Girls' had offered candidates for the 1968 trial examination and might claim the right to be identified as the 'first' IB school in England (Bunnell, 2008). Both schools had been formally authorized to offer this 'curriculum and social movement' (Bagnall, 2010, p. 11) immediately after the experimental period (1970–1976) had ended, though Richard Pearce (pers. comm.) has reported that ISL actually started teaching the IBDP in September 1976. Leach (1969, p. 151) was confident the IB 'experiment' would work and prophesized that '[i]t is not inconceivable that by 1977…7,500 candidates will be using the IB successfully each year'.

The early history of the IBDP has been extremely well told of late (e.g. Hill, 2010; Tarc, 2009a). But, it is worth telling the story of the initial development of the IBDP as it involved an interesting historical coincidence. The first IB course, in Contemporary History, emerged out of the Conference for Teachers of Social Studies in International Schools, held at the International School of Geneva from 26th August to 1st September 1962 (Hill, 2010, p. 37). The role of the Geneva school cannot be over-stated: 'The initial work was undertaken by teachers at the International School of Geneva, rightly considered the place where the IB was spawned' (Hill, 2010, p. 35). In fact, there were two events occurring in the summer of 1962. Coincidentally, an attempt was being made at the United World College of the Atlantic, in its castle base in south Wales, to create a broad and balanced 'baccalaureate'-type programme. Here, Alec Peterson was working with Robert Blackburn, the school's deputy headmaster; 'During the summer of 1962, Peterson worked with him on the curriculum for the new school' (Hill, 2010, p. 42). In other words, the summer of 2012 was in effect the 50th anniversary of the IBDP, although this significant event attracted little, if any, scholarly attention. It is worth commemorating that, in fact, the term 'IB' was first used by Robert Leach in a report he drew up 50 years ago for the Geneva-based International Schools Association (ISA): 'Until an international baccalaureate is operative, the essential ideal of the international school falls down in practice' (Leach, 1962, cited in Hill, 2010, p. 36).

The year 2012 was also the 40th anniversary of the publication of a seminal book by Alec Peterson about the IB as an 'experiment in international education'. This chapter will use this book as a key source of material as it also (alongside Leach, 1969; Mayer, 1968; Peterson, 1987) provides a good account of the operational context of international schooling as it had emerged by the early 1970s. The IB in 1972 had involved just 19 schools in 11 countries, 5 of which were state schools (i.e. 80% were classified as private international schools), aiming to demonstrate 'that it actually worked in practice on a small scale and was capable of expansion' (Peterson, 1987, p. 24). By 1972, a total of 1,544 candidates had been entered in cumulative total for the IBDP exam, but of whom only 170 had actually passed the full Diploma (Hill, 2010, p. 91). Five schools were reported in 1972 to be close to phasing out national examinations in favour of the IBDP (Hill, 2010, p. 92). By the time ISL formally joined in 1977, a total of 9,000 candidates had taken the IB exam and approximately 6,000 were currently involved (Hill, 2010, p. 109). The IB World in England was still relatively small even a decade later. By 1986 there were 18 schools authorized to offer the IBDP in the UK (Peterson, 1987, p. 236), 16 of them were in England, and 6 of them are still members of the main 'local' association – the London International Schools Association (LISA).

The current scene

The IB was never in fact assured of survival. This statement is an important one to make when considering the role of the 'pioneer' schools. As Hill (2010, p. 12) stated, 'the road to its current achievements has at times been rocky and on at least one occasion it seemed likely the good idea would not make it'. Like any infant, the IB required a fair degree of parenting, and this fact now deserves some recognition. The IB did survive and it involved 500 schools in 70 countries in 1997 (Hayden and Wong, 1997). The number of countries hosting an IB school globally subsequently increased from 113 in 2005 to 144 in March 2013. The huge growth of the IB between 2005 and 2013 has seen it passing a succession of milestones. The 4,000th programme had appeared on 25th June 2011 when the Taihu International School in China was duly authorized. The IB was officially educating 1 million children by March 2012. A year later there were over 3,500 IB schools, including 2,400 schools offering the IBDP. Of these, 188 were in England and 1,400 in the US. Significantly, in February 2013 both IB Primary Years Programme (PYP) and the Middle Years Programme (MYP) had hit the 1,000-school mark. It is worth noting that the MYP was not an IB 'product' as such but began life as the International Schools Association Middle Years Curriculum, and was 'adopted' by the IB in 1992. The PYP had been first discussed at an ECIS conference in Rome in 1990, and became the International Schools' Curriculum Project 3-12 (ISCP) in 1992.

To complete an already complex picture, the 'IB continuum' was joined by yet another programme, the Career-Related Certificate (the IBCC) in 2011, and it came fully on-stream in September 2012. In January 2012 the

IB began a revamp of the MYP, with moves to bring in external assessment (examination) at end of Year 5. The 'new' MYP begins proper in 2014. In April 2012 the IB announced the 'IB Open World Schools' pilot project. This was to involve four 'IB World Schools' (International School of Berne, Riverview High School in Florida, Yokohama International School and the Adrian Public Schools in Florida) which were selected to operate as 'IB Open World Schools', and they were allowed in September 2012 to enrol non-IB candidates at non-IB schools to undertake IBDP courses online. In July 2012 the four IB programmes were developed as 'sub-brands', sitting alongside the IB 'corporate brand', each with their own logo and colour design. By this method the IB has created a framework for distinguishing between different groups of schools. The diverse body of 3,500 'IB World Schools' that existed at the end of 2012 can itself now be fragmented and sub-branded, beginning with a distinct (perhaps superior) 'IB Open World School'.

This development is an important one in the context of this chapter, which will argue the case for another category to emerge, to be named the 'IB Pioneer World School', encompassing schools that have been involved continuously with the IB since the early 1980s. In fact, the IB itself has presented a framework for identifying some schools as 'pioneers'. The IB in a presentation to the United World Colleges in 2003 advanced the notion of a 'pioneer model' type of school, characterized as the 'first public school reached or within reach' (IBO, 2003, p. 11). Establishing contact with this type of school allows the IB to build up good relations with the local authorities and build recognition of the IB programmes. In IB planning parlance, contact with such schools allows a country or region to attain 'Band 2' status, where the IB has the strongest potential to grow. The IB in 2003 was looking towards attaining this status in Germany, Lithuania and Texas (IBO, 2003, p. 12). In other words, the concept of 'pioneer' can be applied equally to a 'first school in the country' as well as to a 'school long-established with the IB'. The concept is clearly multi-dimensional in practice.

To add weight to the assertion that ISL is a 'pioneer', it is worth noting that it was authorized to offer the PYP in 2004, and became a 'continuum' school (offering all three main IB programmes) four years later. Significantly, it was still in 2012 one of only five 'continuum' schools in the UK (alongside four other international schools: ACS Egham International School, Dwight School London, International Community School London and Southbank International School). Moreover, by 2012 these five schools had been joined by just another 145 in the world. To add to the historical picture it is worth noting that the IB could possibly reach its 2006-set target of 2.5 million children in 10,000 schools by 2020 (Beard, 2006), although a more recent publication (Guy, 2011, p. 141) has predicted 2.0 million children in 10,000 schools by 2020, reflecting a slight slowdown in annual compound growth, as one might expect mathematically.

The conceptual context

Conceptualizing significant periods in time

The significance of the early 1980s

Several frameworks exist for conceptualizing the growth and development of the IB. Tarc (2009a; 2009b), for example, has offered a four-period interpretation from 1962 until 2009. Within this framework, ISL joined the IB during the 'second period', which had existed between 1973 and 1989, and which Tarc called the 'Growth and Sustainability' period. An earlier useful framework had come from Wallace (1999), who presented a 'lifetime' analogy. It was proposed by Wallace that the period until 1983 be regarded as the 'infancy' period of the IB. This period saw two IB directors general (Alec Peterson, 1968–1977 and Gérard Renaud, 1977–1983). The 15-year period that saw Roger Peel as director general (1983–1999) was labelled the 'youthful' period. George Walker's period as director general (1999–2006) was described as being the 'adulthood' period of the IB. Presumably, the current period (starting with Jeffrey Beard's appointment in 2006) is a 'middle-aged' or 'maturity' one. This chapter will take the end of the 'infancy' period as being the 'pioneer' stage. This would be about 1983, when there were about 300 IBDP schools, that is, about 15% of the 2012 complement.

It is actually very difficult to gauge exactly how many schools have offered the IB during the past 40 years. Many have dropped the programmes and some have even dropped it and then come back on board later in time (e.g. Grennaskolan in Sweden was involved in 1970 but did not renew its links until 20 years later). Also, school names change, and some schools have since merged. For example, in May 1972, 19 schools had entered 631 candidates. However, ten of these (i.e. almost half) had dropped the IBDP by 1992. This story in itself is interesting, revealing the fact that many of the initial 'pioneer' schools had only a short historical linkage with the IB. For instance, the Iranzamin International School in Tehran, one of the first seven involved in the 1968 trial exam was disbanded in 1980 and re-emerged later in Spain. Southampton College and International College Beirut were both part of the May 1972 cohort, yet they dropped the IBDP around the same time that ISL was officially authorized. This gives schools like ISL an even greater significance, still offering the IBDP in 2012 after 35 *continuous* years.

The most objective means of gauging when schools became involved with the IB 'project' comes from the date they were authorized and the examination code that was duly assigned. Copenhagen International School, for example, also took part in the 1968 trial exam and has the examination code 000004. Frankfurt International School was involved in the May 1969 exam session and has code 000007. There is no doubting the early 'pioneer' nature of a school with a code number like this. St. Clare's Oxford, the longest-running IB school in England, was authorized in January 1976 and has the code 00041. The official IB website tells us that there were only about 150 programmes being offered in the early 1980s. However, it has been asserted (Hill, 2010, p. 129) that there were 313 schools in 1986, and 545 in 1994, and these figures seem more closely aligned with the 'authorization code'. In November 1983, the Booker T. Washington High School (Tulsa, Oklahoma) had been authorized (code: 000297), and in March 1984 ISL was joined in London by Southbank International School (code: 000309).

The early 1980s was definitely a very significant period for the IB. The IB added offices in Buenos Aires and Singapore in 1982. By 1980, there was concern that the IBDP was beginning to be perceived as 'Euro-centred' (Fox, 1998). A seminar was convened in Singapore, and the issue of 'Euro-bias' of certain subjects was tackled at the 1982 Standing Conference of Heads in New York. Blackburn (1983) reported on the increasing interest in the IBDP in 'developing' countries but highlighted several barriers. In 1984, a seminar took place in Nairobi, to deal with these issues. Significantly, the year 1983 saw Spanish join French and English as 'working' languages of the IBDP. More interestingly, this was also the time when the proportion of IB schools that were 'international schools', which had hitherto been in a majority, fell below 50% for the very first time. A presentation by the IB Director General to the ECIS Annual Conference (19th November 2004) had revealed there were 1,215 IBDP schools and since it was also stated around that time that 18% were 'international schools' we can deduce that about 300 IB schools were of this type in 2004. This figure has fallen dramatically as a proportion from 80% in 1972 to 58% in 1979, 18% in 2004 and is expected to be just 5% by 2020 (see the presentation by Beard and Holloway, 2010), although 3% might be more realistic given current growth trends. The linkage between the IB programmes and international schools has gone from being virtually *synonymous* in 1972 to being in 2012 almost *tenuous*.

The significance of the late 1990s

The late 1990s was certainly also a very significant time. The IB moved noticeably much further away from its international school base after entering the 'adulthood' phase. The link is still a strong one, but Hayden and Wong (1997, p. 352) seemed to conceptualize this development well when they noted that the IBDP had moved from 'being a programme for international schools, to being an international programme for schools'. Wallace (1999, p. 8) had also stated the IB was entering a 'new era', having moved from a period of 'expansion' to 'consolidation'. This comment now seems to have been a little premature since the 'IB World' actually doubled in number from 1999 to 2004 (from 1,000 to 2,000 schools). In other words, there was still huge expansion to come, but Wallace was certainly correct in 1999 to sense a change of direction, and the arrival of a different era. In particular, the IB World moved significantly *away* from international schools *towards* national ones. Towards the end of the 'youthful' period, at a conference of the International Schools Association in 1997, IB Director General Roger Peel had spoken of the 'coming of age' of international schooling: 'The thesis that international education has come of age is the growing confirmation that international teaching and learning is no longer the private domain of International Schools' (cited in Hill, 2010 p. 142). George Walker, the succeeding director general, talked of the IB having moved from 'contact' (with international schools) to 'connections' (with national schools) (see Walker, 2007). The IB has undergone enormous expansion in American public schools during the 'connections' phase, although the growth has not always been welcomed (Bunnell, 2012). The IBDP added (IBO, 2003, p. 6) almost 32,500 students between 1997 and 2002. Of these, almost half (15,544) were located in North American public schools, plus another 3,440 were in private schools in North America. In fact, 58% of the student expansion between 1997 and 2002 had occurred in schools in North America. Significantly, at the end of 2012, 40% of all IB schools were in the US.

Conceptualizing the emergence of the 'pioneer' schools

The 'first batch' of schools

Some educators had envisaged a very small membership emerging: 'The IB project is a small-scale project experiment in international education designed to solve certain very limited problems at present facing international schools. Could it lead to something more substantial?' (Peterson, 1972, p. 122). There was no initial consensus on the need for a large-scale body of schools. The original concept (as envisaged in 1964 by Georges Panchaud, Professor of Education at the University of Lausanne) was for an 'experiment' limited to only about a dozen schools (recalled Peterson, 1987, p. 207). Peterson remarked how some people (such as Panchaud) 'initially conceived of the experiment as a piece of applied educational research' (Peterson, 1987, p. 61). The IB started life as a remarkably small organization (initially called the International Schools Examination Syndicate, ISES), reliant at first solely upon voluntary involvement: 'At first, all involved with the ISES were unpaid enthusiasts for international education' (Hill, 2010, p. 40). Martin Mayer remarked that 'the organization was very weak and needed considerable financial support to strengthen it' (Mayer, 1968, p. 4). Even up until 1973 the IB was operating out of a small office in west London (Hill, 2010, p. 69).

The small-scale 'experiment' required some 'laboratories'. The IB had three prominent 'founding laboratories'. The work of the Geneva school and Atlantic College is well known, but the United Nations school in New York (UNIS, founded in 1947) was another prominent body: 'the third of the major international schools to join in the planning' (Peterson, 1972, p. 16). Indeed, the New York school was the first, in 1968, to adopt the IBDP as the sole basis of curriculum. Fox (1998, p. 70) had remarked that 'UNIS was thus in an optimum position to serve as a laboratory for the IB experiment'. The first official IBDP exam session was held in May 1971. Twelve schools in 10 countries entered a total of 601 students. The 'laboratory schools' began to be gradually authorized. The British Schools of Montevideo was officially authorized in January 1971 as were Atlantic College, Frankfurt International School, International School of Geneva and UNIS. The Goethe-Gymnasium in Frankfurt was officially authorized in January 1972 as was Copenhagen International School. St. Catherine's School-Moorlands School in Argentina came on board the 'project' in January 1973.

Paul Tarc (2009b) saw 1973 as being the end of the first of four periods, entitled 'The Creation and Experiment Period'. Thus, using Tarc's framework, the 'first batch' of IB schools involved, from 1962 to 1973, just 12 schools in a largely liberal-humanist 'project'. The United World College of the Pacific (Lester B. Pearson College) became the first IB school in Canada in January 1974. The Antwerp International School was the first school in Belgium, authorized in January 1975. In January 1976, the first school in India appeared: 'In educational terms, however, the decision by Kodaikanal International School to join a small cadre of schools worldwide in adopting and trialling the DP marked a watershed in educational terms' (Ashworth, 2011, p. 179).

The 'second batch' of schools

The seven experimental exams (1970–1976) had involved about 40 schools. The 'experiment' by 1974 had a waiting list of about 80 schools (Hill, 2010, p. 102), and thus probably had a lot more by 1976. The next 'batch' of schools duly began to appear relatively quickly. There was now not a need for a controlled sample of schools, but a need for a greater diversity and broader geographical platform. Peterson (1987, p. 65) noted that there was an initial debate about 'whether the IBO should seek to recruit an internationally balanced group of schools…or should simply respond to demand'. However, the more practical response in 1977 was to simply go for growth *per se*: 'the first essential was to recruit a sufficiently diverse group of schools to demonstrate that the project was feasible and filled a need'. The view that emerged was that '[t]he more schools the better, irrespective of their nature and the more schools, the more income' (Peterson, 1987, p. 207).

ISL was joined in January 1977 by the Kungsholmens Gymnasium (Stockholm), Washington International School, International School Moshi (the first in Africa), United World College Singapore (the first in Singapore) and International School of Brussels (code: 000050). Also in January 1977, the Colegio Colombo Británico in Colombia became the first authorized IB school in the Andean region. In March 1977, the American International School (Vienna) was authorized as was the Anglo-European School (Ingatestone, Essex). The IB was now growing at a significant rate of about five schools per month. The second Inter-Governmental Conference in London, 15–16 February 1978, recommended that the IB now undertake a 'carefully controlled expansion'. That same month, Narrabundah College became the first school in Australia to be authorized (code: 000092). St. John's International School (Brussels) and the French American International School (San Francisco) were also authorized in February 1978. In June 1978, the prestigious private Sevenoaks School came on board (code: 000102), revealing that the IB had hit the 100-school mark. In September 1979, the American School of Paris was authorized, followed by the Colegio Anglo-Colombiano (Bogota) in February 1980 (code: 00149). December 1981 saw the 200-school mark appear (St. Leonard's College, Victoria, Australia; code: 00196). The 250-mark was hit around March 1983 (The Overseas School of Colombo, Sri Lanka, became 000245). For information, Canyon High School in California was authorized in August 1988 and became 000500.

Moving the issue forward

The moral case for recognition

This chapter offers a new framework for conceptualizing the role of the early IB schools. To briefly summarize, although the diverse body of IB schools are equally branded 'IB World Schools', a historical analysis of the initial growth of the IB reveals that 'batches' of schools can be identified. The very first schools involved in the experimental IBDP period until 1976 can be classified as being the 'laboratory schools', voluntarily testing the largely hidden 'experiment' and allowing it to have a scale (no more than 500 students per year) and base (about 40 reputable schools worldwide) for experimentation. This 'first batch' mainly consisted of international schools (who now constitute only about 10% of the total 'IB World', and is expected to fall to 5% by 2020). The schools that subsequently came on board the IBDP project provided a showcase and each acted as a champion for the fledgling curriculum at a time when it was still a 'risk' and largely an innovative 'experiment'. As the period until 1983 was the 'infancy' period, we can use this as a convenient cut-off point for identifying the 'pioneer' schools, numbering approximately 300 (i.e. about 8% of the current 'IB World').

This gives scope for a controversial perspective to appear. The role of the long-established 'pioneer' IB schools, acting voluntarily as early 'champions' of the IBDP, arguably gives this type of international school a more important and prestigious role that subsequent schools do not have. The IB may now see all its member schools as equal 'customers', yet there is a strong case for arguing that the early 'pioneers' have a greater case for historical and moral 'ownership' of the IBDP than the others. This chapter concludes that the role of many international schools in the historical growth and development of the IB needs re-assessing and their current role as 'IB World Schools' needs re-evaluating.

There is a strong moral and historical case for differentiating between 'batches' of IB schools. The early pioneers have a particularly strong case for special identification. It is true that (since 1976) each school pays the same annual fee irrespective of the size of the school. However, the 'price' they pay does not reflect the real cost of making the programmes (i.e. it does not reflect the input from teachers and other educators, mainly volunteers, over the years): 'The making of IB depended upon grass-roots volunteerism on the part of committed teachers, school leaders and influential "friends"' (Tarc, 2009a, p. 11). Along this line, Hayden (2010, p. 14) suggested that educators should consider 'an admiration for the early pioneers who had the "good idea", who with courage and determination put energy, enthusiasm and time into persuading others of the "good idea", and who managed to secure funding to enable that "good idea" to be put into practice'. Hill (2010, p. 12) has reminded us that 'the success that is taken for granted some 40 years on may well have been won in earlier days'. Most recently, it has been noted (Hayden and Thompson, 2011, p. 9) that the IBDP owes its existence 'to the inspiration and selfless commitment of a dedicated group of far-sighted educators from the middle of the last century'.

In fact, the 'good idea' owes its survival in 1976 to relatively few people. It is an under-reported fact that it had long been planned to 'hand over' the IB to the United Nations (UN); 'negotiations have started already for the permanent establishment of the International Baccalaureate after 1975 under UN control' (Peterson, 1972, p. 31). But, on 14th May 1976 the UNESCO Executive Board had rejected this notion, and '[t]he future of the IB became critical from that moment' (Hill, 2010, p. 108). At the peak of the ensuing funding crisis, Alec Peterson had called a meeting at his London office (4th June 1976) to discuss saving the IB. Peterson (1987, p. 94) described how as 'an emergency measure, representatives of ten of the schools most concerned to keep the IB going met in London'. It was here that the annual school subscription of 10,000 Swiss Francs was (unanimously) agreed upon. Peterson had written to schools in 1976 and stated that 'an additional $130,000 a year for the years 1977 and 1978' was needed, or the 'decision to close down the project' would be taken (Hill, 2010, p. 108). In other words, after 1976 the IB required quickly many more schools on-board. This story is remarkable in revealing just how intimate and close-knit the IB was at that point in time. The subsequent growth and development of the IB depended in 1976 upon the (voluntary) actions of fewer than a dozen people, mainly educators working in international schools. The IBDP had taken an initial 'slippery path' (Hayden and Thompson, 2011, p. 16) with 'the new creation threatened on a number of occasions by lack of funds and questions of recognition and credibility'.

The role of the early 'laboratory schools' in particular cannot be overstated: 'By 1975, heads, teachers, university admissions officers and government ministries were accepting the IB Diploma on the basis of its initial success in a number of schools around the globe' (Hill, 2010, p. 26). The vital and essential role of the initial body of international schools as voluntary laboratories was acknowledged by Peterson when he stated that '[t]he fact that their proposals would actually be tried out in the international schools provided something akin to an international laboratory situation which could not have been provided by any other means' (Peterson, 1972, p. 89). One reason to be grateful for the participation of these initial schools is that the IB was not only an experiment but was a risk: 'The schools that had agreed to try IB were taking a gamble' (Mathews and Hill, 2006, p. 38). Alec Peterson (1987, p. 27) recalled how he had 'set out on a tour' of schools in Africa, Middle East and South America: 'It included a swing through Nigeria, Ghana, Uruguay, Chile and the USA.' Peterson visited schools that had been identified in 1967 by Martin Mayer as 'possibles'. Several schools visited by Peterson (e.g. St. George's, Rome) decided not to join the project: 'The process of decision is a complicated one and was then much more complicated since the IB was an untried venture' (Peterson, 1987, p. 27).

The practical case for recognition

It seems important to mention here that the relationship between the IB and international schools (as represented by bodies such as the Academy of International School Heads, AISH) has become a problematic and seemingly quite tense one. Some educators in the dwindling bloc of international schools now clearly take offence at being seen as regular 'customers' (rather than 'members' or 'creators'). This issue arose publicly during late 2008 (e.g. Matthews, 2009a, 2009b; Toze, 2008), alongside a view that growth was compromising quality in terms of the consistency and reliability of the IB. In some ways, this is a reasonable stance to take. As we have seen, the IB in 1976 faced the real possibility of not continuing, without the authorized schools fully funding it, and the mainly international schools who came on board to save the project at that time (about 80 appeared in 1976–1979 alongside the initial 40 or so) have a particularly strong moral case for asserting 'ownership' or 'parentship' of the IBDP. The issue of an emerging 'ownership tension' can be conceptualized as an extension of a wider 'operation tension' (Tarc, 2009a). Put bluntly, there does seem to be a practical need for giving some of the international schools a more prominent role and 'badge' of distinction. As discussed earlier, the IB itself has begun in 2012 to create a platform for distinguishing between groups of schools and seemingly acknowledges that some schools are strategically more important than others. A parallel case can be made in historical terms.

One aspect of the early IB that comes through the writing such as Peterson (1972; 1987) is that the IBDP benefited from a high degree of innovation and experimentation, especially from the international schools. Peterson (1987, p. 37) noted that 'the great advantage which the IBO has enjoyed over national systems has been the willingness of teachers...to experiment'. Furthermore, Peterson (1987, p. 38) said that 'The teachers involved in the IB have been mainly self-selected innovators.' Within these comments lies a fundamental role for international schools; free from national control they can afford to experiment and innovate. This seems a valuable role that needs in 2012 to be readdressed and re-evaluated. Giving some of the early international schools a badge of distinction (as 'pioneer' schools), whether literally or in spirit, might help to rekindle the innovation and experimentation flame.

References

Allen, K. (2002), 'Atolls, seas of culture and global nets', in M. Hayden and J. Thompson (eds), *International Education in Practice: Dimensions for National and International Schools*. London: Kogan Page, pp. 129–144.

Ashworth, G. (2011), 'Taking forward the IB Diploma in India: context and challenges', in M. Hayden and J. Thompson (eds), *Taking the IBDP Forward*. Suffolk: John Catt Educational Limited, pp. 179–196.

Bagnall, N. (2010), *Education without Borders: Forty Years of the International Baccalaureate 1970–2010*. Saarbrucken, Germany: Verlag Dr. Muller.

Bates, R. (2011), 'Introduction', in R. Bates (ed), *Schooling Internationally: Globalisation, Internationalisation and the Future for International Schools*. London: Routledge, pp. 1–21.

Beard, J. and Holloway S. (2010), 'Head to head: a session for IB heads of school'. Presentation at IB Heads of Schools Conference, Singapore, 25 March 2010.

Beard, J. (2006), 'Where the IB is heading...'. Presentation by IBO Director General Jeffrey Beard, IB Asia-Pacific Regional Conference, 6–9 October.

Blackburn, R. (1983), 'The International Baccalaureate in developing countries', *International Schools Journal*, 5, 7–13.

Bunnell, T. (2008), 'The International Baccalaureate in England and Wales: the alternative paths for the future', *Curriculum Journal*, 19(3), 151–160.

Bunnell, T. (2012), *Global Education Under Attack: International Baccalaureate in America*. Frankfurt, Germany: Peter Lang.

Fox, E. (1998), 'The emergence of the International Baccalaureate as an impetus for curriculum reform', in M. Hayden and J. Thompson (eds), *International Education: Principles and Practice*. London: Kogan Page, pp. 65–76.

Guy, J. (2011), 'Challenges to access', in G. Walker (ed), *The Changing Face of International Education: Challenges for the IB*. Wales: IBO, pp. 139–158.

Hayden, M. (2010), *The International Baccalaureate: Pioneering in Education*. Suffolk: John Catt Education Limited, pp. 11–14.

Hayden, M. and Thompson, J. (2008), *International Schools: Growth and Influence*. Paris UNESCO.

Hayden, M. and Thompson, J. (2011), *Taking the IBDP Forward*. Suffolk: John Catt Educational Limited.

Hayden, M. and Wong, C. (1997), 'The International Baccalaureate: international education and cultural preservation', *Educational Studies, 23*(3), 349–361.

Hill, I. (2010), 'The International Baccalaureate: pioneering in education', *The International Schools Journal Compendium, Volume IV*. Suffolk: John Catt Educational Limited.

IBO (2003), 'Driving pro-active growth at the IB'. Presentation to United World Colleges, 23 June 2003.

Leach, R. (1969), *International Schools and Their Role in the Field of International Education*, Oxford: Pergamon Press.

Matthews, M. (1989), 'The scale of international education: part 1', *International Schools Journal*, 17, 7–17.

Matthews, M. (2009a), 'Another head weighs in on the IB raised in Toze letter', *The International Educator, 23*(3), 28.

Matthews, M. (2009b), 'The International Baccalaureate: common myths, real concerns', *The International Educator, 24*(1), 11, 17.

Mathews, J. and Hill, I. (2006), *Supertest: How the International Baccalaureate Can Strengthen Our Schools*. Chicago, IL: Open Court.

Mayer, M. (1968), *Diploma: International Schools and University Entrance*. New York: The Twentieth Century Fund.

Peterson, A. (1972), *The International Baccalaureate: An experiment in international education*. London: George G. Harper and Co. Ltd.

Peterson, A. (1987), *Schools across Frontiers – The Story of the International Baccalaureate and the United World Colleges*. Chicago, IL: Open Court.

Ronsheim, S. (1970), 'Are international schools really international?' *Phi Delta Kappan* 7(2), 43–46.

Sylvester, R. (1998), 'Through the lens of diversity', in M. Hayden and J. Thompson (eds), *International Education: Principles and Practice*. London: Kogan Page. pp. 184–196.

Sylvester, R. (2002a), 'The "first" international school', in M. Hayden, J. Thompson and G. Walker (eds), *International Education in Practice: Dimensions for National and International Schools*. London: Kogan Page. pp. 3–17.

Sylvester, R. (2002b), 'Mapping international education: a historical survey 1893–1944', *Journal of Research in International Education, 1*(1), 91–126.

Tarc, P. (2009a), *Global Dreams, Enduring Tensions: International Baccalaureate in a Changing World*. New York: Peter Lang.

Tarc, P. (2009b), 'What is the "International" in the International Baccalaureate? Three structuring tensions of the early years (1962–1973)', *Journal of Research in International Education, 8*(3), 235–261.

Terwilliger, R. (1972), 'International schools – cultural crossroads', *The Education Forum, 36*(3), 359–363.

Toze, D. (2008), 'Concerns about IB exam results undermining confidence in program', *The International Educator,* 23(2), 6.

Useem, R. and Downie, R. (1976), 'Third-culture kids', *Today's Education,* 65(3), 103–105.

Walker, G. (2007), 'International education: From contacts to connections'. Speech delivered at IB Asia Pacific Annual Regional Conference, Singapore, 4 January 2007.

Wallace, E. (1999), 'New directions', *IB World* December 22, 8–11.

Wilkinson, D. (2002), 'International education and issues of governance', in M. Hayden, J. Thompson and G. Walker (eds), *International Education in Practice: Dimensions for National and International Schools.* London: Kogan Page, pp. 185–196.

Wylie, M. (2011), 'Global networking and the world of international education', in R. Bates (ed), *Schooling Internationally: Globalisation, Internationalisation and the Future for International Schools.* London: Routledge. pp. 21–39.

CHAPTER TEN

Dilemmas of International Education: A Bernsteinian Analysis

James Cambridge

Introduction

Various dilemmas face international education, as it is embodied in the programmes of the International Baccalaureate (IB). The IB currently experiences the same 'enduring tensions' that were present at its inception (Tarc, 2009). A theory of pedagogic discourse is used as a heuristic device to develop and frame critical questions (Bernstein, 2000). Three case studies are presented to illustrate and discuss the dilemmas and tensions relating to distributive rules, exemplified by open access versus academic selection in IB Diploma programmes; pedagogic recontextualization rules, inscribed in the IBDP international history curriculum and history for the purposes of (re)producing docile, governable citizens; and evaluative rules, inscribed in the tension between performance and competence modes of educational assessment, and the proposed changes in store for the IB Middle Years Programme.

This chapter begins by considering the historical tensions which have been part of the IB since its inception (Tarc, 2009). This is followed by discussion of Basil Bernstein's (2000) theorization of educational relationships in terms of the *pedagogic device* that comprises discursive rules for the distribution, recontextualization and evaluation (i.e. assessment) of knowledge. Pedagogic recontextualization constitutes the ways in which the products of academic research are selected, sequenced and paced as they are converted into a form useable in school lessons (Singh, 2002). The pedagogic device is then used as a lens for the description and analysis of dilemmas and tensions in the context of the implementation of IB programmes of study.

Reflecting upon the outcomes of the conference of educators held at Sèvres in the spring of 1967 that led to the formal institution of the IB, ADC 'Alec' Peterson, the founding director general of the IB, wrote:

> Two questions of great importance for the future of the examination were discussed and settled at this meeting. Was it to be a 'pass/fail' or a graded examination? And would any certificate or diploma be offered to those who either did not pass in the full range of six subjects or did not offer the full range? It was clear that the pass/fail concept, which is acceptable within some national systems where the pupils entering for the university entrance examination are, through a process of pre-selection, homogeneous in terms of academic ability and seeking qualification at a common level, would not be suitable for an international examination. Here provision must be made for pupils seeking to enter colleges and universities with very different admissions standards, and no pre-selection could operate. There was also a possibility that countries of the Third World might wish to make use of the examination for more limited purposes than entry to the most selective universities overseas. It was therefore agreed that the grade in each subject should be recorded and that the issue of the full Baccalaureate diploma would depend on a satisfactory level of achievement in the whole range of six subjects...On the other hand, candidates who passed in only a limited number of subjects would receive a 'certificate' or 'attestation', stating exactly the grade which they had received in each subject. Such certificates would provide both an objective element in a school-leaving diploma and a basis for admission by colleges that did not require the full Baccalaureate. (Peterson, 1972, p. 16)

It is justified to quote this source at length because the text draws attention in fine detail to issues to be discussed throughout this chapter. Furthermore, while it is important to avoid making anachronistic claims that link statements to explanatory theories developed by different theorists at different times, it is possible to draw parallels between the direction of Peterson's thinking, as exemplified in the passage above, and the theory of pedagogic discourse proposed by Bernstein (2000). For instance, it is evident that Peterson discusses the implementation of boundaries in a variety of ways here. The difference between 'passing' and 'failing' an examination constitutes one type of boundary. Another example can be seen in the entry requirements to be attained in order to gain admission to higher education; such requirements constitute a threshold – that is, a boundary – which must be crossed by the successful college or university applicant. Yet another boundary is inscribed in the contrast between developed and less developed or Third World countries.

Bernstein (2000) addresses discursive boundaries in the abstract, but what forms can they take? In the context of organization studies, Hernes (2004) argues that boundaries may be physical, normative or cognitive. Building on this typology, as Cambridge (2012a) proposes, physical boundaries can be recognized in terms of the walls and fences surrounding a school. However, many international schools are enclaves in which business is conducted in a language not used in the surrounding community. Language constitutes a normative social boundary between those who speak it and those who do not. The discursive boundaries between different school subjects can be considered to be cognitive boundaries that allow different forms of official knowledge (i.e. knowledge identified as the legitimate content of formal educational assessment) as well as drawing a distinction between official knowledge and unofficial knowledge. Moreover, Bernstein (2000) discusses how the strength of boundaries *between* and *within* curriculum contents – 'classification' and 'framing' respectively – contribute to the production of collection codes (pedagogic discourse characterized by strong classification and strong framing) and integrated codes (with weak classification and weak framing). Peterson (1972) describes the IB Diploma in terms of what Bernstein would refer to as a collection code. That is to say, the IB imposes strict rules concerning the number and combinations of academic subjects that are eligible for the award of the full IB Diploma. This is a conclusion that may be triangulated with other studies, for example Remillard (1978). However, the imposition of such strict rules is mitigated by acknowledgement that award of IB certificates is allowed with respect to more limited suites of subjects. The award of IB certificates rather than the full IB Diploma may be interpreted as a weakening of the collection code (Cambridge, 2012b). Richard Caffyn discusses boundaries in greater detail elsewhere in this volume.

In his book *Global Dreams, Enduring Tensions*, Paul Tarc (2009) explores the ways in which discourse about international education produced by the IB has changed and developed over the course of its history. The 'global dreams' of the title refer to the aspirations of the IB 'as a growing transnational movement, aimed at creating a better world through education' (Tarc, 2009, p. 1). The 'enduring tensions' refer to the gap between such aspirations and their practical implementation – 'the contradictions at work between the wider normative dreams of the IB (internationalism, making a more modern and peaceful world) and how the IB actually operates in the world' (Tarc, 2009, p. 24). Tarc proposes that such tensions were present at the origin of the IB and have endured, albeit in changed and developed forms, to the present day.

The propagation of international understanding has been identified as the central aim of international education since the earliest days of the IB. However, the term is left undefined in policy documents, and Tarc (2009, p. 16) proposes that it functions 'as a floating signifier of the global dreams of the IB'. Consequently, this hollowed-out semiotic space has been filled with a variety of meanings according to context when the need has arisen.

Tarc (2009, pp. 97–8) argues that, by the turn of the twenty-first century, 'international understanding' had lost its former meta-status in IB discourse. With the growth of the IB in state sectors, international education has become recast from an educational programme of 'international schools' into a kind of philosophy and mission that any school, including one situated in a national educational system, could adopt and attempt to enact.

Another enduring tension relates to the contradictions between the instrumental aims of education for the (re)production of national cultural identity and the production of the global citizen. This embraces not only the tension between 'national' and 'international' or 'global' contexts for citizenship but also calls into question the concept of citizenship itself. What is the relationship between the citizen and the state? Is the role of the citizen to serve the state, or is the role of the state to serve the citizen? Is citizenship a legal status that is conferred by states or is it produced by the participation of active citizens cooperating together in civic practices of negotiation and transformation (Tully, 2008)? In the light of such questions, how and for what purpose are the IB founding values of 'the will to act' and 'social service' to be implemented? Action, service and self-empowerment can be interpreted as techniques of governmentality so that 'engaging in service is altered from a moral or ethical obligation to an attribute of self-conduct desirable, in its own way, to governments, institutions and individuals' (Tarc, 2009, p. 103). The study of history in school is considered to play an important role in the production of citizens of many national societies, and this will be examined as an example below.

What might be the impact of implementing IB programmes in one school that is part of a wider educational system? How might implementation affect competition between schools for students or teachers? Tarc (2009, p. 105) observes that 'the IBO's relationship to neoliberal school reform remains, at best, unreflexive'. It may be argued that the recent growth of the IB is a direct consequence of neo-liberal 'post-welfare' policies of the developed economies that have introduced private sector involvement and sharpened market competition in the public sector, including education (Ball, 2007; Clarke et al., 2000; Tomlinson, 2001). The growth of the IB over the past decade or more has been facilitated by the establishment of global trade agreements that have encouraged the extension and spread of cross-border services in education (i.e. by a weakening of classification or boundary strength between states). The development of a global market in the services offered by a variety of non-governmental educational service providers including the IB has been enabled by the ways in which the national frontiers have become more permeable between states that are signatories to the agreements of the World Trade Organization (WTO). National education systems have been forced to become less protectionist and more open to market competition.[1]

Robertson (2003, p. 263) explains that education services are viewed as falling into five main categories under the WTO General Agreement on Trade in Services (GATS). The categories comprise primary education, secondary education, higher education, adult education and 'other' educational services. In terms of the nature of the activity that is legally protected under GATS, four main modalities of trade in education are recognized:

- *Cross-border supply* including any type of course provided through distance education or the Internet, any type of testing service and education materials which can cross borders.

- *Consumption abroad* involving the education of foreign students and the most common form of trade in education services.

- *Commercial presence* being the actual presence of foreign investors in a host country, for example foreign universities setting up courses or entire institutions in another country.

- *Presence of natural persons* being the ability of people to move between countries to provide education services.

The penetration of national markets by international education providers may be expected to include all four of the modalities outlined here, but the relaxation of restrictions involving 'cross-border supply' and 'commercial presence' is most likely to facilitate growth in the transnational education market including international schools. Furthermore, it may be argued that 'presence of natural persons', that is to say, the cross-border movement of people rather than objects or capital, has facilitated the expansion of international schools not only in terms of the supply of students and their families seeking their services but also in terms of the supply of professionally qualified teachers. The expansion of international schools, and the concomitant expansion of international education, may be interpreted as a response to the demands of a growing market of globally mobile workers. This demand in the market was identified early in the present era of economic globalization for, as Sutcliffe (1991, p. 34) expresses it, 'by the 1970s, the problems of the mobile and expatriate families were sand, not oil in the wheels of international trade. An international academic passport was required.'

What of the impact on national educational systems of the demand for international school teachers? It has been estimated that 'the number of teaching staff needed by international schools in 2020 could be approximately double what it was in 2009' (Hayden and Thompson, 2011, p. 90). Nicholas Brummitt and Anne Keeling in this volume discuss the growth of the international schools market. Research on the impact of international teacher migration on schooling in developing countries in the context of Southern Africa (Appleton et al., 2006) may be relevant to understanding the employment policies of international schools in certain regions of the world. Teachers trained in poorer countries are attracted to become expatriate workers employed in richer economies. Whilst such teachers enjoy personal gain as a consequence of their employment, patterns of employment such as this constitute a 'brain drain' that can further impoverish the less developed economies supplying the globally (or more accurately regionally) mobile workforce. It may be argued that, in many parts of the world where they are growing in number, international schools constitute a 'magnet' that can distort teacher supply and demand. Many international schools seek to employ trained teachers from Anglophone developed countries such as Great Britain, the US, Canada, Australia and New Zealand (Hayden, 2006), but, nevertheless, it has also been observed by assorted commentators that there are complex and segmented labour forces at work in many schools that may be characterized variously as 'host country nationals, local expatriates and overseas hire expatriates' (Garton, 2000, p. 87), 'childless career professionals, career professionals and mavericks' (Hardman, 2001) or 'the administrative core, the professional contractual fringe, and the flexible labour force' (Cambridge, 2002, p. 163). Expatriate teachers from Anglophone developed countries, on the one hand, and those from less developed countries, on the other, may be represented disproportionately in certain of these categories. If the number of international schools, and other schools offering international education, continues to increase as expected, the demand for teachers will also expand. This is likely to have a profound impact on the diversity of nationalities of teachers recruited in such schools in certain locations as competition between international schools and national education systems increases.

The present book has been written with the intention of reviewing changes and developments in international education throughout the four-decade history of the International School of London. Such a review might be expected to take the position that progress and improvement have taken place over time. This appears to be the perspective propagated by the former IB Deputy Director General Ian Hill (2012) in his discussion of the evolution of 'international mindedness' in international education. However, in contrast to the critical approach adopted by Tarc (2009), it may be argued that Hill (2012) presents a 'Whig interpretation' of the history of the IB (Butterfield, 1931). That is to say, Hill argues for a narrative discourse that makes assumptions of improvement and progress towards enlightenment. This narrative discourse is exemplified by the content of the table, labelled Figure 1 in Hill (2012, p. 252), that contrasts 'traditional' and 'progressive' educational trends up to the 1960s. However, this assertion is contested. Implicit in the selection and presentation of these data is the assumption that each pair of terms constitutes a binary opposition with a hierarchy of positions, such that the 'progressive' criterion-referenced educational assessment practised by the IB represents an improvement over 'traditional' norm-referenced assessment, or that 'progressive' child-centred teaching represents an improvement over 'traditional' teacher-centred styles of teaching. However, this dichotomy between 'progressivism' and 'traditionalism' is a mystification that invokes what may be described as 'invented tradition'. It may be more productive theoretically to interpret the dichotomy as a contrast between discursive positions. The former perspective sees student-centred learning as an end in itself, whereas the latter sees education as the means to an end. 'In the context of the IB, the desire to provide a liberal education "of the whole person" is enabled but also constrained by the demands of developing a diploma of acceptable standards for university admissions in multiple countries' (Tarc, 2009, p. 24).

Current practical or 'operational' tensions experienced by the IB, according to Tarc (2009), focus on its 'representativeness' and 'access' to its programmes. The atheoretical, apolitical and ahistorical perspectives of the IB are highlighted here. For example, Tarc (2009, p. 42) argues that 'Western metaphysical assumptions [made by the IB] of being and learning are naturalized and thus made universal'. The issue of access to IB programmes is also highly problematic. 'While the content of many of the IB's courses and the IBO's mission statements correspond to the idealist orientation, the provision and uptake of IB tends to privilege the market-values orientation' (Tarc, 2009, p. 105). Doherty (2010, p. 6) describes the implementation of IB programmes in Australia as an 'ironic marriage of neo-conservatism (re-asserting centralised power) and neo-liberalism (divesting power from the centre to the market)' in which the IB Diploma 'thrives in this ideological space of being both a market/choice strategy and a fashionably conservative solution at the same time'. In other words, even an apparently 'non-ideological' position is replete with ideology, in the form of underlying assumptions, and inbuilt structural and philosophical givens. These are the 'unknown knowns' of discourse – 'the disavowed beliefs and suppositions we are not even aware of adhering to ourselves' (Žižek, 2008, p. 457).

In view of recent comments by the UK Secretary of State for Education Mr Gove concerning reform of educational assessment in England (Hansard, 2012), it may be argued that Hill's (2012) linear model of educational reform from 'traditional' to 'progressive' ideologies might be better interpreted as swings of a pendulum between contrasting positions. Whilst this view of educational reform might be considered to be local to England, it may also be argued that it forms part of a global discourse signalling a move in the developed economies towards the establishment of standards and measurable goals in national systems of education in response to international comparative studies of educational attainment such as PISA, TIMSS and PIRLS (Crossley and Watson, 2003; Davies, 2011; OECD, 2013; Phillips and Schweisfurth, 2006; TIMSS, 2013). To take an example external to the English national context, Engel and Olden (2012) review the conflicting demands for internationalization and standardization in the US education system. Curriculum innovation and implementation are being carried out against a background of core standards and mandated educational assessment. Educational standards are themselves globalized, through international comparative assessment exercises such as those listed above. Engel and Olden (2012, p. 89) conclude that the imposition of standards and mandated testing 'limit a global dimension of learning in two ways: first, to a skills-based approach (i.e. the skills required to compete in a global economy), and second, to a nationalistic perspective of culture and cultural difference, rooted in a more superficial form of multiculturalism rather than a critical understanding about global citizenship and cosmopolitanism'. An international curriculum and assessment organization such as the IB could hardly be expected to be immune from such pressures to embrace a neo-liberal ideology of performativity in teaching and learning (Ball, 2003). The benchmarking of educational performance of learners in international schools by the International Schools' Assessment (ISA), conducted by the Australian Center for Educational Research (ACER, 2013), may be interpreted as a driver calling for a response by the IB to perceived demands for standards and measurable goals in the form of a change from competence modes of assessment, exemplified in the current IB Primary Years and Middle Years Programmes, towards performance modes, exemplified by written or online examinations.

Having explored the policy environment in which international education is implemented, pedagogic discourse will now be introduced as a heuristic device for developing critical questions about international education.

Pedagogic discourse

Singh (2002, p. 572) characterizes Bernstein's pedagogic device as 'a model for analysing the processes by which discipline-specific or domain-specific expert knowledge is converted or pedagogised to constitute school knowledge (classroom curricula, teacher-student talk, online learning)'. The pedagogic device comprises discourse that organizes the distribution, recontextualization and evaluation (i.e. assessment) of knowledge. Knowledge, as it is created in universities and other places of research and knowledge production, must be selected, sequenced and paced in order to be made available to learners in schools. This process is called pedagogic recontextualization or pedagogization of knowledge (Singh, 2002). Cambridge (2010) proposes that curriculum and assessment organizations such as the IB are agents of pedagogic recontextualization. The recent history of educational reform in many parts of the world has traced a shift in control over pedagogic recontextualization, away from decentralized bodies independent of direct governmental control, such as examination boards, towards increasing centralization and direct control by government (Fitz et al., 2006; Grace, 2008). Such centralized control of the curriculum is referred to by Bernstein as the 'Official Recontextualisation Field' (Singh, 2002). Curriculum development in the international context is becoming increasingly complex, particularly with regard to interactions with the multiplicity of Official Pedagogic Fields of different states, all of which have to be negotiated with in order to gain official recognition for international programmes of study (Cambridge, 2010), and which may be interpreted as constituting an upward search for approval.

In addition to rules of discursive order that govern the form and content of *what* is to be learned, Bernstein recognizes rules of social order inscribed in regulative discourse that govern *how* learning is to proceed:

> Rules of social order refer to the forms that hierarchical relations take in the pedagogic relation and to expectations about conduct, character and manner. This means that an acquirer [that is, a learner] can be seen as a potential for labels. Which labels are selected is a function of the framing. Where framing is strong, the candidates for labelling will be terms such as conscientious, attentive, industrious, careful, receptive. Where the framing is apparently weak, then conditions for candidature for labels will become equally trying for the acquirer as he or she struggles to be creative, to be interactive, to attempt to make his or her own mark. (Bernstein, 2000, p. 13)

In these terms, the *IB Learner Profile* (IB, 2006), as a specification for the ideal IB learner, valorizing qualities such as being inquiring, knowledgeable, thinking, communicating, principled, open-minded, caring, risk-taking, balanced and reflective may be interpreted as an explicit example of the regulative discourse promoted by the IB.

> In PYP schools teachers are required, on behalf of all students, to assess and report on progress in the development of the attributes of the learner profile. This is done by using the learner profile for self and peer assessment, as the basis for teacher/student/parent conferences and through reporting to parents. MYP and Diploma Programme schools are expected to focus on monitoring student development in light of the profile in as many ways as possible, by engaging students and teachers in reflection, self-assessment and conferencing. Each IB World School, as a whole, is also encouraged to reflect on the success of the implementation of the learner profile. (IB, 2006, p. 3)

As the passage above indicates, the regulative discourse inscribed in the Learner Profile exerts discipline over not only learners but also their teachers and schools in terms of how they should produce the specified outcomes of learning.

Distributive rules

Distributive rules of discourse govern the ways in which knowledge is made accessible to different groups in society (Bernstein, 2000). A common way of implementing differential access to knowledge in school is to impose some form of educational selection. Cambridge (2011a, p. 48) proposes that a school might identify the IBDP as a programme of study that is most appropriate for 'Gifted and Talented' students. Only those deemed to be in this category would be considered capable or worthy of having access to the IBDP. 'Gifted and Talented' programmes may be organized as a 'school within a school' (Matthews and Kitchen, 2007). In other words, certain students may attend a particular school but be segregated from their fellows as a consequence of curriculum arrangements. This is an example of the relationship between 'the formal organization of the school and the disciplinary organization of knowledge' (Siskin, 1994, p. 37). The way in which a school is organized reproduces and embodies discourse about the structure of knowledge, in terms of the composition of academic subject departments. Hence, implementation of IB programmes inevitably has the effect of reproducing and embodying discourse about division of labour and social stratification by regulating access to knowledge, academic subjects and programmes of study.

Students following the IBDP in different schools may not be pursuing the same programme of study because 'one school might be non-selective, offering an open access whole-school programme, whereas another might be selective, offering a restricted access school-within-a-school programme. The values and assumptions underlying the criteria for entry on to the programmes of study are different in either case' (IB, 2008, p. 22). Cambridge (2010, p. 211) explains this distinction in Bernsteinian terms by proposing that 'the non-selective, open access approach is inscribed with a discourse of weak classification and weak framing, whereas the restricted access, school-within-a-school represents a discourse of strong classification and strong framing'.

The curriculum can be used to widen access to and participation in education by weakening classification. For instance, Kugler and Albright (2005) discuss how the IBDP can be used as a means of broadening access to high school education for 'underserved' (e.g. Afro-American and Hispanic) communities in the US. They describe how the IBDP was introduced into a public high school with the intention of increasing inclusion by encouraging greater enrolment from 'minority cultures' in high school classes. This was achieved by changing policy 'from the "Gifted and Talented" model that admitted students mainly on the basis of their performance in standardized tests to an "honors" approach that focused on students' motivation and performance in class' (Kugler and Albright, 2005, p. 43). The adoption of this approach meant rejecting the implementation of 'a diploma-only program as a school-within-a-school' (Kugler and Albright, 2005, p. 43). However, Cambridge (2011a, p. 49) argues that a conclusion that may be drawn from this example is that a quality such as 'inclusiveness' is not implicit in a programme of study such as the IBDP but is an outcome of the policy environment in which the programme is implemented and not an attribute of the programme itself. Under different circumstances and in different contexts, different policy outcomes could be achieved using a similar programme of study. In other words, the school a student attends and the policies it implements are (at least) as important as the programme of study followed by that student.

What empirical evidence might be used to test the hypothesis that the IB Diploma is implemented in contrasting ways in different parts of the world? Under rubric 11, the annual DP Statistical Bulletins (IB, 2009, 2010, 2011, 2012a) enumerate 'Number of candidates registered by category, gender and IB region'. What are regional variations in candidate enrolment on the IB Diploma programme? It is proposed that such data provide quantitative evidence of the differentiated implementation of IB programmes in different parts of the world. Diploma Programme candidates must register in one of four categories (International Baccalaureate, 2012a, p. 4):

- Diploma: candidates intending to complete the requirements for the award of an IB Diploma.

- Retake: previous IB Diploma candidates who are seeking to improve their results. The highest grade obtained for a subject will contribute towards the IB Diploma.

- Certificate: candidates taking one or more subjects who are not seeking the award of the IB Diploma.

- Anticipated: candidates intending to complete the requirements for one or two standard-level subjects (excluding languages *ab initio* and pilot subjects) at the end of their first year of the Diploma Programme. They must complete all remaining IB Diploma requirements in the corresponding examination session in the following year.

The relative frequencies of registrations in the 'Anticipated' and 'Retake' categories are generally low when compared to those in the 'Diploma' and 'Certificate' categories. Table 10.1 indicates that Certificate registrations are lower in the Africa, Europe and Middle East (IBAEM) and Asia Pacific (IBAP) regions than in the Americas (IBA) region. Table 10.1 also indicates that Diploma registrations in the Africa, Europe and Middle East (IBAEM) and Asia Pacific (IBAP) regions are double the level of Diploma registrations observed in the IB Americas region. Furthermore, in three of the years enumerated here, the frequency of Certificate registrations in the IBA region exceeds the frequency of Diploma registrations, but this is not observed in the data from IBAEM and IBAP.

There is a methodological challenge to valid and reliable data analysis in the form of how the 'anticipated' registration category is implemented in the IB Americas region, and how it stands in relation to the other enumeration categories and to the other regions. How many candidates registered in the 'anticipated' category in one year go on to complete the Diploma the following year? To what extent are the component parts of the IB Diploma implemented as discrete courses in one academic year, for example with

Table 10.1: Certificate (C) and Diploma (D) registrations per cent by IB region (sources of primary data: International Baccalaureate 2009, 2010, 2011, 2012a)

Year	IBAEM		IBAP		IBA	
	C	D	C	D	C	D
2009	18.53	70.45	19.99	67.79	33.98	34.44
2010	18.11	71.50	20.17	69.22	35.80	34.23
2011	19.07	71.09	19.51	71.13	35.91	35.14
2012	19.86	70.67	19.06	72.57	36.97	35.09

standard-level subjects studied in year 1 and higher-level subjects studied in year 2 of a two-year programme? The stated intention of the IB is that learning in the Diploma Programme should be concurrent across all subjects, such that 'students deal each year with a balanced curriculum in which the required subjects are studied simultaneously' (Marshman, 2010, p. 3), but this may not always be implemented in practice.

Notwithstanding this methodological challenge, a variety of hypotheses may be proposed that account for these observations. One hypothesis is that students with a wider range of academic ability follow IB programmes of study in the IBA region, so that consequently a lower proportion of candidates are registered for the full Diploma, and a greater proportion entered for Certificates. A second hypothesis, linked to the first, is that schools in other parts of the world are more selective in terms of IBDP course admissions, as compared to IBA schools. In other words, the pedagogic discourse implemented in schools in the IB Americas region practises weaker classification in terms of distributive rules governing access to programmes. As discussed above, there is evidence to indicate that IB programmes of study are used in the US to widen access by students from a variety of social and economic backgrounds to senior high school education (Kugler and Albright, 2005). A third hypotheses is that college or university entrance in North America is not contingent upon achieving the IB Diploma, so fewer students feel compelled to enter for it. That is to say, the pedagogic discourse implemented in colleges and universities in the IBA region is inscribed with weaker classification in terms of distributive rules governing entry to courses. A fourth hypothesis is that, against a backdrop of state-mandated testing in the context of No Child Left Behind legislation, IB programmes are utilized as magnets to attract students and as drivers of school improvement policies. There is evidence that the IB has attempted to position its programmes as the means for schools to improve standards (IB, 2005). A fifth hypothesis is that paternalistic attitudes concerning breadth and balance in the curriculum that are implicit in structure and content of the IB Diploma (i.e. strong framing) are relatively weakened in the face of competing market forces (Cambridge, 2011b, p. 137). That is to say, students would rather pick and choose their own combinations of school subjects even if they do not contribute to a Diploma and not have their subject choices prescribed for them.

Finally, it may be the case that the IBDP is in competition with the College Board Advanced Placement (AP) and its implementation is convergent with its competitor. Competitive pressure on curriculum and assessment organizations such as the IB and AP may be interpreted in terms of neo-institutional theory. This is a theory from the field of organization studies that addresses the observation that business organizations in a competitive field appear to resemble each other (DiMaggio and Powell, 1983). Organizations in competition with each other might be expected to have distinctive differences that give each a 'unique selling point'. However, in practice their organizational arrangements, publicity materials and other features frequently appear to show convergence. Neo-institutional theory proposes that such organizations are subject to processes leading to similarity. When disparate organizations in the same line of business are structured into a field, by competition, the state or the professions, powerful forces emerge that lead them to become more similar to one another. Processes leading to convergence are identified as different types of isomorphism. Isomorphism is 'a constraining process that forces one unit to resemble other units that face the same set of environmental conditions' (DiMaggio and Powell, 1983, p. 149). DiMaggio and Powell (1983, p. 150) identify three mechanisms of isomorphic change:

- Coercive isomorphism that stems from political influence and the problem of legitimacy;

- Mimetic isomorphism resulting from standard responses to uncertainty; and

- Normative isomorphism associated with unifying professional practice.

Coercive isomorphism results from both formal and informal pressures exerted on organizations by other organizations upon which they are dependent and by the cultural expectations in the society within which organizations function. Local legislation and politics will influence the structure and activities of schools in particular contexts. Mimetic isomorphism results from organizations tending to model themselves after similar organizations in their field that they perceive to be more legitimate or successful. In other words, nothing succeeds like success; organizations aspiring to success imitate the attributes of other organizations that they consider to be successful. Two aspects of professionalization are important sources of normative isomorphism. 'One is the resting of formal education and of legitimation in a cognitive base produced by university specialists; the second is the growth and elaboration of professional networks that span organizations and across which new models diffuse rapidly' (DiMaggio and Powell, 1983, p. 152). It may be argued that organizations involved in curriculum development and assessment services are influenced by all of these types of isomorphism. However, the tendency to imitate one's competitors – mimetic isomorphism – is probably the strongest. It is evident that further research is required to identify the factors that determine how IBDP is implemented in different locations and settings.

Recontextualizing rules

Pedagogic recontextualization refers to the processes of curriculum development by which knowledge is produced for reproduction and assessment in school. As Cambridge (2012b) argues, echoing Scott (2008), the critical issues for the production of international curriculum for use in the context of international education lie in *what* knowledge is recognized as official knowledge, *who* makes the selection of such knowledge and *by what criteria* the selection is made. These issues are apparent in the different ways in which history is recontextualized for contrasting purposes.

In a chapter discussing the early development of the International School Examination Syndicate History Subject Guide (i.e. the direct antecedent of the IB), Leach (1969, p. 202) offers a variety of phrases that help to distinguish IB philosophy of history education: 'to train the mind rather than impart information; to learn how to learn; knowledge of the world rather than just knowledge etc. Every teacher is conscious of the dangers of mere accumulation of facts or of premature specialization.' Furthermore, history in the IB is 'conceived not only as dealing with a world outlook but is so constructed as to involve students in historical procedures' (Leach, 1969, p. 207). It is evident that such language resembles the 'progressive' axis of the typology of educational trends outlined by Hill (2012, p. 252) and is reflected in it. Hence, terms listed by Hill (2012) such as 'critical thinking', 'range of skills testing', 'constructivist', 'pro-active participation' and 'multiple perspectives' can be identified with the approach that employs weak framing of pedagogic discourse discussed by Leach (1969).

The role of the IB in the pedagogic recontextualization field with respect to the early development of the history curriculum is neatly summarized by Hill (2010, p. 39):

History was chosen as the starting point for an international programme because it was recognised as a subject particularly prone to national and ideological biases…The successful development of an international history course would pave the way for other courses less plagued by patriotic interpretations, whether imposed by a government or not. It was not the content of the contemporary history course that was to differentiate it from its national counterparts, it was its pedagogical approach. The fundamental premise required students to analyse, explore and appreciate the different interpretations of the same event by various historians operating in diverse cultural contexts. Understanding the complex reasons why a particular interpretation exists, without necessarily agreeing with it, gives legitimacy to other points of view.

Nevertheless, the huge growth of the IB in the North American market in particular has engendered specific problems in the context of history education in the IB Diploma. A driver contributing to this growth may be identified with education policies such as the 1994 *Goals 2000: Educate America Act* that stated that 'every adult American will possess the knowledge and skills necessary to compete in a global economy' (Bunnell, 2012, p. 12) and the 2001 *No Child Left Behind Act*. This latter act is based on the premise that setting high standards, establishing measurable goals and implementing a regime of rigorous educational assessment can improve individual outcomes in education. Many school districts in the US have identified the programmes of the IB as levers for achieving such policy outcomes, and indeed the programmes have been promoted as such by the IB itself (IB, 2005). However, it may be proposed that opportunities such as these have led to uneven growth and 'mission creep' as the IB has arguably abandoned its core niche audience of the international schools community in pursuit of expansion into a single national market in the US.

Lewis (2006, p. 57) observes that, of 18,712 students throughout the world who sat for the May 2005 IB Higher Level History examination, 'ninety-eight percent...pursued either the history of the Americas or the history of Europe as their optional topic...In other words, less than 3% of all Higher Level history students concentrated upon Asia, Oceania, the Middle East or Africa'. Bunnell (2008, p. 418), commenting on this statistic, points out that 62% of the students took the history of the Americas option. Lewis (2006, p. 57) concludes that 'we can only explain this imbalance as a reflection of the dominant Anglo-European elements within our schools and a belief that non-Western regions are less important'. However, it may be argued that, while it is sincere, Lewis presents a jejune and apolitical proposition. What argument is Lewis attempting to make? Is implementation of the IB history course being criticized because candidates, or more likely their teachers, elect *not* to study the history of a region other than where they are resident? Whereas a wholeheartedly pure 'internationalist' approach to international education might involve such an arrangement, the state of affairs reflected in the statistics may be interpreted as representing a pragmatic approach. For instance, why should American students not tend to opt for history of the Americas? Lewis (2006, p. 58) argues critically that the current model of international education 'seems to place examinations as the driver of secondary education, leaving our global reality and mission statements on the sideline', but a more nuanced view beyond citing an abstraction in the form of 'Anglo-European elements' is possible. An explanatory theory alternative to that offered by Lewis (2006) would contrast the varied aims and purposes of history education in international education and national education systems.

As Cambridge (2012a) argues, a central function of education in national systems is the (re)production of docile (that is to say, educable), governable citizens. A review comparing the College Board AP and the IBDP, conducted on behalf of the Thomas P. Fordham Institute, a conservative education policy think-tank based in Washington DC, identified the strengths of IB World History at Standard Level with 'demanding, well-constructed, content-rich exams; strong content within narrowly defined course parameters' (Byrd et al., 2007, p. 14). However, it also stated that a weakness of the course was that 'US students in IB programs could miss exposure to almost all core US History content; even as a world history course, its 20th century focus is too narrow; lacks emphasis on important chronological knowledge' (Byrd et al., 2007, p. 14). While an Americas option, covering US, Latin American and Canadian history is available, the report noted that 'this option contains some good information, but because it includes much more than US history, the course inevitably slights important topics, events, and people that all US high school students should know' (Byrd et al., 2007, p. 15). Consequently, it may be concluded that a crucial role of American history in US high school education continues to be for the (re)production of American citizens. Any programme of study that does not fulfil this specific role cannot be valid for the production of citizens in this context. From this perspective, it may be concluded that the history curriculum in the US embodies an encyclopaedist ideology, promoting the memorization of 'inert ideas…pre-structured interpretations of ideas given by the teacher to the student' (Peterson, 2003, p. 38). This constitutes a pedagogic discourse with stronger framing when compared with the historiographic approach favoured by the IB. Hence, there are points of contradiction between discourses of international education programmes that aspire to promote 'international mindedness' through critical evaluation of sources – and which are therefore considered to be 'un-American'– and national programmes of education that aspire to (re)produce national citizens through the propagation of national historical narratives.

Evaluative rules

Evaluative discourse refers to the ways by which the knowledge relayed and reproduced by pedagogic discourse is assessed. Educational assessment exerts a backwash effect on pedagogic practice. How learning of the curriculum is assessed has a strong influence on how it is taught. Bernstein (2000) identifies contrasting modes of pedagogic practice with a focus on assessment of *performance* and *competence* respectively. The performance mode 'places the emphasis upon a specific output of the acquirer [i.e. the learner], upon a particular text the acquirer is expected to construct and upon the specialised skills necessary to the production of this specific output, text or product' (Bernstein, 2000, p. 44). The performance mode of assessment is 'the dominant, established model…with the focus upon acquirers' past and future accomplishments, with strong apparent progression and pacing, evaluation focused on what was missing from their texts in terms of explicit and specific criteria of which they were made aware' (Fitz et al., 2006, p. 6). On the other hand, in a competence mode of pedagogic assessment practice, learners 'apparently have a great measure of control over selection, sequence and pace…The emphasis is upon the realisation of competences that acquirers already possess, or are thought to possess' (Bernstein, 2000, p. 45). Competence modes may be identified with 'liberal/progressive', learner-centred approaches to education (Fitz et al., 2006, p. 7). However, the competence mode may be criticized on the grounds that it is expensive to produce and maintain because of the time required for the development of resources, communicating with students and parents, and personalizing the learning of individuals (Bernstein, 2000).

The contrast between the integrated code of primary and junior secondary education and the collection code of senior secondary education appears to be commonplace. Fitz et al. (2006, p. 100) observe:

> As Bernstein noted…the strong preference, particularly of the new middle class, was for primary classrooms where boundaries between work, play and the subjects were weak and pedagogy 'invisible', aiding teacher discovery of the multiple talents of their progeny while, for secondary schools, their preference, given that their abilities had now been made explicit, was for strong subject boundaries in traditional knowledge domains.

Following on from this argument, Cambridge (2012b) proposes that IB programmes of study are characterized by contrasting degrees of integration and collection. Compared with the IBDP, the IB Middle Years (MYP) and Primary Years (PYP) programmes show weaker classification and framing and, hence, greater integration. This is exemplified by the transdisciplinary themes that underpin the IB PYP. There are currently no mandated formal examinations in the IB PYP and MYP. Educational assessment in the PYP and MYP may be identified with a competence model, with school-based judgements about learning based on students' project work in integrated 'areas of interaction'. Joint moderation of MYP coursework by groups of teachers reinforces integration between them. In contrast, assessment in the IBDP may best be identified with a performance model, with judgements about students' learning made independent of the school in the context of formal examinations in 'traditional' academic subjects.

However, an interesting development in IB assessment practice is indicated in *MYP: The Next Chapter project* (IB, 2012b). Proposed changes will see an end to MYP subject moderation and its replacement by e-assessment (IB, 2012b, p. 11). This assessment will take the form of a concept-based, summative test that may be interpreted as being in the performance mode. Hence, there appears to be a policy change in assessment practice in the MYP that constitutes a shift away from the competence mode towards the performance mode:

> The assessment will require students to apply a key concept in discussing a choice of topics from the discipline, providing support with discipline-related concepts. A range of question types will elicit conceptual understanding, including extended response; short answer; three- to four-sentence answers; drag and drop; manipulating graphs and data; proposals/presentations; diagrammatic responses; website creation, or blogging. (IB, 2012b, p. 11)

Furthermore, there also appears to be the proposed implementation of a collection code, in common with the IBDP, in the award to MYP certificates:

> In order to gain 'full' certification (IB MYP Certificate), students sit at least six disciplinary and one interdisciplinary e-assessments. The disciplinary e-assessments must be from six different subject groups, which must include a language and literature subject, a language acquisition subject (or two language and literature e-assessments), mathematics, a science discipline and a discipline from individuals and societies. (IB, 2012b, p. 11)

Such changes in assessment practice may be interpreted as a pragmatic response on the part of the IB to growth in the market that makes the external moderation of the work of an increasing number of schools unsustainable. The policy to produce a seamless continuum between different phases of the IB is evidently also a driver of this change in assessment practice. Moreover, this change in policy appears to promote a shift in the pedagogic discourse of the IB MYP, not only from competence to performance, but also from integration to collection. From this perspective, it may be argued that profound changes in the ideology of educational assessment and pedagogical practice are in train, and that a shift from the established values of the IB towards a new set of principles is imminent.

Conclusion

The preceding discussion has concentrated on the tensions and dilemmas relating to implementation of IB programmes, described and analysed in terms of three aspects of Bernstein's theory of pedagogic discourse.

Distributive rules of discourse that address the access of different categories of learners to various types of knowledge have been exemplified by reference to open access policies to IB Diploma programmes in some schools and academic selection for entry in others. The contrast between the IBDP history curriculum and the teaching of history for the purposes of (re)producing docile, governable citizens in national systems has been identified as a tension in terms of pedagogic recontextualization rules. The changes in assessment proposed for the IB MYP may be interpreted as a shift in evaluative rules from a competence mode to a performance mode of assessment.

There has been considerable change in the implementation of IB programmes throughout the world during the course of the history of the International School of London. The IB Diploma programme started as a niche course confined to the United World Colleges, serving students from the worldwide community, and institutions such as the International School of London, serving students from a local catchment with a more restricted geographical range. As has been pointed out elsewhere in this volume, the International School of London was an early adopter of the IB (Peterson, 2003). However, the linkage between international education, as exemplified by the programmes of the IB, and international schools has become uncoupled in recent years. As Bunnell (2011, p. 163) expresses it:

> A presentation by the IB Director General to the Annual Conference of the European Council of International Schools (19 November 2004) revealed there were 1215 IBDP schools. As it was also stated around that time…that 18% were 'international schools' we can therefore deduce that about 300 IB schools were 'international schools' in 2004. This figure has fallen dramatically as a proportion from 58% in 1979 and is expected to be just 5% by 2020.

To what extent does an organization such as the IB, as it is currently constituted, continue to serve the needs of international schools and their students? As the IB continues to penetrate national systems, and adapts its distributive, recontextualizing and evaluative practices in order to accommodate the demands of local, national, official, pedagogic recontextualization fields, a critical question needs to be asked: Will the programmes of the IB continue to be fit for the purpose of international education, as practised in international schools?

Note

1 The author discussed 'Public–Private Partnerships: the WTO General Agreement on Trade in Services as a Context for the IBO Strategic Plan' at the Alliance for International Education conference, Düsseldorf, October 2004.

References

Acer (2013), *International Schools' Assessment* (ISA). http://www.acer.edu.au/tests/isa (Accessed 25 January 2013).

Appleton, S., Sives, A. and Morgan, W.J. (2006), 'The impact of international teacher migration on schooling in developing countries – the case of Southern Africa', *Globalisation, Societies and Education,* 4(1), 121–142.

Ball, S. (2003), 'The teacher's soul and the terrors of performativity', *Journal of Education Policy,* 18(2), 215–228.

Ball, S. (2007), *Education plc: Understanding Private Sector Participation in Public Sector Education.* London: Routledge.

Bernstein, B. (2000), *Pedagogy and Symbolic Control: Theory, Research, Critique (Second edition).* Lanham, MD: Rowman & Littlefield Publishers, Inc.

Bunnell, T. (2008), 'The global growth of the International Baccalaureate Diploma Programme over the first 40 years: A critical assessment'. *Comparative Education* 44(4), 409–424.

Bunnell, T. (2011), 'The International Baccalaureate and "growth scepticism": A "social limits" Framework', *International Studies in Sociology of Education,* 21(2), 161–176.

Bunnell, T. (2012), *Global Education under Attack: International Baccalaureate in America.* Frankfurt am Main: Peter Lang Verlag.

Butterfield, H. (1931), *The Whig Interpretation of History.* http://www.eliohs.unifi.it/testi/900/butterfield/ (Accessed 19 January 2013).

Byrd, S.Ellington, L., Gross, P., Jago, C. and Stern, S. (2007), *Advanced Placement and International Baccalaureate: Do They Deserve Gold Star Status?* Washington, DC: Thomas B. Fordham Institute. http://edexcellence.net/foundation/publication/publication.cfm?id=378 (Accessed 25 January 2013).

Cambridge, J. (2002), 'Recruitment and deployment of staff: A dimension of international school organisation', in M.C. Hayden, J.J. Thompson and G. Walker (eds), *International Education in Practice.* London: Kogan Page, pp. 158–169.

Cambridge, J. (2010), 'International Baccalaureate Diploma Programme and the construction of pedagogic identity: A preliminary study', *Journal of Research in International Education,* 9(3), 199–213.

Cambridge, J. (2011a), 'Pedagogic discourse: A language for the description and analysis of international curriculum implementation', *International Schools Journal,* 31(2), 45–52.

Cambridge, J. (2011b), 'International curriculum', in Bates, R. (ed), *Schooling Internationally: Globalisation, Internationalisation and the Future for International Schools.* Abingdon: Routledge, pp. 121–147.

Cambridge, J. (2012a), 'International Education research and the sociology of knowledge', *Journal of Research in International Education,* 11(3), 230–244.

Cambridge, J. (2012b), 'IB Diploma Programme as pedagogic discourse', in M. Hayden and J.J. Thompson (eds), *Taking the IB Diploma Programme Forward.* Woodbridge: John Catt Educational, pp. 65–76.

Clarke, J., Gewirtz, S., and McLaughlin, E. (2000), *New Managerialism, New Welfare?* London: SAGE Publications.

Crossley, M. and Watson, K. (2003), *Comparative and International Research in Education: Globalisation, Context and Difference.* London: Routlege Falmer.

Davies, B. (2011), 'Why Bernstein?', in D. Frandji and P. Vitale (eds), *Knowledge, Pedagogy and Society: International Perspectives on Basil Bernstein's Sociology of Education*. Abingdon: Routledge, pp. 34–45.

DiMaggio, P.J. and Powell, W.W. (1983), 'The Iron Cage revisited: Institutional isomorphism and collective rationality in organizational fields', *American Sociological Review,* 48(2), 147–160.

Doherty, C. (2010), 'Re-centring the curricular market: Pedagogic identities in IB Diploma programs in Australia', Paper presented at the International Basil Bernstein Symposium 2010, Griffith University, Brisbane, Australia, 30 June–3 July 2010. http://www.griffith.edu.au/__data/assets/pdf_file/0008/221759/Doherty-RT.pdf (Accessed 2 March 2013).

Engel, L. and Olden, K. (2012), 'One size fits all', in B.D. Shaklee and S. Baily (eds), *Internationalizing Teacher Education in the United States*. Lanham, MD: Rowman & Littlefield, pp. 77–92.

Fitz, J., Davies, B. and Evans, J. (2006), *Educational Policy and Social Reproduction*. London: Routledge.

Garton, B (2000), 'Recruitment of teachers for international education', in M.C. Hayden and J.J. Thompson (eds), *International Schools and International Education*. London: Kogan Page pp. 85–95.

Grace, G. (2008), 'Changes in the classification and framing of education in Britain, 1950s to 2000s: An interpretive essay after Bernstein', *Journal of Educational Administration and History,* 40(3), 209–220.

Hansard Parliamentary Reports (2012), 17 Sep 2012, Column 653: Exam Reform. http://www.publications.parliament.uk/pa/cm201213/cmhansrd/cm120917/debtext/120917-0001.htm (Accessed 2 March 2013).

Hardman, J. (2001), 'Improving recruitment and retention of quality overseas teachers', in S. Blandford and M. Shaw (eds), *Managing International Schools*. London: Routledge Falmer, pp. 123–135.

Hayden, M.C. (2006), *Introduction to International Education*. London: Sage.

Hayden, M.C. and Thompson, J.J. (2011), 'Teachers for the international school of the future', in R. Bates (ed), *Schooling Internationally: Globalisation, Internationalisation and the Future for International Schools*. Abingdon: Routledge, pp. 83–100.

Hernes, T. (2004), 'Studying composite boundaries: A framework of analysis', *Human Relations,* 57(1), 9–29.

Hill, I. (2010), 'The International Baccalaureate: Pioneering in education' International Schools Journal Compendium 4. Woodbridge: John Catt Educational.

Hill, I. (2012), 'Evolution of education for international mindedness', *Journal of Research in International Education,* 11(3), 245–261.

IB (2005), *A Look at North American IB Legislation*. http://www.ibo.org/ibna/document lation.pdf (Accessed 25 January 2013).

IB (2006), *IB Learner Profile Booklet*. Cardiff: International Baccalaureate.

IB (2008), *A review of research relating to the IB Diploma Programme*. Cardiff: International Baccalaureate. http://www.ibo.org/programmes/research/resources/dpresearchreview.cfm (Accessed 25 January 2013).

IB (2009), *IB Diploma Programme Statistical Bulletin, May 2009 Examination Session*. Cardiff: International Baccalaureate.

IB (2010), *IB Diploma Programme Statistical Bulletin, May 2010 Examination Session*. Cardiff: International Baccalaureate.

IB (2011), *IB Diploma Programme Statistical Bulletin, May 2011 Examination Session*. Cardiff: International Baccalaureate.

IB (2012a), *IB Diploma Programme Statistical Bulletin, May 2012 Examination Session*. Cardiff: International Baccalaureate.

IB (2012b), *MYP: The Next Chapter. Development Report (October 2012)*. Cardiff: International Baccalaureate.

Kugler, E.G. and Albright, E.M. (2005), 'Increasing diversity in challenging classes', *Educational Leadership*, 62(5), 42–45.

Leach, R.J. (1969), *International Schools and Their Role in the Field of International Education*. Oxford: Pergamon Press.

Lewis, C. (2006), 'International but not global: How international school curricula fail to address global issues and how this must change', *International Schools Journal*, 25(2), 51–67.

Marshman, R. (2010), *Concurrency of Learning in the IB Diploma Programme and Middle Years Programme*. Cardiff: International Baccalaureate.

Matthews, D. and Kitchen, J. (2007), 'School-within-a-school gifted programs: Perceptions of students and teachers in public secondary schools', *Gifted Child Quarterly*, 51(3), 256–71.

Oecd (2013), *Programme for International Student Assessment (PISA)*. http://www.oecd.org/pisa/ (Accessed 25 January 2013).

Peterson, A.D.C. (1972), *The International Baccalaureate: An Experiment in International Education*. London: George Harrap.

Peterson, A.D.C. (2003), *Schools across Frontiers* (second edition). La Salle, IL: Open Court.

Phillips, D. and Schweisfurth, M. (2006), *Comparative and International Education: An Introduction to Theory, Method and Practice*. New York: Continuum.

Remillard, R. (1978), *Knowledge and Social Control in a Multinational Context: An Analysis of the Development, Content and Potential of the International Baccalaureate*. Unpublished PhD thesis, State University of New York at Buffalo, NY.

Robertson, S.L. (2003), 'WTO/GATS and the global education services industry', *Globalisation, Societies and Education*, 1(3), 259–266.

Scott, D. (2008), *Critical Essays on Major Curriculum Theorists*. London: Routledge.

Singh, P. (2002), 'Pedagogising knowledge: Bernstein's theory of the pedagogic device'. *British Journal of Sociology of Education*, 23(4), 571–82.

Siskin, L.S. (1994), *Realms of Knowledge: Academic Departments in Secondary Schools*. Washington, DC: Falmer Press.

Sutcliffe, D. (1991), 'The United World Colleges', in P. Jonietz and D. Harris (eds) *World Yearbook of Education 1991: International Schools and International Education*. London: Kogan Page, pp. 25–37.

Tarc, P. (2009), *Global Dreams, Enduring Tensions: International Baccalaureate in a Changing World*. New York: Peter Lang Publishers.

Timss (2013), *TIMSS and PIRLS International Study Center*. http://www.timss.org/ (Accessed 25 January 2013).

Tomlinson, S. (2001), *Education in a Post-welfare Society*. Buckingham: Open University Press.

Tully, J. (2008), 'Two meanings of global citizenship: Modern and diverse', in M.A. Peters, A. Britton and H. Blee (eds), *Global Citizenship Education: Philosophy, Theory and Pedagogy*. Rotterdam: Sense Publishers, pp. 15–39.

Žižek, S. (2008), *In Defense of Lost Causes*. London: Verso.

CHAPTER ELEVEN

Boundaries and Boundary Management in International Schools: Psychodynamics and Organizational Politics

Richard Caffyn

Introduction

Borders and boundaries are an intricate part of organizational and everyday life. These complex and multifaceted locations represent many things: entry, exit, dialogue, identity, vulnerability, change, preservation and understanding. Such structures are at once paradoxical but always about discourse and interaction, be it conflict or synergy. In the 1945 film *I Know Where I'm Going*, written, produced and directed by Michael Powell and Emeric Pressburger, the heroine journeys through numerous boundaries, including national, social, class, emotional and physical (Cook, 2002). She travels north from Manchester to the Hebrides, passing from 'England', the urban, the predictable and the safe (essentialist) into 'Scotland', the wild, the strange and the threatening (constructivist). The nexus between boundaries forms its essence: the physical landscape and national borders, emotional states of being and the perceived chaos and threat. Even language, English to Gaelic, is part of the individualized and 'self' constructed boundary discourse within the film. It is essentially about perception and interaction, the possible and the unpredictable that can occur on boundaries, places that should, in theory, be about control and order. These highly charged physical, social and emotional landscapes are fraught with the power to threaten and change. Likewise, in transferring this cinematic paradigm to organizational theory, it is the organization and especially the school that also has complex and varied boundaries where interaction and dialogue are at their most rich, but also at their most problematic.

Boundaries and their significance

'Schools as organisations may be viewed as a complex network of independent subsystems where boundaries are continually being reinforced and attacked, where boundaries overlie each other and where "boundary rules" are frequently violated' (James et al., 2006, p. 51).

In understanding the complexities of schools as organizations and social systems, it is useful to consider social systems theory, and in particular, the idea of both external and internal boundaries. A boundary separates a system from its environment and acts as a means to control and manage the kinds of exchanges that pass between the system and its environment (Hernes, 2003; Dunning et al., 2005). This concept can also be extended internally to the component substructures and subcultures found within an organization. Boundaries are, as Hernes (2004) argues, not fixed or static but fluid. Boundaries and borders are subtly different from each other: a border is a specific place of movement, a gate, across a boundary. However, for this chapter I make limited distinction between the meanings.

Boundaries affect not just the organizational structure of the school but also how the curriculum is perceived and who has responsibility. Leadership is critical to this in ensuring that boundaries are secure, but in turn do not become barriers (James et al., 2006). The dual nature of a boundary is important in enabling a school to function, have clarity of purpose and policies, and enable both control and discourse. In considering the external boundaries of the school, it is also useful to understand how far a boundary extends and where the borders are set (Handy and Aitken, 1986). It is in managing the boundaries of the whole organization, and especially those between groups, individuals, subcultures and locations of power, that many of the challenges to social interaction in schools lie.

International schools are intrinsically complex and unique; often isolated and diverse entities that have numerous boundaries with their locations and internally between groups and subcultures. The need among many stakeholders for identity, and the vulnerability international schools have due to differing cultures, subcultures, expectations and emotional needs, means that there is a great likelihood for cross-boundary exchange and conflict. International expatriate society constantly interacts on complex boundaries for identity and control over icons and space (Lave, 2003). It is initially useful to look at organizational theory and how it applies to how boundaries are formed, how these are manifest and how such theory can be applied to understanding schools.

Theorizing boundaries

By using the work of James et al. (2006), Hernes (2003, 2004) and Foucault (1977), a model of understanding international schools as organizations can be applied, where the importance of both psychodynamics and organizational micropolitics is stressed in conceptualizing boundaries (Caffyn, 2011). Paulsen (2003) argues that organizations are social dynamic systems, especially in relation to their external environment. Individuals belong to multiple groups and these are organic, changing and shifting according to changes in the organization as Marshall (2003) suggests.

> Organisations are constituted as a dynamic and complex social system with independent networks of interpersonal and intergroup relationships. Within this social milieu, issues of control, power and influence, status, competition over resources, and boundaries between groups inevitably emerge and are contested. (Paulsen, 2003, p. 16)

Hernes (2003) argues for a dualism in boundaries where opportunity and control create a paradoxical reality. The boundary both constrains and enables; and this ambiguity is further expanded by Marshall (2003). Marshall suggests that organizations are not fixed or structured, but are shifting and temporal, open to changing goals, subjective views and social interaction. Organizations are both social and political: places of struggle, 'power, knowledge and identity formation' (2003, p. 69).

The types of boundaries in organizations are numerous and there is extensive discussion as to how to categorize each. Hernes (2004) argues for three kinds of boundaries: mental, social and physical. These are broad dimensions and he also expands on these as having substructures. A physical boundary can be viewed as being either tangible and material or made of rules and regulations (Hernes, 2003). The social boundary is constructed from 'informal social networks' (Hernes, 2003, p. 39), whilst the mental boundary is made of complex codes, icons, rituals and communication. Even in the mental boundary, emotion and vulnerability can create discourses of identity and power. 'Mental boundaries are also guarded by stakeholders who wish to maintain them as a basis for power and who wish to impose their definitions of reality on the group or the organization...' (Hernes, 2003, p. 40–41).

Marshall (2003) discusses various metaphors to explain boundaries in organizations. He addresses the idea of containment, an essentialist concept seeing the unproblematic dualism of the organization and its environment. However, Marshall dismisses containment as illusory and goes on 'the outward-facing boundaries of organizations are considered less like the solid walls of a container and more like a permeable membrane or zone of interaction' (2003, p. 59). This idea of an open, organic and contested zone made up of emotions, power and complexity suggests a far more constructivist and unordered organizational state beneath the visible formal structure.

In taking these various concepts of organizational boundaries further, it is useful to see these structures as myriad and organic in nature. Boundaries are dualistic and paradoxical, not just because they are about containment and access, but because they are political structures and, at the same time, located around emotions, culture and social interaction. These categories are different from each other and each interacts with the other in diverse complex ways.

Allan (2002) suggests that there is potential for conflict on cultural boundaries within an international school, particularly where dominant and host country cultures impact the school's culture and subcultures. This idea can be extended to the internal boundary divisions where subcultures, departments and individuals have both history and experience that creates complex cultural identity. Individual identity in international schools is not necessary with one culture or national group but is marked by background where cultural interaction, background, experience and familial structure collide to create immense cultural diversity.

Power has an impact on boundaries (Robertson, 2000) and operates in relation to who can dominate, access and position themselves through the boundary. Power and emotions (James, 1999) are important factors in understanding the operation and nature of boundaries. Much of the issue of emotions in organizations such as schools is linked to perceptions and questions of vulnerability and identity (Evans, 1998). How groups and individuals perceive themselves and their organization can become problematic and affect others, especially where perception of the reality is distorted and individuals isolated. Morgan (1997) argues that individuals and groups can create their own reality and this controls how they act and interact with others. International schools are possibly prone to this phenomenon where insecurity compounds and locates such discourses too firmly in isolated and vulnerable locations.

Those with formal power, the management and the leadership of a school, can impact teacher boundaries through domination and controlling teacher autonomy (Eden, 2001). Achinstein suggests that boundary politics is about negotiation and constant questioning, where challenge and contesting claims for control are commonplace.

> Fostering a culture of collaboration within a teacher professional community may spark conflict. Communities are often born in conflict because they demand substantial change in school norms and practices, challenging existing norms of privacy, independence, and professional autonomy, and may question existing boundaries between cultures and power groups at school sites. They remain in conflict as their valued norms of consensus and critical reflection, of unity and discord, are oftentimes incompatible. (Achinstein, 2002, p. 425)

Achinstein sees schools as conflict orientated, and the impact of either power as formal authority or as influence (Lukes, 1974) can create extensive interplay on border zones between groups and individuals, particularly over control and dominance. Those in power can place pressure on boundaries, transgressing borders and causing conflict. In previous research into international schools, I argue that micropolitical problems were often caused by the isolation of the school and the pressure created by those with power who penetrated borders, especially through dominance (Caffyn, 2010). Lareau (1997) suggests that parents can impact boundaries of control in schools where they have a status and class position that allows them to transcend such boundaries. This kind of conflict can occur considerably in international schools where parents can have exaggerated power due to the fee-paying nature of the school, higher economic and class position in the community and positional access to board control.

Boundaries give security to subcultural groups where categories can be used to normalize, control or exclude the other (Gunter, 2006). Emotional interplay on these boundaries as border politics and organizational psychodynamics has the possibility to reinforce group structures and can project negative or positive feelings on others. As Dunning et al. (2005) argue, categorizing others and projecting feelings and emotions on them is important to understand in boundary management and group or subcultural identity. 'The conscious and unconscious predisposition to projections has important implications for the way individuals and groups in schools manage their boundaries' (p. 256).

This concept of classification, control and normalization is common in organizations such as schools where identity and vulnerability deepen boundaries between groups.

> Class, race, age, sexuality, do not exist as normalised truths about who we are but are created classifications and as such are used to systemise and hence control sharing and staring across boundaries. This is evident in how typing is used by the self and others to include or exclude individuals and groups from particular social, political, cultural and economic practices. The challenge for educational organisations is how they may replicate or resist such structures that do harm to human beings through the actions of human beings. (Gunter, 2006, p. 257)

Boundary complexity in international schools

International schools are often isolated and vulnerable places, possessed with issues of social identity and standing (Caffyn, 2010). Boundaries in such schools can be diverse, depending on the school and focused as much on culture and emotions as organizational structure. Both Ogbu (1992) and

Inokuchi and Nozaki (2005) offer interesting and related discussions of cultural boundary problems between US students and other nationals, and the students' views on orientalizing other cultures or deepening boundaries with them. Diverse national groups and an external boundary which faces an alien host country location can in turn create both emotional and political pressures on an international school.

Boundaries between cultural groups cause problems of perception and misunderstanding, where expression and behaviour can create friction. Differing attitudes and cultural norms, especially in behaviour, can lead different national groups to view internal boundaries as permeable or fixed. Shamir and Melnik (2003), in a study of US and Israeli workers in various multinational companies in Silicon Valley, found that there was a different attitude towards hierarchy, the home/work boundary and language in the workplace. Yet, boundary access is open to more than just cultural variables and the reality has greater complexity where attitudes and behaviour are affected by multiple factors and these interplay on the diverse boundary structures in an organization.

Hernes' (2004) conceptualization of boundaries as a multi-dimensional typology of states of being is important and underlines the organic and shifting nature of such systems. Who has control of a boundary, how is crossing the boundary undertaken, and what the power relationships are and how rituals become manifest are considerations when understanding the dualism of the boundary as both fixed and contestable. It is this very ambiguity that causes complexity and problems for an organization. Schools perhaps suffer more from this inherent ambiguity as these organizations have numerous boundaries, both internal and external, that are contested and crossed constantly, whereas prisons, international border locations (e.g. ports, airports, railway stations) and, to a lesser extent, hospitals have greater regulation and power in controlling movement. Power distance between the school and clientele is often challenged and is less fixed, compared to the stronger professional power found in other professions. Fee-paying, board control and the flexible access to schools for clientele enable greater power and traffic across external boundaries. International schools serve diverse, often contradictory, parental interests and goals (Allan, 2002).

Schools have diverse borders shrouded in historical, locational and cultural ritual, and due to their often loose coupling (Bush, 1995) nature, these are open to interpretation, perception and challenge. The school becomes a place of political and social discourse, a focal point where emotions, views, philosophy, needs, identity and insecurity thrive. With an international school, these kinds of issues can multiply, especially where the school becomes surrogate family, community and centre for many disparate and complex individuals and groups. Yet, with globalization and the ideological premise of an international school as a borderless structure, is it, like modern organizations, to be regarded as more a network of relationships, systems and social interaction (Marshall, 2003, p. 63)? Boundaries become more hidden, less pronounced and marked by ritual and abstract detail. These zones become places of negotiation and bargaining: locations that are undefined, open to interpretation, access and risk (Hope, 2007).

Boundaries are social, cultural and political places, similar in concept to the idea of bargaining zones (Abell, 1975), where movement and control are open to negotiation. A border reflects issues of power, ritual, classification, identity and control. These spaces become locations where 'the other' is limited and controlled, where individuals are often unsettled, insecure and observed, and where difference is significant (Foucault, 1977).

Morgan (1997) discusses the importance of boundary relations between the organization and its subsections with their environments (p. 112). He stresses the impact of the boundary, its nature and structure, and the issue of knowledge. Who has knowledge to access the boundary or of the differing environments and zones either side? How is knowledge interpreted and reality perceived? 'One can also control transaction across boundaries by performing a buffering function that allows or even encourages certain transactions while blocking others' (Morgan, 1997, p. 181).

Power is significant to borders and boundaries in schools. Position (Caffyn, 2009) extends the idea of power as just authority and influence (Lukes, 1974), by underlying the location of power in such zones. For example, a secretary or caretaker has positional power to control boundaries of knowledge and information (secretary) or resources and building access (caretaker). This access to power on borderlands also implies autonomy and independence, and much conflict occurs due to competing and contesting control between the structure and other groups, individuals and subcultures. 'Boundary transactions are thus often characterised by competing strategies for control and counter control' (Morgan, 1997, p. 182).

Leadership is central to the issue of power as it 'creates and sustains boundaries' (James et al., 2006, p. 159). Relationships between different groups and individuals are often marked by access to resources, tasks, status and communication. How different groups relate to each other, especially to leadership, can determine the kind of problems or synergy on their borders. This is particularly true of internal school departments where power builds up around individuals, subcultures, space and nature (Ball, 1987). Departments and subcultures can develop into city states, highly independent, powerful and historically determined (Caffyn, 2008). These boundaries are made up of organizational needs, political power and both social and cultural symbolism. As Marshall suggests, in analysing boundaries as complex metaphors, such internal divisions are dualist, marked by meaning, tradition and history. 'They can imply security, solidarity, and belonging, but equally, and often simultaneously, they are about exclusion and alienation' (2003, p. 61). Organizational structures such as departments and social and emotional structures such as subcultures (Caffyn, 2011; Lave, 2003) develop their own boundaries and both rituals and rules of access based on identity, protection and needs.

External boundaries are highly idiosyncratic in international schools. Protection of school boundaries is often in reaction to the shift from exclusivity of schools as an almost isolated 'monastic' place to accountability and external influence (Williams, 1989). Parental influence and power are a significant force and pressure on external boundaries. Watkins (1989) suggests that such influence and access should be strongly encouraged and that boundaries should, in turn, be permeable. This creates a double-edged binary consequence in that parental influence can be positive and synergistic, but also has the possibility to be critical and negative. Parental power, as an example of the growing political and consumerist control of the client or customer, is a constant boundary pressure.

In an international school parental power can be both political and psychodynamic in that parents as customers demand value for money yet are also affected by issues of identity, vulnerability and displacement (Caffyn, 2009). This latter social factor creates unrest and the school as focal point in a limited social network can bear the brunt of this. Lave (2003) describes the pressure and impact of parental identity discourses on the local international school in Porto. The school becomes vulnerable and is open towards an inflated and prominent place in an anxious and contested locality (Allan, 2002). Its boundaries are exposed to diverse claims for access because it has a higher level of emotional and political prominence in the expatriate community. Such a home–work boundary is made up of tangible structures, artefacts or icons, individual views and cultural boundaries – all in fact caught in interwoven social and political dynamics (Nipper-Eng, 2003, p. 263). The permeability between the home and work is significant in international schools where many staff have a closer and emotional link to the workplace as surrogate family and social support system than with their current residential neighbourhood.

Foucault discusses border places extensively, seeing some locations such as prisons as having fixed and controlled borders where the 'self' is forced inwards (1977, p. 239). Surveillance and knowledge are factors in such locations where architecture is power and control. Borders are firmly established and ritual becomes an aspect of how power and control are endemic to the place. In schools, borders are less fixed or centrally controlled, and more open to influence and challenge. The boundary is a zone of dualism; at once about control, discipline and surveillance, but also about movement, dialogue and unease. Both prisons and hospitals have greater boundary control, security and established rituals of border negotiation. This preserves and reinforces the professional culture and allocates more power to central control. In the school, there is the added emotion of 'the child' as the resource closest to the parent. This aspect and the weaker boundary structure then create political and psychodynamic traffic across the borders. The borders themselves are often highly permeable and leadership has problems of containment. For example, in the second of the case-study examples I discuss in this chapter, cross-boundary traffic was extensive particularly from host country legislation and powerful expatriate parents. This factor caused both political pressure on school leadership and a kind of 'culture shock' for new management and staff in coming to terms with the nuances and uniqueness of the school.

Boundaries, therefore, can be physical, psychological, structural, cultural, external and political (Figure 11.1). This conceptualization can be used as a heuristic device to further explore and investigate international schools' social and organizational structure. It goes beyond the positivist ontological concept of organizations as fixed and objective, arguing that reality is subjective and perceived individually.

Boundary	Detail
Physical	⅄ Building design ⅄ Use and ownership of space ⅄ Rules and regulations
Psychological	⅄ Mental ⅄ Social
Structural	⅄ Hierarchical and disciplinary ⅄ Curriculum and pedagogic
Cultural	⅄ Subcultures
External	⅄ Clientele ⅄ Local environment ⅄ International organizations ⅄ Host country
Power	⅄ Political ⅄ Access and position

FIGURE 11.1: *A heuristic model to conceptualize boundaries in international schools*

Boundaries exist in time and place, and can both change and develop, reflecting the organization as a living organism (Morgan, 1997). The boundaries are also interchangeable and interact with each other, adding to the complexity and intricate nature of the school. International schools operate with some similar boundary issues to national schools, though with added complexity in terms of their immediate external environment and location, and the number of possible internal subcultures created through isolation, history and locational impact (Caffyn, 2008, p. 2010).

Boundary case studies

To gain a closer, contextual understanding of boundaries in action within international schools, three brief case-study vignettes from my previous research are discussed. These vignettes are part of wider case-study investigations of schools and offer a view on diverse aspects of boundary management complexity.

Case study 1: Isolated campuses and diverse social boundaries

I looked in detail at several international schools and their micropolitics, trying to ascertain why politics occurred (Caffyn, 2009). In one, Kitezh International School in Eastern Europe, the school had four campuses with differing locations, building designs, staff and ritual. It had originally been a Canadian school but had become more international and diverse in staff nationality over time. One of the campuses, Bachynsky, was typical of the autonomous sections of the school, identified through its unique cultures, fragmented groups and isolation. Nationality, arrival year in the school and home location in the city of Kitezh marked boundaries between staff. These groups grew with different levels of ownership, power and positional control. Each had their own social and political zones in the school, marked by subtle codes and ritual, but developed as singular subcultures. Boundaries in Bachynsky were between these groups and were about identity in a difficult and strange host locality. One such subculture was a group of Canadian teachers: middle-aged, arriving at the school in the same year and living in the same housing block (Caffyn, 2010). This group was separated from others, politically in terms of control and power, and psychologically in terms of social structure and insecurity. They were pulled together as a subculture and their group boundary was controlled by powerful individuals and group ritual which protected the group. The strong boundary was caused in part in reaction to the alien, complex local environment, and emotion and history affected this to enable social boundaries to be secure (Caffyn, 2009, p. 131). Tajfel (1982) argues that groups are formed to create social identity and to counter external threats. Attributing individual behaviour to the group and categorizing group behaviour (Hewstone and Jaspers, 1982) are of interest in understanding the social dynamics of international schools. How far does individual action become a reflection of the self or of group identity?

Case study 2: Camps, cigarettes and cultural control

The other case study that is discussed is the Ruritanian International School (RIS), a very large single campus school well established in a Northern

European country (Caffyn, 2009). One interesting incident looked at in depth was of the issue and clash of cultures to do with staff smoking in the evening during school camps. Staff members were required to assist with camps and may have become influenced by the local Ruritanian culture which was relaxed about smoking, especially during work time. This practice caused considerable indignation and concern with expatriate parents and created a problem between long-term staff and the more transient leadership. Leadership was more influenced by expatriate business practices and Anglo-Saxonization (Ferner and Quintanilla, 1998). This caused conflict on the borders of the locally influenced long-term staff where this issue became a political emic *cause célèbre* which developed binary splitting and projecting (Dunning et al., 2005) onto leadership and parents as antagonistic and 'wrong'. Such a significant issue was a threat to autonomy, the hybrid long-term staff school culture and ownership, and was marked by protection of identity, rights and freedom in the face of limited control. It was also part of the frustrations of the terminus feeling many long-term staff in international schools can suffer from when they are stuck in a location for personal, familial and economic reasons and these frustrations act to generate conflict and power claims within the school itself. The clash of cultures, views, perceptions and rights on these social and political borderlands becomes enshrined in the fabric of the school: its history, codes of practice and structure. These boundaries are complex, full of emotion and political power, and create distance, misunderstanding and difference (Hernes, 2003). There was limited discussion or negotiation as each side became entrenched in their perceived rights, power and identity. Such issues can become synergistic and boundary clashes can certainly develop and strengthen organizations. However, the clash between long-term staff and both leadership and expatriate parents became a struggle for legitimacy, autonomy and cultural identity. This clash built around a perceived boundary icon or artefact as Rafaeli and Vilnai-Yavetz (2003) suggest. Such icons, like cigarettes or camps, channel emotional interplay, cultural discourse and power plays. These become mental boundaries, as Hernes (2003, p. 40) outlines.

Case study 3: Parent demands for language support

The final case study is an older unpublished investigation into parental perceptions and demands for extra mother tongue language support based on local bylaws. This took place in a small Central European international school (CEIS) located well outside the capital city of the country. The school had been set up by local business firms to enrich and develop the location as a centre for international and national economic growth. It had 160 students and 30 staff, and most of the clientele were local. The issue developed from a parental demand by a small group for mother tongue language support for students as was common in state system schools. The problem was that there was no knowledge of whether the school could have this support as it was classified as international and outside the state system though still supported by the state. This meant it was an anomaly. Certain parents were active in their demands that the school leadership investigate this issue, and this became a clash of power and boundary infiltration based on perceptions of who had power, ownership and voice in the school. The parental experience of the state system and local knowledge became a powerful voice and clashed with the professional and international background of much of the leadership. It also became an issue of who had rights to cross fragile boundaries of knowledge and control. The ability to influence and have status or rights was historical, and certain parents' perceptions and expectations were that their views and demands should be listened to, especially as they had longevity in the school. The leadership of the school, for some parents, appeared to be seen as 'wrong' and emotional feelings were projected so that all their actions were classified as bad; the splitting of good and bad, and the projecting of bad onto groups or individuals (Dunning et al., 2005; James et al., 2009).

Discussion of the case-study findings and developing boundary theory

In each of the three case studies discussed, there are issues of boundary conflict based on perceptions, culture, expectations, power and identity. These factors can be regarded as political, such as power, voice and ownership, or psychodynamic where the concerns are focused on emotions, insecurity and the self. The latter factor, the self, is important to consider and place within an international expatriate and local host country environment. The myriad of physical, organizational and psychological borders at play within the international school that impact on the self, the individual, are significant. Individuals cross borders and boundaries; they span different groups and subcultures, and have multiple identities (Hernes, 2004).

For leadership in these three case studies, boundary management seemed to follow one of the following paths where each became a discourse of border control:

- Coercion
- Collusion
- Confrontation
- Closure

The latter is a state where the border is closed and discourse completely restricted. These paths demonstrate the complexity and problems of organizational boundaries for leadership, where schools have to control, negotiate and regulate permeability and interference (James et al., 2006). To control this impact, individuals and groups are often coercively assigned into categories and become orientalized. This enables regulation and the labelling of problem individuals as the 'other', to ensure control. In international schools, individuals can easily become classified or dismissed as 'different', maverick or difficult due to not being the same or not following established traditions, either from the locality or school. Staff are often viewed as essentialist, objects to classify and codify, thus attempting to normalize, predict and control behaviour (Hardman, 2001).

Exiles and expatriates can be regarded as distinctive exclusive groups (Gold, 2001), more defined by borders than other social groups. These groups are positioned distantly from their immediate location through exclusivity, social structure, emotional distance and isolation. Thus, such groups have a more psychological, contested and short-term relationship with the locality and other groups. These factors can distance expatriates from other groups and extends, as Turner (1982) suggests, the in-group and the out-group juxtaposition. Added problems such as the quest for identity, vulnerability to the other, changes of structure and insecurity create a shifting dynamic that can have limited stability. Distance and isolation are hugely important in considering why boundaries become so problematic in expatriate groups and for international schools. Groups and individuals pressurize the school as a focal point, a place of social cohesion, and perceived stability. These groups and subcultures can be highly flexible, insecure and organic in nature, often focused on questions of identity and on temporal social or psychological interdependence (Turner, 1982).

The final area to discuss from these case studies is the nature of professionalism in education. The professional distance in schools as emotional, social and child-centred organizations is usually far less than organizations such as hospitals or prisons. Teaching as a profession is often compromised by the easier social interaction across boundaries of professionalism. In an international school, clientele power can permeate easily and the nature of international schools as the 'other' in the host country can also distance staff from professional support structures. Even where union or professional associations are powerful, isolation and difference can render the school an anomaly – a different place, problematic to categorize. Staff can be, in turn, affected by this cross-border traffic and lack of professional respect and from being at the lower end of the expatriate class structure (Caffyn, 2009).

International schools have permeable boundaries in numerous areas and face diverse emotional and political actors and groups. There are zones of control and places of complex bargaining that school management needs to be aware of. The added dimension of the psychodynamic complexity of displaced and powerful groups means that social and emotional interaction can be significant. In the case of the camps at RIS and the extra language support at CEIS, political control and cultural emotions impacted significantly and caused distance and conflict. Emotion became a factor in extending political power and ensuring identity. There can also develop 'perceptions of criticality', where how one person perceives an issue, environment, statement or incident is markedly different to another, and this state of being can create enormous friction and conflict. Individuals attribute different senses of importance and significance to diverse issues. Consequently, misunderstandings, behavioural problems and long-term vendettas can develop that become historically embedded in the psyche and social fabric of the school and its community.

Boundaries and border imply differing zones: within and without, us and 'the other'. In the isolation and difference that much dialogue signifies in international education, and therefore international schools, the 'other' is seen as problematic, dangerous and alien. Authorization and accreditation in schools also designate those approved or accepted and those who are not. This can be regarded as a disciplinary system (Foucault, 1977) creating boundaries between groups and surveying those attempting to cross boundaries of acceptance. It is part of the dualist nature of quality assurance, creating norms and regulation for quality whilst developing restriction. Exclusivity and difference are commonplace in international education and this kind of discourse also isolates, controls and classifies. The 'other', whether perceived as the maverick teacher (Hardman, 2001), the risk-taking local parent who chooses the international school instead of the state school or the rogue school that challenges existing 'accepted' international education norms, is vulnerable. Both internally and externally to the school, the 'other' becomes categorized and disempowered, a victim of discourses of orientalism. Individuals can risk social isolation in moving into an international school, be these individuals, parents or teachers. They run the risk of loss of identity, diffusion of culture, dominance by others and future insecurity. These are still perceptions, sometimes based on reality, but exist as boundaries crossed when joining the international school community. Threat and risk make crossing such boundaries difficult and emotion and fear can easily affect interrelationships and politics. Fragmentation can occur on these boundaries, where organizations and communities break apart and identity becomes more defined due to issues of expectations, experience and vulnerability (Caffyn, 2007).

Summary

Boundaries can be regarded as omnipresent in all organizations, and an organization is, in effect, a 'boundary maintaining system' (Hernes, 2003, p. 35). Such divisions are physical, mental, cultural, political and power based. As I have argued elsewhere, the complexities and both social and political interplays and nuances of international schools with their unique locations (Caffyn, 2010) and histories (Caffyn, 2008) make them particularly prone to diverse boundary movement and, consequently, problems. Synergy is an aspect of the discourse of boundaries but difference and the strong emotional insecurity created by isolation, transience and power imbalances lean towards a more complex problematic dialogue. Efforts by individuals and groups, be this school leadership, host country staff, transient expatriates, state employees, managers, boards or parents, tend towards trying to make sense of these complexities, idiosyncrasies and diversity. This is often done through coercive assignment, categorization, surveillance and discipline.

Boundaries are active and paradoxical, essentially complex locations where groups and organizations collide and contest power and control. Negotiation, power and the ability to bargain are key aspects of these places. International school boundaries are negotiated zones of interaction dependent on positional power, emotion and socio-cultural behaviour (Caffyn, 2011). These are places where identity is formed and where culture is reinforced and contested and where organizations can fragment into defined groups (Caffyn, 2007). For leadership and management in international schools, external and internal boundaries are the frustrating paradoxical reality of social and political interaction.

References

Abell, P. (1975), *Organisations as Bargaining and Influence Systems*. London: Heinemann.

Achinstein, B. (2002), 'Conflict amid community: The micropolitics of teacher collaboration', *Teachers College Record*, 104(3), 421–455.

Allan, M. (2002), 'Cultural borderlands: Cultural dissonance in the international school', *International Schools Journal*, 21(2), 42–53.

Ball, S. J. (1987), *The Micro-Politics of the School: Towards a Theory of School Organisation*, London: Routledge.

Ball, S.J. (ed) (2004), 'The sociological of education: A disputational account', in *The Routledge Falmer Reader in Sociology of Education*. London: Routledge Falmer, pp. 1–12.

Bush, T. (1995), *Theories of Educational Management*. London: PCP.

Caffyn, R. (2007), 'Fragmentation in international schools: A micropolitical discourse of management, culture and postmodern society', in M.C. Hayden, J.J. Thompson and J. Levy (eds), *The SAGE Handbook of Research in International Education*. London: Sage, pp. 339–350.

Caffyn, R. (2008), 'Understanding the historical context: History as an investigative lens in studying the micropolitics of international schools', *International Schools Journal*, 27(2), 29–36.

Caffyn, R. (2009), *Micropolitics of International Schools*. Saarbrucken: VDM.

Caffyn, R. (2010), 'We are in Transylvania, and Transylvania is not England': Location as a significant factor in international school micropolitics', *Educational Management, Administration and Leadership*, 38(3), 320–340.

Caffyn, R. (2011), 'International schools and micropolitics: fear, vulnerability and identity in fragmented space', in R. Bates (ed) *Schooling Internationally:*

Globalisation, Internationalisation and the future for International Schools. Abingdon: Routledge, pp. 59–82.

Cook, P. (2002), *I Know Where I'm Going.* London: British Film Institute.

Dunning, G., James, C. and Jones, N. (2005), 'Splitting and projection at work in schools', *Journal of Educational Administration,* 43(3), 244–259.

Eden, D. (2001), 'Who controls the teachers? Overt and covert control in schools', *Educational Administration Management and Leadership,* 29(1), 97–111.

Evans, L. (1998), *Teacher Morale, Job Satisfaction and Motivation.* London: Sage.

Ferner, A. and Quintanilla, J. (1998), 'Multinationals, national business systems and HRM: The enduring influence of national identity or a process of "Anglo-Saxonisation"', *The International Journal of Human Resource Management,* 9(4), 710–731.

Foucault, M. (1977), *Discipline and Punish: the Birth of the Prison.* London: Allen Lane.

Gold, S.J. (2001), 'Gender, class and network: Social structure and migration patterns among transnational Israelis', *Global Networks,* 1(1), 57–78.

Gunter, H.M. (2006), 'Educational leadership and the challenge of diversity', *Educational Management Administration and Leadership,* 34(2), 257–268.

Handy, C. and Aitken, R. (1986), *Understanding Schools as Organisations.* London: Penguin.

Hardman, J. (2001), 'Improving recruitment and retention of quality overseas teachers', in S. Blandford and M. Shaw (eds), *Managing International Schools.* London: RoutledgeFalmer, pp. 123–135.

Hernes, T. (2003), 'Enabling and constraining properties of organisational boundaries', in N. Paulsen and T. Hernes (eds), *Managing Boundaries in Organisations.* Basingstoke: Macmillan, pp. 35–54.

Hernes, T. (2004), 'Studying composite boundaries: A framework of analysis', *Human Relations,* 57(1), 9–29.

Hewstone, M. and Jaspers, J. (1982), 'Intergroup relations and attribution processes', in H. Tajfel (ed), *Social Identity and Intergroup Relations.* Cambridge: CUP, pp. 99–133.

Hope, A. (2007), 'Risk taking, boundary performance and intentional school internet "misuse"', *Discourse: Studies in the Cultural Politics of Education* 28(1), 87–99.

Inokuchi, H. and Nozaki, Y. (2005), '"Different than us": Othering, orientalism, and the US middle school students' discourses on Japan', *Asia Pacific Journal of Education,* 25(1), 61–74.

James, C.R. (1999), 'Institutional transformation and educational management', in T. Bush, L Bell, R. Bolam, R. Glatter and P. Ribbins (eds), *Educational Management: Redefining Theory, Policy and Practice.* London: PCP, pp. 142–154.

James, C.R., Connolly, M., Dunning, G. and Elliott, T. (2006), *How Very Effective Primary Schools Work.* London: PCP.

Lareau, A. (1997), 'Social-class differences in family-school relationships: The importance of cultural capital', in A.H. Halsey, H. Lauder, P. Brown and A. Stuart Wells (eds), *Education: Culture, Economy and Society.* Oxford: Oxford University Press, pp. 703–717.

Lave, J. (2003), 'Producing the future: Getting to be British', *Antipode,* 492–511.

Lukes, S. (1974), *Power: A Radical View.* London: Macmillan.

Marshall, N. (2003), 'Identity and difference in complex projects: Why boundaries still matter in the "boundaryless" organisation', in N. Paulsen and T. Hernes (eds), *Managing Boundaries in Organisations*. Basingstoke: Macmillan, pp. 55–75.

Morgan, G. (1997), *Images of Organisation*. London: Sage.

Nipper-Eng, C. (2003), 'Drawing the line: Organisations and the boundary work of "home" and "work"', in N. Paulsen and T. Hernes (eds), *Managing Boundaries in Organisations*. Basingstoke: Macmillan, pp. 262–280.

Ogbu, J.U. (1992), 'Understanding cultural diversity and learning', *Educational Researcher*, 21(8), 5–13.

Paulsen, N. (2003), '"Who are we now?": Group identity, boundaries, and the (Re)organising process', in N. Paulsen and T. Hernes (eds), *Managing Boundaries in Organisations*. Basingstoke: Macmillan, pp. 14–35.

Rafaeli, A. and Vilnai-Yavetz, I. (2003), 'Discerning organisational boundaries through physical artifacts', in N. Paulsen and T. Hernes (eds), *Managing Boundaries in Organisations*. Basingstoke: Macmillan, pp. 188–210.

Robertson, S.L. (2000), 'Teachers' labour, class and the politics of exchange in international studies', *Sociology of Education*, 10(3), 285–283.

Shamir, B. and Melnik, Y. (2003), 'Some organisational consequences of cultural differences in boundary permeability', in N. Paulsen and T. Hernes (eds), *Managing Boundaries in Organisations*. Basingstoke: Macmillan, pp. 281–301.

Tajfel, H. (ed) (1982), 'Instrumentality, identity and social comparisons', in *Social Identity and Intergroup Relations*. Cambridge: CUP, pp. 483–507.

Turner, J.C. (1982), 'Towards a cognitive redefinition of the social group', in H. Tajfel (ed), *Social Identity and Intergroup Relations*. Cambridge: CUP, pp. 15–40.

Watkins, C. (1989), 'The caring functions', in J. Sayer and V. Williams (eds), *Schools and External Relations: Managing the New Partnerships*. London: Cassell, pp. 15–32.

Williams, V. (1989), 'Schools and their communities: Issues in external relations', in J. Sayer and V. Williams (eds), *Schools and External Relations: Managing the New Partnerships*. London: Cassell, pp. 46–64.

AUTHOR INDEX

SUBJECT INDEX